THE UNIVERSITY OF
CHESTER

REVOLUTIONARY ACTS

REVOLUTIONARY ACTS

Amateur Theater
and the Soviet State,

1917–1938

L Y N N   M A L L Y

CORNELL UNIVERSITY PRESS

Ithaca and London

First published 2000 by Cornell University Press

Printed in the United States of America

Library of Congress Cataloging-in-Publication Data

Mally, Lynn.
  Revolutionary acts : amateur theater and the Soviet state,
1917–1938 / Lynn Mally.
      p. cm.
Includes bibliographical references.
  ISBN 0-8014-3769-5 (alk. paper)
  1. Amateur theater—Soviet Union—History—20th century.
I. Title.
  PN3169.S65 M27 2000
  792'.0222'094709041—dc21

                                        00-009282

Cornell University Press strives to use environmentally
responsible suppliers and materials to the fullest extent
possible in the publishing of its books. Such materials include
vegetable-based, low-VOC inks and acid-free papers that are
recycled, totally chlorine-free, or partly composed of nonwood
fibers. Books that bear the logo of the FSC (Forest
Stewardship Council) use paper taken from forests that have
been inspected and certified as meeting the highest standards
for environmental and social responsibility. For further
information, visit our website at www.cornellpress.cornell.edu.

Cloth printing   10 9 8 7 6 5 4 3 2 1

For Bob and Nora

Contents

Preface

THIS BOOK began as a study of the Leningrad Theater of Working-Class Youth, known by its acronym TRAM. But as my work on this theater and its Moscow affiliate continued, I discovered that these popular youth stages were simply the most visible representatives of a much wider phenomenon of amateur theater that blossomed in the early Soviet period. My research then grew to include the amorphous network of impromptu stages that inspired, imitated, and eventually outlasted TRAM. Expanding this project beyond TRAM, which has its own archives and extensive secondary literature, made this book much harder to write. I hope that the end product has more to say about the place of theater and the amateur arts in the cultural transformation begun with the October Revolution.

At the early stages of this project I was taken under the wing of two remarkable experts on Russian theater, Vladislav Ivanov and Maria Ivanova. They introduced me to a new field and gave me invaluable bibliographic assistance. What began as a professional relationship ended as a friendship. Their book-lined apartment was a haven for me on my trips to Moscow. The Internet has made the work of writing a little less solitary. I was bolstered by good-natured criticism and cyber pep talks from Louise McReynolds, who tried to hem in my natural tendencies toward social history. Susan Larsen has been a wonderful reader, both on the 'Net and off. Evgeny Dobrenko aided me with his broad knowledge of mainstream Soviet culture. Susanna Lockwood Smith shared her insights into the world of amateur music. Alice Fahs and I shared many conversations on theater, popular culture, and writing, all of which helped me to refine my thoughts. The friendship and bibliographic assistance of Joan Ariel and Ellen Broidy were very important to me. Two theater lovers, Carroll Smith-Rosenberg and Alvia Golden, helped me see this project in a broader perspective. I am particularly grateful to Alvia for thinking up the title.

Many colleagues have given me comments on individual chapters, including Jim von Geldern, Lewis Siegelbaum, and Anne Walthall. A convivial group of Russian scholars in southern California, including Robert Edelman, Choi Chatterjee, Arch Getty, Georg Michels, Elise Wirtschafter, and Mary Zirin, read versions of assorted chapters. Laurie Bernstein saw me through a research trip to Moscow. Stan Karas smoothed my way through Soviet newspapers of the 1930s. Viktorina Lefebvre helped me to compile the bibliography and the notes. My warmest thanks go to John Ackerman of Cornell University Press. I received research support for this project from the International Research Exchange Board (IREX), the Social Science Research Council, and the University of California, Irvine.

It is customary for authors to thank their families, but I believe that I have special reasons to do so. Robert Moeller has always been my first and final reader. I am grateful for his erudition, patience, and most of all his sense of humor. And my daughter Nora deserves a special mention because she continues to teach me about the passion and commitment that go into amateur theater.

Portions of chapter 4 were previously published in "The Rise and Fall of the Soviet Youth Theater TRAM," *Slavic Review* 51, no. 3 (Fall 1992) and "Performing the New Woman: The Komsomolka as Actress and Image in Soviet Youth Theater," *Journal of Social History* 30, no. 1 (Fall 1996). I gratefully acknowledge the permission of the American Association for the Advancement of Slavic Studies and the *Journal of Social History* to reprint them here. Chapter 5 includes revised sections of two published articles. I thank the Ohio State University Press for allowing me to incorporate sections of my "Autonomous Theater and the Origins of Socialist Realism: The 1932 Olympiad of Autonomous Art," *The Russian Review* 52, no. 2 (April 1993). Copyright 1993 by Ohio State University Press. All rights reserved. The journal *Russian History* gave me permission to include parts of "Shock Workers on the Cultural Front: Agitprop Brigades in the First Five-Year Plan," *Russian History* 23, no. 1–4 (1996).

REVOLUTIONARY ACTS

Introduction

"THE YEAR since the last festival of the October Revolution will enter the history of Russian theater," proclaimed Adrian Piotrovskii, a prominent Leningrad scholar, cultural activist, and local bureaucrat, in 1924. "It is the first year that the triumph of the mass movement known as amateur theater [*samodeiatel'nyi teatr*] has become apparent." Piotrovskii listed what he believed were amateur theater's significant accomplishments, including its influence over the most progressive professional stages. "Maybe this coming year will lead us to a long awaited, unified theatrical style, rooted in the 'amateur' performances of Soviet youth."[1] For Piotrovskii, amateurs were the main source of creativity in Soviet theater and he was not alone in his convictions. Many observers expected a new, participatory socialist culture to emerge from the amateur stage.

This book examines amateur theaters as a distinctive medium of urban organization and entertainment in the first two decades of Soviet power. Amateur theaters served a variety of functions for their participants, audiences, and sponsoring institutions. They provided avenues of artistic and political self-expression for their mainly youthful actors. Housed in local gathering spots and workplaces, they offered a vital

---

1. A. I. Piotrovskii, "God uspekhov," in his *Za sovetskii teatr! Sbornik statei* (Leningrad: Academia, 1925), 67–68. Unless otherwise indicated, all translations are my own. On Piotrovskii's career, see Katerina Clark, *Petersburg, Crucible of Cultural Revolution* (Cambridge: Harvard University Press, 1995); James von Geldern, *Bolshevik Festivals, 1917–1920* (Berkeley: University of California Press, 1993); and E. S. Dobin, ed., *Adrian Piotrovskii: Teatr, kino, zhizn'* (Leningrad: Iskusstvo, 1969).

form of entertainment for urban neighborhoods. State agencies used them to disseminate political information and mark important celebrations. Finally, they constituted a popular forum to help shape a unified and widely accepted Soviet theatrical repertoire.

Focusing on the two capital cities, Moscow and Petrograd/Leningrad, I argue that the study of amateur theater allows us to trace crucial transformations in Soviet cultural life from the early revolutionary years to the late 1930s: the growing status and prestige of artistic experts; the articulation of a unified Soviet artistic canon; and efforts to control spontaneous forms of cultural expression by the lower classes. I aim to show that amateur theaters are an important—and understudied—form of cultural production and consumption in the Soviet Union.[2] This work also adds to a lively conversation about how the population at large contributed to the formation of the Stalinist aesthetic doctrine of socialist realism.

Early Soviet amateur stages were extremely diverse. Some inhabited beautiful halls and offered elaborate training programs; others were fly-by-night operations. Some played home-made propaganda sketches; others staged Chekhov and Schiller. What united them was their community base and nonprofessional standing. Participants did not earn a living from their cultural work. The Russian language offers two common words for amateurism: *liubitel'stvo*, rooted in the verb *to love* (as *amateur* is rooted in the Latin *amare*); and *samodeiatel'nost'*, literally translated as "doing-it-yourself."[3] Although the words can be used interchangeably, Soviet writers increasingly distinguished between the two. *Liubitel'skii teatr* came to stand for all that was bad in amateur activities. *Samodeiatel'nyi teatr*, by contrast, represented all that was good in

2. For overviews of Soviet amateur theater, see S. Iu. Rumiantsev and A. P. Shul'pin, eds., *Samodeiatel'noe khudozhestvennoe tvorchestvo v SSSR*. 2 v. (Moscow: Gosudarstvennyi institut iskusstvoznaniia, 1995); V. B. Blok, "Khudozhestvennoe tvorchestvo mass," in A. Ia. Zis', ed., *Stranitsy istorii sovetskoi khudozhestvennoi kul'tury* (Moscow: Nauka, 1989), 11–42; V. Ivashev, ed., *Ot "zhivoi gazety" do teatra-studii* (Moscow: Molodaia gvardiia, 1989); V. N. Aizenshtadt, *Sovetskii samodeiatel'nyi teatr: Osnovnye etapy razvitiia* (Kharkov: Khar'kovskii gosudarstvennyi institut kul'tury, 1983); and N. G. Zograf et al., eds., *Ocherki istorii russkogo sovetskogo teatra v trekh tomakh* (Moscow: Akademiia nauk, 1954–60), v. 1: 467–78, v. 2: 460–78. On the significance of amateur theater to postwar educational institutions, see Anne White, *Destalinization and the House of Culture* (London: Routledge, 1990), esp. 70–79.

3. E. Anthony Swift coined this inventive translation. See his "Workers' Theater and 'Proletarian Culture' in Pre-Revolutionary Russia, 1905–1917," *Russian History* 23 (1996): 94.

the Soviet approach, including collective interaction and productive social results.

As the Soviet state took shape, amateur theaters opened everywhere,
created by soldiers, workers, peasants, students, and the unemployed.
They were a path for participants to claim a public role. "The country
had never been attacked by such violent theater fever as during the first
years of the revolution," recalled the director and critic Pavel Markov.
"Every district, every army unit, every factory had its own 'theater-cir-
cle,' watched over and developed with the greatest care and attention."[4]
By the late 1920s trade unions alone were supporting a national network
of some twelve thousand amateur stages.[5]

Amateur theaters provided a venue where performers, the audience,
and political overseers intersected. They were located primarily in clubs,
initially impromptu gathering spots carved out of urban spaces. Soviet
clubs offered participants a chance to meet their daily needs, gain valuable information about work opportunities and state regulations, and
discover opportunities for relaxation and amusement. These multiple
tasks—combining necessity with pleasure—quickly made them a focus
of attention for those committed to creating a Soviet public sphere, a
realm where private needs could be met in a shared collective space.
Cultural activists called clubs a "public hearth" in a world where private
hearths were linked to the old bourgeois past. They believed clubs had
the power to nurture a sense of common purpose and common identity.
In the words of the artist El Lissitzky, "The club ought to become a gathering place where the individual becomes one with the collective and
where he stores up new reserves of energy."[6]

Clubs offered a wide range of amusements, but theatrical events of
various kinds—classical plays, improvisations, recitations, and staged
games—were among the most popular forms of participatory cultural
activity in the early Soviet years.[7] In the minds of club advocates, discov-

4. P. A. Markov, *The Soviet Theatre* (London: Victor Gollancz, 1934), 137.
5. *Novye etapy samodeiatel'noi khudozhestvennoi raboty* (Leningrad: Teakinopechat', 1930),
11.
6. El Lissitzky, *Russia: An Architecture for World Revolution*, trans. Eric Dluhosch (Cambridge: MIT Press, 1970), 44.
7. On clubs in general, see Gabriele Gorzka, *Arbeiterkultur in der Sowjetunion: Industriearbeiter-Klubs, 1917–1928* (Berlin: Arno Spitz, 1990); John Hatch, "Hangouts and Hangovers:
State, Class and Culture in Moscow's Workers' Club Movement, 1925–1928," *Russian Review* 53, no. 1 (1994): 97–117; idem, "The Formation of Working Class Culture Institutions
during NEP: The Workers' Club Movement in Moscow, 1921–1923," *Carl Beck Papers in*

ering the right kind of inclusive and engaging theatrical work was a crucial step in creating a successful gathering spot. Thus amateur theaters
were doubly blessed (or burdened) with the tasks of community building; they were deemed the ingredient most effective in transforming the
bare walls of an occupied storeroom into a new kind of public space.

After the first chaotic years of the revolution, Soviet state agencies devoted considerable resources to clubs. Trade unions, their primary sponsor, began to construct new buildings devoted solely to club activities.
For Soviet architects, these new spaces offered special challenges; it was
a chance to create an environment that could embody the collectivist
principles of the Russian revolution. So important were these problems
to Soviet designers that a club interior—Alexander Rodchenko's model
workers' club—was chosen to represent the Soviet Union at the International Festival of Industrial Arts in Paris in 1925.[8] Inventive club buildings, most constructed in the late 1920s, served as the premier examples
of Soviet constructivist architecture. The size, form, and placement of
the stage, so central to club activity, became a key issue for a new generation of architects.[9]

No matter where they were staged, amateur performances helped to
legitimize the Soviet state. By seizing on the pressing issues of the day,
many works encouraged army enlistment, mobilized participants for Soviet celebrations, and informed audiences about international events.
Those stages that chose a repertoire of familiar prerevolutionary plays
helped to provide viewers with the rudiments of cultural literacy. Because of their popularity and ability to transmit political and cultural values, amateur stages were extremely useful to the government. At a time
when film equipment was scarce and illiteracy was high, theaters spread
the political message of the revolution. They were also evidence that the
revolutionary state was committed to a mission of enlightenment.

These humble stages even contributed to the Soviet Union's cultural
influence abroad. This was especially true during the years of the First
Five-Year Plan (1928–32), when Soviet industrial expansion provided a

Russian and East European Studies, no. 806 (Pittsburgh: University of Pittsburgh Center for
Russian and East European Studies, 1990).

8. Selim O. Khan-Magomedov, *Rodchenko: The Complete Work* (Cambridge: MIT Press,
1987), 178–86.

9. On club architecture, see V. Khazanova, *Klubnaia zhizn' i arkhitektura kluba.* 2 v.
(Moscow: Rossiiskii institut iskusstvoznaniia, 1994); and Frederick Starr, *Melnikov: Solo Architect in a Mass Society* (Princeton: Princeton University Press, 1978), 127–47.

vivid contrast to capitalist nations trapped in a global depression. The openly agitational, politicized style of amateur performance in this period inspired emulation by many Communist theater groups, from the Chicago Blue Blouses to the Red Rockets in Berlin.[10] Soviet amateurs offered their Western counterparts a model of cultural creation through confrontation with the past, an approach radically opposed to the ideas of the Social Democrats, who still tried to offer workers access to their cultural heritage.[11] Communists everywhere proclaimed that their art would be a "weapon in the hands of the working class." Yet despite this common expression of theater's role, and despite the many similar forms employed, there is one striking difference between agitational theater in Western nations and the Soviet Union. Soviet theaters were agitating for a state that already existed; in the West they were fighting for a state that was yet to be.

Although most Soviet amateurs embraced their agitational tasks, they could still run afoul of the political apparatus. State institutions invested considerable resources to oversee their work, but ultimately it could not be completely controlled. In the 1920s, scripts were prepared and altered at the performance site by individual instructors and the actors themselves. Even government-approved plays could be staged in unexpected ways. One critic writing in the early 1930s was offended by a performance of Nikolai Gogol's satirical play poking fun at the tsarist bureaucracy, *The Inspector General*, because the theater dared to draw parallels with the Soviet bureaucracy.[12] Amateur performances were public forums where participants could express their own political and social visions. As such they always carried the potential for subversion.

10. On Soviet influence, see Richard Stourac and Kathleen McCreery, *Theatre as a Weapon: Workers' Theatre in the Soviet Union, Germany and Britain, 1917–1934* (London: Routledge, 1986); Richard Bodek, *Proletarian Performance in Weimar Berlin: Agitprop, Chorus, and Brecht* (Columbia, S.C.: Camden House, 1997); David Bradby, "The October Group and Theatre under the Front Populaire," in *Politics and Performance in Popular Drama*, ed. David Bradby et al. (Cambridge: Cambridge University Press, 1980); Stuart Cosgrove, "From Shock Troupe to Group Theatre," in *Theatres of the Left, 1880–1935*, ed. Raphael Samuels (London: Routledge, 1984), 168–69; and Ira A. Levine, *Left-Wing Dramatic Theory in the American Theatre* (Ann Arbor: UMI Research Press, 1985), 100–104.

11. On Social Democratic approaches to theater in the 1920s, see Cecil W. Davies, *Theater for the People: The Story of the Volksbühne* (Manchester: Manchester University Press, 1977); Helmut Gruber, *Red Vienna: Experiment in Working-Class Culture, 1914–1934* (New York: Oxford University Press, 1991), ch. 4; and W. L. Guttsman, *Workers' Culture in Weimar Germany: Between Tradition and Commitment* (New York: Berg, 1990), chs. 2 and 8.

12. A. Kasatkina, "Problemy klubnogo repertuara," *Teatr i dramaturgiia* 8 (1933): 52.

Pre-Revolutionary Origins

Soviet amateur theaters drew on the experience, repertoire, and personnel of the Russian popular theater movement. Efforts to democratize the theater and broaden its social base were evident all over Europe in the last decades of the nineteenth century.[13] In Russia, popular theaters (*narodnye teatry*) were sponsored by government agencies, progressive intellectuals, and sometimes even factory owners who built stages at the work site. Supporters believed that edifying forms of entertainment would help to transform the tastes and habits of the lower classes. In addition, some were motivated by altruistic aims. For them Russian elite culture, including the works of Gogol, Anton Chekhov, and Alexander Ostrovsky, was a national treasure that should be shared with all the people.[14]

Advocates of peoples' theater hoped their efforts would counteract less enlightened forms of popular entertainment. They specifically targeted a long tradition of fairground theaters, erected during the spring and winter holiday seasons. Called *balagany*, these temporary wooden structures offered a wide range of works, from comic sketches, to peep shows, to Petrushka plays, the Russian version of Punch and Judy. Initially presented free of charge, with donations requested by performers, these festivities became increasingly commercialized by the late nineteenth century. Entrepreneurs added roller-coaster rides and sometimes even short films to the attractions. They also varied the theatrical repertoire, offering patriotic plays, pantomimes, and scenes from works common on professional stages.[15] Often rowdy affairs enlivened with drinking bouts and fist fights, such entertainments were placed under ever more watchful control by the tsarist government in the last decades of

13. See David Bradby and John McCormack, *The People's Theatre* (London: Croom Helm, 1978), esp. 15–29.

14. On Russian people's theater, see Gary Thurston, *The Popular Theatre Movement in Russia, 1862–1919* (Evanston, Ill.: Northwestern University Press, 1998); idem, "The Impact of Russian Popular Theatre, 1886–1915," *Journal of Modern History* 55, no. 2 (1983): 237–67; E. Anthony Swift, "Theater for the People: The Politics of Popular Culture in Urban Russia, 1861–1917" (Ph.D. dissertation, University of California, Berkeley, 1992); and G. A. Khaichenko, *Russkii narodnyi teatr kontsa XIX-nachala XX veka* (Moscow: Nauka, 1975).

15. On fairground theaters, see Catriona Kelly, *Petrushka: The Russian Carnival Puppet Theatre* (Cambridge: Cambridge University Press, 1990), 19–55. On their transformation in the late nineteenth century, see Al'bin M. Konechnyi, "Popular Carnivals During Mardi Gras and Easter Week in St. Petersburg," *Russian Studies in History* 35, no. 4 (Spring 1997): 52–91, esp. 72–82; and A. F. Nekrylova, *Russkie narodnye gorodskie prazdniki, uveseleniia i zrelishcha* (Leningrad: Iskusstvo, 1984), esp. 163–75.

the regime. Officials moved them away from the central urban areas and even banned alcohol to make them more respectable.[16]

After the revolution of 1905, which stimulated the growth of proletarian institutions, workers began to create their own theaters, often located in clubs and Peoples' Homes funded by the trade union movement. As Anthony Swift's work has shown, Russian workers' theaters did not aim for an experimental or self-generated repertoire. However, participants did insist on deciding for themselves which works would be presented. By and large, they chose from a store of Russian and Western European classics. In particular workers were drawn to plays they felt had a progressive message to convey, such as Ostrovsky's *Poverty Is No Crime*, interpreted by worker audiences as a critique of capitalism, and Gerhart Hauptmann's *The Weavers*, an homage to workers' rebellion.[17]

Rural Russia had its own forms of theatrical entertainments. Drawing on both pagan and Christian traditions, Russian peasants participated in a wide range of ritualistic dramas associated with planting, harvesting, and the important life passages of birth, marriage, and death. Peasants also engaged in scripted games and improvisations. At least by the nineteenth century, these improvisations had evolved into more developed plot outlines for non-ritualistic dramas. Often performed at Lenten festivals, these included short satirical works and longer plays distinguished by their episodic structure and their free relationship to historical material. The best known of these works, *The Boat* (*Lodka*) examining a trip down the Volga, and *Tsar Maksimilian*, offering a moving confrontation between a tsar and his son, served as bases for improvised entertainment well into the Soviet period.[18]

Soviet amateur theaters drew on these different traditions of popular theater. Many cultural circles designed to foster amateur theatricals continued their work almost unchanged after the revolution. The famous Ligovskii People's Home in Petrograd/Leningrad, founded in 1903, served as an educational base for a generation of worker authors. After the revolution, it continued to sponsor the well-known traveling theatrical troupe led by Pavel Gaideburov, a director devoted to spreading the classics of Russian and world theater to the lower classes. The set de-

---

16. Von Geldern, *Bolshevik Festivals*, 106–7; Swift, "Theater for the People," 259–60.

17. Swift, "Workers' Theater," 67–94. See also Mark D. Steinberg, *Moral Communities* (Berkeley: University of California Press, 1992), 241.

18. Elizabeth Warner, *The Russian Folk Theatre* (The Hague: Mouton, 1977), esp. 127–76; A. F. Nekrylova and N. I. Savushkina, "Russkii fol'klornyi teatr," in L. M. Leonov, ed., *Narodnyi teatr* (Moscow: Sovetskaia Rossiia, 1991), 5–20.

signer Vasilii Polenov assumed control of an organization to aid workers' and peasants' theater in 1912. His center continued its work after
1917, now under the auspices of the Soviet state's cultural ministry,
Narkompros.[19] These artists shared many Bolsheviks' respect for established high culture, as well as their contempt for the commercialism of
the capitalist marketplace.[20] Thus, amateur theater provided a way for
sectors of the old intelligentsia to find an institutional home under the
new regime.

Amateur Theater in Soviet Cultural Debates

As an art form directly involving the lower classes, the very population the Bolsheviks claimed to serve, amateur theaters found themselves
at the center of controversies concerning the form and function of revolutionary culture. Bolsheviks were passionately committed to bringing
about a wide-scale cultural transformation or, in their words, a "cultural
revolution" that would solidify the gains of the political upheaval.[21] But
this was hardly a straightforward process, since they did not share a
common vision of what the cultured Soviet citizen should be like.

Nonetheless, one assumption the new state's leaders did share was
that theater would be an important tool in crafting this new individual.
Theater was, in the words of Katerina Clark, "the cradle of Soviet culture."[22] As an art form that could unify actor and audience, theater was
believed to have special abilities to create shared community values. It
did not rely simply on words but melded language with color, light,

19. On Polenov's center, see "Sektsiia sodeistviia ustroistva derevenskikh, fabrichnykh i
shkol'nykh teatrov," 15 February 1915, GARF, f. 628 (Tsentral'nyi Dom narodnogo tvorchestva im. N. K. Krupskoi), op. 1, d. 1, ll. 22–24, and "Shtaty Doma teatral'nogo
prosveshcheniia im. V. D. Polenova" (1921), ibid., d. 104, l. 2.

20. On the shared values of the prerevolutionary intelligentsia and the Bolshevik leadership, see Jeffrey Brooks, *When Russia Learned to Read: Literacy and Popular Literature,
1861–1917* (Princeton: Princeton University Press, 1985), esp. 295–353.

21. By "cultural revolution," I do not mean the limited period of cultural radicalism during the First Five-Year Plan. Rather, I am referring to the broad Bolshevik project of cultural transformation that included literacy, cleanliness, and improved standards of health,
as well as distinctly Soviet art forms. See Michael David-Fox, "What Is Cultural Revolution?" *Russian Review* 58 (April 1999): 181–201, for a discussion of the history and significance of this concept.

22. Clark, *Petersburg*, 104. On the centrality of theater to early Bolshevik cultural projects, see also Julie Anne Cassiday, "The Theater of the World and the Theater of the State:
Drama and the Show Trial in Early Soviet Russia" (Ph.D. dissertation, Stanford University,
1995), ch. 1.

music, and movement. By integrating the intellect and the emotions, theater had the power to create new patterns of behavior. Acting on these premises, the Bolsheviks moved quickly to nationalize important professional theaters and monitor the work of impromptu stages.

Questions about performance space and repertoire drew amateur actors, often unwittingly, into the long-running controversy between advocates of realism and the theatrical avant-garde. Avant-gardists contended that amateur theaters were uniquely situated to accomplish one of their most cherished goals—to erase the division between performers on the stage and the passive viewer audience. Vsevolod Meyerhold, the nation's most famous experimental director, opened a "Club Methodological Laboratory" to train directors and writers for club theaters.[23] His students endorsed stylized, episodic performances that could be altered through group participation. Many amateurs embraced this direction as a way to make their performances directly relevant to local struggles. These methods, they argued, provided them with an avenue for self-expression and self-determination.

For proponents of realism, the amateur stage had a different purpose, namely "to illuminate life, satisfy spiritual longing, and aid in further education," in the words of one commentator.[24] Professionals from the Moscow Art Theater taught Stanislavsky's acting techniques in order to help amateurs create persuasive characters. Realist playwrights presented stories that would teach an inspiring history of the revolution, offering actors and viewers positive role models to emulate. Supporters of this direction believed their work nurtured a socialist consciousness, while the loosely structured plays inspired by the avant-garde only confused audiences. Their insistence on uplifting tales and stellar heroes, still very fluid in the 1920s, eventually solidified into the fixed rules of socialist realism.

As competitors for an urban audience, amateur theaters were also drawn into debates over the continuing existence of commercial culture in the Soviet Union. In the years of the New Economic Policy (1921–28), when limited capitalist enterprise was permitted, Russian cities saw a growth in restaurants, dance halls, and movie theaters playing foreign films. A segment of the cultural bureaucracy saw this as a threat to socialism, questioning the value and indeed the morality of "purely enter-

23. On this studio, see Iurii Kobrin, *Teatr imeni Vs. Meierkhol'da i rabochii zritel'* (Moscow: Moskovskoe teatral'noe izdatel'stvo, 1926), 35, and ch. 2.

24. A. M., "Kakim dozhen byt' rabochii teatr," *Novyi zritel'* 11 (1926): 5.

taining" forms of amusement. Their strict position was opposed by others who insisted that work designed for educational purposes alone would alienate audiences and drive them away. This controversy, which Denise Youngblood has called the "entertainment or enlightenment debate," raged for much of the 1920s.[25] It was hardly unique to Soviet Russia, as left-leaning cultural leaders everywhere questioned how best to approach popular entertainments such as adventure films and variety shows that were generated in the capitalist marketplace.[26]

As self-styled educators of their audiences, amateur performers tried to mix enlightenment and entertainment. During the 1920s, potential viewers had many other choices for an evening on the town. Innovators tried to devise politically acceptable works that incorporated appealing elements of urban mass culture. They integrated slide shows into performances to make them approximate films. They used melodies popular in cafés and night clubs. These efforts met with derision from puritanical critics, who found them at best frivolous and at worst a dangerous concession to capitalist decadence.

In addition, amateur theaters were plagued by an even more fundamental problem that went to the heart of Soviet social organization: What should these theaters' relationship to professionals be? This question was highly politicized in the early Soviet years, not only in the arts but also in the army, trade unions, and education. Everywhere, the revolution provoked hard-fought battles over the status of experts and the significance of expertise, battles that sought to determine the meaning of social equality in the world's first socialist state.[27]

Participants in amateur theaters had no easy answers to these accursed questions, proposing two contradictory models for the cultured Soviet citizen. Some practioners were inspired by ideas reminiscent of the young Karl Marx and Friedrich Engels, who claimed: "The exclusive concentration of artistic talent in a few individuals and its consequent suppression in the large masses is the result of the division of labor. . . . In a communist organization of society there are no painters; at most there are people who, among other things, also paint."[28] According to

25. Denise J. Youngblood, *Movies for the Masses: Popular Cinema and Soviet Society in the 1920s* (Cambridge: Cambridge University Press, 1992), 35–49.

26. Gruber, *Red Vienna*, 123–35; Andreas Huyssen, "The Hidden Dialectic: Avant-garde—Technology—Mass Culture," in his *After the Great Divide: Modernism, Mass Culture, Postmodernism* (Bloomington: Indiana University Press, 1986), 3–15.

27. See Richard Stites, *Revolutionary Dreams* (New York: Oxford University Press, 1989), 124–44.

28. Karl Marx and Friedrich Engels, *The German Ideology*, in Karl Marx and Friedrich Engels, *Literature and Art* (New York: Progress Publishers, 1947), 76.

this ideal, if amateur theatrical work spread widely among the population, established stages might eventually be abandoned altogether. Others insisted, however, that the Soviet system would show its superiority by discovering talented workers who would pass through amateur theaters to a career on the professional stage. These models were based on conflicting ideas of theater itself—was it a participatory activity infusing all of life or a skilled profession to be learned?

"Do-it-yourself theater" aptly describes amateur activity during the Bolshevik revolution and the Civil War, the subject of chapter 1. Central control was weak, accounting in part for the remarkable diversity of repertoire during this chaotic period. Original agitational works were common, particularly in the influential theaters of the Red Army. In addition, prerevolutionary classical plays as well as less edifying potboilers found their actors and audiences. Civil War amateur theater was in large part a battle for public visibility—with actors seizing the right to new public roles. Unlikely urban environments were transformed into performance spaces—restaurants, basements, and, most symbolically, gathering spots for the former privileged classes. The quality of performances was usually indifferent; actors took little time to prepare and they had few props or costumes. But a polished presentation was not essential for audience or actors—the important thing was that the performance was taking place at all.

In the early years of the New Economic Policy (NEP), many amateur actors and directors wanted to continue what they regarded as the real accomplishments of the Civil War, especially its improvisational, politicized theatrical experiments. Chapter 2 examines efforts to make "small forms"—skits, mime, circus techniques, and loosely connected episodic works—the main focus of amateur work. Its proponents claimed that the amateur theater of small forms was more innovative and invigorating, and more closely tied to daily life, than anything performed on professional stages. A few took these ideas to extremes, rejecting any kind of professional involvement. Enthusiastic voices in favor of an amateur theater of small forms found a broad public forum in the early 1920s, as theater circles experimented with methods to educate and entertain audiences simultaneously.

By the late NEP period, however, there were clear signs that small forms were beginning to lose their constituency. Chapter 3 investigates a turn away from small forms after 1925. Criticism came in part from the viewing audience, especially select worker-reporters (called *rabochie korrespondenty*, or *rabkory*), who had grown tired of well-worn stereotypes and predictability.[29] The debate over the repertoire of club theater, generally restricted to specialized journals in the early 1920s, began to emerge as a topic of national discussion. Cultural bureaucrats insisted that positive changes in professional theaters had made the oppositional stance of amateur stages obsolete; now they advanced the idea of a *smychka*, or union, between the amateur and professional arts.[30] They advised amateurs to turn to larger works and perhaps even to try the same plays that were gaining audiences on professional stages.

Chapter 4 offers a case study of a particularly influential amateur theater, the Leningrad Theater of Working-Class Youth, or TRAM, sponsored by the Leningrad Komsomol. It garnered more national and international attention than any other Soviet amateur stage, in large part because of its original repertoire. Begun in the early 1920s, it initially staged small forms. By the mid-1920s, however, it moved to more sustained plays written by its own youthful members. Helped by the Komsomol press, it soon acquired a national following and local affiliates in other urban centers. Its members saw themselves as separate from and, indeed, superior to professionals in the theater. TRAM members developed what they believed to be the clearest articulation of *samodeiatel'nyi teatr*. They were not actors but rather activists who drew their material from the streets, factories, and dormitories. Their aim was to influence the behavior of viewers.

Yet for all their claims to a radical aesthetics, TRAM theaters still bore many identifying marks of established theater. They performed three- to five-act plays that offered a cohesive narrative. They presented their work on conventional stages, with sophisticated lighting, costumes, and set designs. Chapter 5 examines a much more extreme form of cultural experimentation, the agitprop brigades. These small, mobile, and politically motivated groups flourished during the years of the First Five-Year Plan. Brigades were composed of young enthusiasts from trade unions, clubs, and factories. Touring work sites and the countryside to drum up support for the industrialization and collectivization drives, they prepared agitational skits and short plays from the raw materials at hand— newspapers, public speeches, and production statistics. Brigade participants were distrustful of professional theater workers and playwrights, who allegedly had no knowledge of daily struggle at the workplace. In-

29. See, for example, V. Gomello, "Nuzhna-li p'esa rabochemu klubu?" *Rabochii i teatr* 7 (1925): 19.
30. "Itogi Vsesoiuznogo soveshchaniia pri Glavpolitprosvete," *Zhizn' iskusstva* 1 (1926): 2.

stead, they tried to rely on their own experiences as laborers and political activists. Using aggressive methods inspired by shock workers in
production, the brigades aimed to root out old habits and shame those
who practiced them.[31]

But the dominance of agitprop brigades was brief. Viewers complained about their monotonous repertoire and lack of believable heroes. Perhaps more serious, critics began to call the political reliability of
agitprop brigades into question. By the time that the first National
Olympiad of Amateur Art was held in Moscow in the summer of 1932,
this form of theatrical activism faced overwhelmingly negative criticism
in the cultural press. Judges and journalists advised amateur circles to
attempt works by contemporary Soviet playwrights and also to take on
classical plays. When addressing political themes, amateur theaters had
to learn to do so "artistically," which was only possible with the intervention of those trained in technique and familiar with the long history
of Russian and world theater.[32]

The final chapter examines amateur stages in the 1930s. The evolving
doctrine of socialist realism, which was applied to amateur as well as
professional art, brought increased standardization. The methods of a
few professional groups, particularly the Moscow Art Theater, were imported to amateur stages. Established theaters supplied directors and
opened comprehensive training programs for amateur circles. New
stages built in the 1930s looked like their professional prototypes, with
proscenium stages and a clear division between the performers and the
audience. Select clubs in the capital cities now had performance halls
seating thousands, large stages, and healthy financial support, allowing
them to mount elaborate productions.

The acceptable repertoire for amateur stages narrowed precipitously
during the 1930s. At the 1938 Moscow competition of amateur art, the
end point of this book, amateur circles performed a short list of contemporary works along with a limited assortment of prerevolutionary classics.[33] Although participants and critics paid lip service to the independent role of samodeiatel'nyi teatr—its close ties to audiences and ability to
provide insights into everyday affairs—in fact, the biggest compliment
that could be bestowed on an amateur stage in the late 1930s was that its
work met professional standards.

31. L. Tasin, "Blizhaishie zadachi dramkruzhkov," Zhizn' iskusstva 36 (1929): 2.
32. A. Kasatkina, "Iskusstvo millionov," Izvestiia 22 August 1932.
33. L. Subbotin, "Nekotorye vyvody iz smotra teatral'noi samodeiatel'nosti," Kul'turnaia rabota profsoiuzov 12 (1938): 72–77.

Assessing the Amateur

In her study of amateur films in the United States, Patricia Zimmermann traces the emergence of amateurism as a concept important to the late nineteenth century, when professionalization became a dominant force in American public life. Both defenders and critics of amateurism examined this phenomenon through a language of stark dichotomies. The professional worked for money, while the amateur worked for pleasure; the professional labored in public, while the amateur moved largely in the private sphere; the professional expressed commonly shared, rational values, while the amateur injected spontaneous, localized elements into creation. She concludes, "Amateurism deflected the chaotic, the incoherent, and the spontaneous into leisure and private life so that public time could persist as methodical, controllable, and regulated."[34]

These reflections on amateurism's place within capitalism offer a chance to locate its distinctive features in the Soviet system. Certainly, neither Soviet participants nor observers believed amateur theatricals took place in the "private sphere." Clubs were, after all, a "public hearth," valued precisely for freeing participants from the narrow, philistine confines of their private homes. Soviet amateur theaters had very important public responsibilities—to educate their audiences, to mark public holidays, to take part in public demonstrations, and to voice the creative ideas of their constituents. Furthermore, the entire concept of a "private life" was denounced as a bourgeois construct in the early Soviet years. As Eric Naiman's work has shown, early Soviet social discourse had nothing but disdain and fear for the private sphere.[35]

Soviet amateurs were also not separate from the world of work in the same way as their capitalist counterparts. Western amateurs often justified their activities as a way to maintain a spark of individual expression within an increasingly regimented capitalist economy.[36] By contrast, Soviet advocates argued that their style of amateurism revealed the superiority of the socialist system. In their free time, Soviet citizens turned to edifying activities that raised their cultural level and facilitated collec-

34. Patricia R. Zimmermann, *Reel Families: A Social History of Amateur Film* (Bloomington: Indiana University Press, 1995), 1–11, quotation 11.

35. Eric Naiman, *Sex in Public: The Incarnation of Early Soviet Ideology* (Princeton: Princeton University Press, 1997), esp. ch. 2.

36. This is a central theme of Wayne Booth's *For the Love of It: Amateuring and Its Rivals* (Chicago: University of Chicago Press, 1999).

tive interaction. Citizens' performances were designed to inspire workers with civic pride and professional skills. Soviet skits and plays of the
1920s addressed the flaws and accomplishments of the work environment. And even in the 1930s, when models of amateur participation
changed radically, amateur actors asserted that the discipline required
for performances increased their labor productivity.

However, in one important respect Soviet and Western amateurism
held something in common. They both illuminated the differences between regimented professional activity and the spontaneous, self-regu-
lated work of the non-professional. The very term that the Soviets chose
for the amateur—*samodeiatel'nost'*—can be translated as autonomous action.[37] Soviet defenses of amateur theater put forward in the 1920s underscored precisely this aspect of amateur work—that it gave voice to
the local and particular in a way that professionalism never could. Amateurism was the source of inspiration for stagnant professionals, whose
training and repertoire could quickly become stale. Outspoken advocates of amateur theater in the capitalist world have expressed their
ideas in much the same terms.[38]

It was precisely the homemade, unpredictable quality of amateur
work that concerned Soviet regulators. They viewed the amateur stage
as a potential purveyor of low cultural values, degraded language, sexual titillation, and dangerous political ideas. During the 1920s and the
years of the First Five-Year Plan, power shifted back and forth between
those favoring either more spontaneity or more control. However, by
the 1930s many avenues for independent creation had been blocked.
The repertoire was tightly regulated, stages were now constructed along
highly conventional lines, and professional artists supervised essential
elements of training programs. The overseers of amateur theaters took
all possible pains to determine that amateur art would become methodical, controllable, and regulated, eliminating any stark contrast with the
professional.

Yet even under Stalin, amateur theater at times proved difficult to
control. One critic was appalled by a 1936 Moscow amateur production

37. Indeed, I translated the term this way in my first works on this topic. See Lynn
Mally, "Autonomous Theater and the Origins of Socialist Realism: The 1932 Olympiad of
Amateur Art," *Russian Review* 52 (April 1993): 198–212.

38. See, for example, the comments of Bonamy Dobrée, who determined that "the amateur has an extremely important, indeed vital part to play . . . in maintaining just that contact with the common apprehensions of life without which an art becomes stale or thin."
(*The Amateur and the Theatre* [London: Hogarth Press, 1947], 6).

of Nikolai Pogodin's *Aristocrats*, a very popular play depicting the rehabilitation of criminals sent to build the White Sea Canal. According to
this critic, the criminals were portrayed as romantic, tragic figures. By
contrast, their secret police overseers, the intended heroes of the piece,
looked wooden and unconvincing. How could the Moscow trade union
leadership have allowed such a raw and unfinished work to be performed in public, queried the critic in a tone of moral outrage.[39] Although the director meekly denied any illicit intentions, amateur performances still permitted subversive interpretations.

39. M. B., "Dekada samodeiatel'nykh teatrov," *Klub* 6 (1936): 29.

1
The Revolution Loves the Theater

"THEATER IS the self-educator of the people," proclaimed a broadside published by the new state's cultural ministry in 1919. "The revolution loves the theater and in revolutionary times theater comes alive and blossoms."[1] This statement attempted to explain the remarkable proliferation of theaters during the first years of the new regime. Some were sponsored by the central government, like the broad network of Red Army theaters; some had local institutional sponsors, such as regional soviets and city governments; and many were impromptu, spontaneous creations by factory councils, newly formed clubs, and informal groups of friends. Given these new groups' ephemeral nature, a precise count is impossible, but the back pages of local newspapers were filled with advertisements for amateur performances. Enthusiastic Bolshevik supporters used this explosion of theatrical activity as proof of the emancipatory power of the revolution. "Future historians will note that during a time of the most bloody and cruel revolution, all of Russia was acting," opined the art historian Piotr Kogan.[2]

This explosion in amateur theater work provoked anxiety as well as pride. Bewildered Russian intellectuals were at loss for an explanation,

1. "Polozhenie o 1-m Vserossiiskom s"ezde po raboche-krest'ianskomu teatru," *Iskusstvo kommuny* 16 February 1919: 5.
2. P. Kogan, "Sotsialisticheskii teatr v gody revoliutsii," *Vestnik teatra* (henceforth cited as VT) 40 (1919): 3–4. See also N. Krupskaia, "Glavpolitprosvet i iskusstvo," *Pravda* 13 February 1921, cited in *Pedagogicheskie sochineniia*, v. 7 (Moscow: Izdatel'stvo Akademii pedagogicheskikh nauk, 1956), 56.

likening the phenomenon to fevers, epidemics, or even psychosis.[3] Many professionals saw a threat to theater as an art form. They bemoaned the untrained actors, the impromptu repertoire, and the shoddy appearance of amateur performances that took place without their oversight. State cultural bureaucrats charged with supervising theaters worried about their ability to channel this frenetic activity that was only nominally under their control. As one high-ranking central official wrote with some despair about amateur stages, "As yet, we know very little about them."[4]

Although their voices are harder to capture, the participants in this rush to theater appeared to have different standards of judgment. For them, acting was a way to enter the public sphere—and thus to lay claim to a new community in which they would have a voice. Performing new works they had helped to shape gave articulation to their revolutionary visions. But even if the works performed were not new, acting meant seizing a public role. In their accounts of the period, both amateur actors and viewers seemed amazed that the performances were happening at all. Eduard Dune's vivid recollections of the first months of the revolution in a large factory on the outskirts of Moscow give a central place to theater as a builder of community. The wife of a skilled worker discovered her talents as a director, while the sets ("as good as those in any provincial theater") were designed by a factory painter: "It was a real eye-opener for many, who were seeing theater for the first time and were captivated by our simple entertainments."[5]

Dune's sentiments are echoed in the memoirs of theater group members at a Moscow textile factory: "The first performances we did on our own, without a leader. We put on small works from Chekhov and other authors. The very fact that workers were performing on stage, even without a leader, made a huge impression. People were proud and said, 'What a life!' "[6] In these accounts, the amateur standing of the actors, people barely differentiated from the viewing audience, was central to

---

3. See, for example, P. A. Markov, *The Soviet Theatre* (London: Victor Gollancz, 1934), 137; Ilya Ehrenburg, *People and Life, 1891–1921*, trans. Anna Bostock (New York: Knopf, 1962), 321–22; and Serge Wolkonsky, *My Reminiscences*, trans. A. E. Chamot (London: Hutchinson, 1924), vol. 2, 219–20.

4. V. Tikhonovich, "Tochki nad i," VT 66 (1920): 2.

5. Eduard M. Dune, *Notes of a Red Guard*, trans. and ed. Diane Koenker and Steven Smith (Urbana: Illinois University Press, 1993), 40.

6. *Klub, kak on est'* (Moscow: Trud i kniga, 1929), 47.

the performance's appeal. As one newspaper critic determined, "These events eliminated the forced and destructive passivity of the viewer and turned the entire hall—both actors and viewers—into a unified, merged whole."[7]

The links that anthropologists and performance theorists have drawn between "aesthetic drama" and "social drama" offer insights into this enthusiasm for theater in a time of revolution. Aesthetic drama is what usually comes to mind when we think of theater. Its elements are almost entirely prearranged. Actors use a prepared text, perform in a fixed spot, and use established theatrical techniques of staging (lighting, scenery, props, etc.) and acting (declamation and movement). They are separate from their audience. The goal of aesthetic drama is to affect some sort of transformation in the consciousness of the viewers, even if that change is only temporary.[8]

Social dramas are sparked by real-life events. Victor Turner, who developed the concept of the social drama, applied this term to insurrections and revolutions. These moments of rupture arise in conflict situations, especially when groups try to occupy a new place in the social system. The participants act out a crisis in society, which finally results in a re-evaluation of the social order. In the social drama, there is no hard and fast distinction between the actors and the viewers. Both are altered through the process, and the change in this case can be permanent.[9]

Although aesthetic drama functions primarily on the stage and social drama can be played out anywhere, these two forms are nonetheless closely intertwined. As Victor Turner writes:

> The stage drama, when it is meant to do more than entertain—though entertainment is always one of its vital aims—is a metacommentary, explicit or implicit, witting or unwitting, on the major social dramas of its social context (wars, revolutions, scandals, institutional changes.) . . . Life itself now becomes a mirror held up to art, and the living now *perform* their lives, for the protagonists of a social drama, a "drama of living," have been equipped by

7. N. R., "Teatr vchera i segodnia," *Krasnaia gazeta* 7 September 1919.

8. On the elements of aesthetic drama, see Richard Schechner, *Performance Theory*, rev. ed. (New York: Routledge, 1988), esp. 166–72.

9. On social drama, see Victor Turner, "Social Dramas and Ritual Metaphors," and "Hidalgio: History as Social Drama," in *Dramas, Fields, and Metaphors* (Ithaca: Cornell University Press, 1974), esp. 37–41, 99, 123. For explicit comparisons between aesthetic and social drama, see Schechner, *Performance Theory*, 171–72, 187–93, 232.

aesthetic drama with some of their most salient opinions, imageries, tropes, and ideological perspectives.[10]

In an attempt to concretize Turner's abstract language, we might ask what amateur actors were learning from the roles they adopted during the Russian revolution. How did they attempt to apply these lessons to the new life they believed the revolution would bring? Nikolai L'vov, a director of amateur groups before and after 1917, grappled with these issues when he tried to assess why so many people were turning to the amateur stage. He believed that both the theater and the revolution were the creators of new futures: "Now, as new ideas make their way through the population at large, and as people begin to see the possibilities of the new life, the broad popular classes immediately feel the call to the stage. Here they find an avenue for their desire for a brighter life. Here they have a chance to expand their spiritual life with new and unknown experiences."[11]

The Problem of Naming

Before the revolution, theater aimed at the lower classes was commonly called "popular theater" (*narodnyi teatr*). When the Bolshevik government began to oversee professional and amateur theatrical activity, one of the first struggles was over language. What was the new state's Commissariat of Education (known by its acronym, Narkompros) supposed to call the burgeoning impromptu theaters that it hoped to control? Anatolii Lunacharskii, the head of Narkompros, initially stuck with the old appellation.[12] But the term "popular theater" struck many others as anachronistic. They began searching for a new descriptive terminology that bore fewer prerevolutionary connotations. Platon Kerzhentsev, an important cultural figure, tried out a number of alternatives in his influential book *Creative Theater* (*Tvorcheskii teatr*), which went through five editions in the first five years of the new regime. He referred to a vaguely defined "creative theater," a "socialist theater," and a "proletarian theater."[13]

10. Viktor Turner, *On the Edge of the Bush: Anthropology as Experience* (Tucson: University of Arizona Press, 1985), 300–301, cited in Schechner, *Performance Theory*, 191.

11. Nikolai L'vov, "Tiaga na stsenu," VT 56 (1919): 8.

12. Lars Kleberg, " 'People's Theater' and the Revolution: On the History of a Concept before and after 1917," in A. A. Nilsson, ed., *Art, Society, Revolution: Russia 1917–1921* (Stockholm: Almqvist and Wiksell International, 1979), 191–92.

13. P. M. Kerzhentsev, *Tvorcheskii teatr*, 5th ed. (Moscow: Gosizdat, 1923), passim.

In early 1919 Narkompros formed a division of "worker-peasant theater," which marked an initial attempt to find a new terminology for
amateur efforts by the lower classes. Its first leader was the long-time activist in popular theater, Valentin Tikhonovich. For Tikhonovich,
worker-peasant theater was a logical term to embody the art of the laboring classes. Despite the anti-peasant bias of many proletarian-based
organizations like the Proletkult, Tikhonovich believed that these two
social groups shared a lot in common: they both worked, many factory
laborers were not that far removed from the land, and many peasants
spent part of the year in a factory. Rather than turning their backs on society's largest social group, workers should collaborate with peasants to
create a new theater.[14]

The first national conference on worker-peasant theater showed quite
vividly, however, that many were not convinced by this line of argu-
mentation. Difficulties emerged already in the planning stages. At a Petrograd meeting called in April 1919, the main speaker was the theater
historian Vsevolod Vsevolodskii-Gerngross, who was engaged in compiling a detailed history of Russian folk theater. He bemoaned the separation between actor and audience created by the introduction of Western European theater in the eighteenth century; in his view the
revolution's task was to reintroduce native theatrical traditions. This
speech drew a hostile response from the audience, especially from one
speaker who decried the notion of separating art according to class.[15]

After many delays, the worker-peasant theater conference finally
opened in November 1919. It attracted representatives from a wide
range of organizations sponsoring theatrical activity, including
Narkompros, the Proletkult, the Red Army, trade unions, and cooperatives. Given this diverse constituency, it is hardly surprising that they
reached no shared consensus. A majority position emerged at the conference, presenting what could be called an updated version of the mission of popular theaters before the revolution. Supported by provincial
delegates, cooperatives, and professional theater workers, this position
applauded efforts to improve theatrical quality, to make critical use of
progressive elements from the prerevolutionary theatrical heritage, and
to strengthen cooperation between workers and peasants.[16]

14. V. Tikhonovich, "Chto takoe raboche-krest'ianskii teatr," VT 12 (1919): 3.

15. "Gorodskoe soveshchanie po voprosu o raboche-krest'ianskom teatre," *Zhizn'
iskusstva* 3 April 1919.

16. V. Tikhonovich, "Nashi raznoglasiia," VT 45 (1919): 4–5; idem, *Samodeiatel'nyi teatr*
(Vologda: Oblastnoi otdel gosizdata, 1922), 32.

However, a vocal minority, made up of Communists, Red Army representatives, and members of the Proletkult organization, disputed all these points. They refused to endorse any suggestions passed by the majority, insisting instead on a separate set of resolutions.[17] While the majority endorsed cooperation between its two constituencies, the Communist faction believed that peasants could be helpful only insofar as they subordinated themselves to workers. "Proletarian theater," read one of the minority resolutions, "is the task of workers themselves, along with those peasants who are willing to accept their ideology." Faction members also rejected the inclusive attitude the majority had formulated toward the artistic accomplishments of past generations. "[Workers' theater] must devote all its energies to formulating a new repertoire, without any borrowings from the past," they insisted.[18]

Perhaps most provocatively, the minority faction at the conference determined that proletarian theater should not embrace conventional forms of performance. Instead, they should aim for "mass action" (*massovoe deistvo*), by which they meant festivals, processions, demonstrations, and the celebration of new holidays.[19] In essence, they were advocating social dramas that would affect both participants and viewers, as opposed to "old-fashioned" aesthetic drama. The conference chair, Tikhonovich, warned that while new forms were important, conventional plays were still needed. Focusing on festivals alone would mark the end of art. Many provincial delegates felt alienated from the rancorous discussions, complaining that they received little relevant help for the theaters they represented and came away without any clear understanding of what mass action was supposed to be.[20]

The fractious conference on worker-peasant theater ended the tenuous influence of the Worker-Peasant Theater Division over urban amateur stages. Only in existence for another year after the conference, the division spent its last months scrambling for more funds from Narkompros. Meetings were marked by the same ruptures that had split the conference.[21] Without the authority or the staff to guide amateur stages, it continued mainly as an information-gathering body, compiling statis-

17. N. L['vov], "Nedelia o s"ezde," VT 43 (1919): 4.
18. "Deklaratsiia fraktsii kommunistov po voprosu proletarskogo teatra, vnesennaia na sessiiu Soveta RKT 28/IX 1919g." GARF, f. 628 (Tsentral'nyi dom narodnogo tvorchestva im. N. K. Krupskoi), op. 1, d. 2, l. 57.
19. Ibid.
20. L['vov], "Nedelia o s"ezde," 4–5; N. L['vov], "S"ezd po raboche-krest'ianskomu teatru," VT 44 (1919): 2.
21. "Vtoraia sessiia Soveta raboche-krest'ianskogo teatra," VT 57 (1920): 4–5.

tics about the social composition and repertoire of urban and rural amateur groups.[22]

After this debacle, theater activists began looking for a less explosive term for amateur theatrical activities. Tikhonovich and others championed *samodeiatel'nyi teatr*—translated literally as "self-activated" or "do-it-yourself" theater—as a more neutral and inclusive category for all nonprofessional stages. He made the switch himself during the Civil War. In December 1917, Tikhonovich finished *Narodnyi teatr*, an overview of amateur stages. A much amended version (which still had the same basic organizational structure), entitled *Samodeiatel'nyi teatr* was published in 1922.[23] This new term, which I have translated as "amateur theater," was meant to sidestep old definitional quagmires. It was not class specific and thus could be applied equally to workers, peasants, white-collar workers, and students engaged in amateur activity. It removed the troublesome adjective *narodnyi*, associated with the efforts of "bourgeois" intellectuals before the revolution. Users also rejected another Russian term for "amateur," *liubitel'*, rooted (as it is in English) in the verb "to love." In the early Soviet period, *liubitel'skii teatr* connoted all that was bad in amateur activities, such as posturing for good parts and wasting time in frivolous leisure-time pursuits. *Liubitel'stvo* took on all the negative connotations of dilettantism.[24] By contrast, *samodeiatel'nyi teatr* came to stand for a new Soviet approach that would foster collective interaction and bring about productive social results.

Samodeiatel'nost' is an old Russian word for amateurism; it was hardly an invention of Soviet bureaucrats. Long before the revolution, amateur theaters had been called *samodeiatel'nye teatry*. Nonetheless, the term was imbued with new significance in the Soviet era. In its literal meaning of "self-activity," *samodeiatel'nost'* was claimed by the Soviet trade union movement as the embodiment of the spirit of the autonomous working class. The Proletkult also appropriated *samodeiatel'nost'* as one

22. See, for example, its report "Samodeiatel'nye teatral'nye kruzhki v 1919 i 1920 godakh," GARF, f. 2313 (Glavpolitprosvet), op. 1, d. 134, ll. 3–4.

23. V. V. Tikhonovich, *Narodnyi teatr* (Moscow: V. Magnussen, 1918); idem, *Samodeiatel'nyi teatr* (Vologda: Oblastnoi otdel Gosizdata, 1922); Kleberg, " 'People's Theater' and the Revolution," 192–94; V. Filippov, *Puti samodeiatel'nogo teatra* (Moscow: Gosudarstvennaia akademiia khudozhestvennykh nauk, 1927), 57. Filippov credits Tikhonovich with the popularization of the term.

24. See, for example, Adrian Piotrovskii's denunciation of *liubitel'skii teatr* in *Krasnoarmeiskii teatr: Instruktsiia k teatral'noi rabote v Krasnoi Armii* (Petrograd: Izdatel'stvo Petrogradskogo voennogo okruga, 1921), 4. In this study, I have translated *liubitel'skii* as "dilettantish" and *samodeiatel'nyi* as "amateur."

of its cardinal principles. This might help to explain why a term without class specifications was chosen at a time when most people were embracing class labels; workers' organizations had already appropriated this concept as their own.

With its connotations of autonomy and self-expression, *samodeiatel'nost'* carried a potential threat to higher authorities.[25] State leaders wanted to encourage the ambitions and talents of the lower classes, particularly the working class, on which they based their legitimacy. These new historical actors needed to be able to "do things themselves." But what would happen if they acted in ways that offended or challenged the new government? What if their creative work proved difficult to guide and control? The possibility that self-activity might turn into dangerous spontaneity was a constant worry for early Soviet leaders. Spontaneity, *stikhiinost'*, was a negative term in the Bolshevik lexicon, linked to anarchism, mindless rebellion, and ignorance. The lower classes, with their tendency toward spontaneity, needed to be led by the Communist Party toward consciousness.[26]

Autonomous self-activity was a slippery category on the continuum between spontaneity and consciousness. Advanced, "conscious" workers could be trusted to choose edifying pursuits; their activity bolstered the state's own arguments for power. When exercised by the unsophisticated, however, *samodeiatel'nost'* posed a potential threat to order. Thus the Bolsheviks were in the paradoxical position of continually encouraging self-activity while simultaneously trying to control it. Many of the conflicts surrounding Soviet amateur theater were embodied within the very name used to describe it.

The Locus of Performance

Amateur theaters were for the most part situated in clubs, a broad category that could describe anything from a well-appointed center built

---

25. For an examination of the conflicting meanings of *samodeiatel'nost'*, see James von Geldern, *Bolshevik Festivals, 1917–1920* (Berkeley: University of California Press, 1993), 28, 126–27, 146, 209, 216; Lynn Mally, *Culture of the Future: The Proletkult Movement in Revolutionary Russia* (Berkeley: University of California Press, 1990), 36–44, 232–39; Rosalinde Sartorti, "Stalinism and Carnival: Organisation and Aesthetics of Political Holidays," in Hans Günther, ed., *The Culture of the Stalin Period* (New York: St. Martins, 1990), 57–61.

26. There is a large literature on spontaneity and consciousness as important categories in Bolshevik political theory. For a discussion especially relevant for cultural history, see Katerina Clark, *The Soviet Novel: History as Ritual* (Chicago: University of Chicago Press, 1981), 22–24.

before the revolution to a requisitioned noble palace or converted store-room.[27] Although urban clubs for the laboring population existed well before the revolution, they expanded rapidly during 1917 and even more chaotically during the Civil War. Many different organizations were responsible for club formation. One short list of clubs in a Petrograd newspaper identified sponsors ranging from the local Communist party, regional city soviets, individual factories, and trade union organizations.[28] In addition, strong local Proletkult organizations were particularly active in founding clubs, which would eventually pass to the leadership of trade unions and local government educational divisions at the end of the Civil War.[29]

The proliferation of clubs attracted the attention of many observers, who called them "social hearths" and "proletarian homes."[30] During the tumultuous years of revolution and Civil War, many came to clubs because their own apartments had become unlivable. At a time when urban housing was often unheated, clubs that were lucky enough to have access to fuel served as a warm retreat. Club reading rooms operated as centers for crucial information on employment opportunities. Club buffets and cafeterias were a source of nourishment, and many observers noticed lines forming for club services only when buffets were about to open. Newspaper advertisements announcing club events used operating buffets as a way to entice patrons.[31] While club advocates realized that many patrons were turning to these spaces out of necessity, they speculated that clubs would eventually begin to assume many of the functions of the private home, creating a new kind of public space.

Clubs also served as entertainment centers for their local communities. If at all possible, they offered a wide range of activities. Some clubs affiliated with trade unions had already amassed large libraries with tens of thousands of volumes.[32] Even new clubs tried to open libraries and reading rooms. The Third International Club in Moscow, begun in

27. On clubs during the Revolution and Civil War, see Gabrielle Gorzka, *Arbeiterkultur in der Sowjetunion: Industriearbeiter-Klubs, 1917–1929* (Berlin: Arno, 1990), 67–168.

28. "Spravochnyi otdel," *Krasnaia gazeta* 5 September 1918.

29. Mally, *Culture*, 183–91.

30. Mikhail Zverev, "Klub ili obshchestvennyi ochag?" *Griadushchee* 5/6 (1919): 23; M. N. Belokopytova, "Kluby rabochikh podrostkov," *Vneshkol'noe obrazovanie* 1 (1919): 57.

31. E. Lozovskaia, "O raionnom moskovskom Proletkul'te," *Vestnik zhizni* 6/7 (1919): 140–141; R. Myshov, "O rabote v proletarskikh klubakh," *Gorn* 2/3 (1919): 41–42; "Spektakli," *Krasnaia gazeta* 21 June 1918.

32. Evgeny Dobrenko, *The Making of the State Reader: Social and Aesthetic Contexts of the Reception of Soviet Literature* (Stanford: Stanford University Press, 1997), 44.

1918, had collected a library of some three thousand volumes by the following year.[33] Clubs sponsored lectures on many topics, ranging from essential political issues of the day to more ethereal reflections on social thought. The First Worker-Peasant Club of Petrograd offered the following array of lectures during one week in the summer of 1918: "The Importance of Life-Long Learning," "The Meaning of Biogenetic Laws and the Human Spirit," and "Sigmund Freud's Theory of the Subconscious."[34]

Theatrical work was among the most popular club activity, although not all centers could support a theater group.[35] Amateur actors flocked to workshops, and local audiences came to view their offerings. Well-endowed theater workshops with trained staff members could host a serious range of classes on diction, movement, and theater history. But most club theater circles did not have the time (or skills) for elaborate training programs; they instead tried to put on as many performances as possible for club audiences hungry for a constantly changing repertoire. Newspaper advertisements for club events during the Civil War announced upcoming "concert-meetings," with a list of activities to match this eclectic title. A typical club evening would feature some kind of recitation, an improvisation or play, along with lectures, music, and sometimes even dancing.[36]

Few clubs had access to large rooms with raised stages. A limited number of factories, run by enlightened capitalists who saw cultural work as a way of creating an educated labor force, built club spaces with stages before the revolution. After the 1905 revolution, newly empowered labor unions also opened clubs with performance spaces.[37] But the majority of new centers founded after the revolution were opened in urban environments designed for other functions. Not only did they lack auditoria, they had no dressing rooms, space for props, or comfortable seating for the audience. Even when a club could boast an adequate hall

33. Questionnaire from the central Proletkult organization, 1 March 1919, RGALI, f. 1230 (Proletkul't), op. 1, d. 430, l. 1.

34. "Rabochaia kul'tura," *Krasnaia gazeta* 1 June 1918.

35. See an overview of select Moscow clubs conducted in 1919, "Kul'turno-prosvetitel'-naia rabota moskovskogo proletariata," *Gorn* 5 (1920): 71–80.

36. See, for example, O. Zol', "Petrogradskii latyshskii rabochii teatr," *Griadushchee* 9 (1918): 22.

37. On factory theaters, see Eugene Anthony Swift, "Theater for the People: The Politics of Popular Culture in Urban Russia" (Ph.D. diss., University of California, Berkeley, 1985), 170–83; on clubs affiliated with the trade union movement, see Victoria E. Bonnell, *The Roots of Rebellion* (Berkeley: University of California Press, 1983), 328–34.

for performances, many different groups laid claim on the space. Trade unions, the official sponsor of many clubs, needed auditoria for professional meetings and conferences. Music circles demanded room to practice and perform. This meant that theater groups had to discover other rooms—or hallways—for rehearsals.[38] Some groups moved often to search for better accommodations. One Petrograd circle changed quarters four times in a two-year period.[39]

But raised stages, costumes, and assigned seating were not necessary ingredients of Civil War theater. "Just as a farm is a field where edible foods are grown, so a theater is a place where transformations of time, place, and persons . . . are accomplished," notes the director and theater historian, Richard Schechner.[40] Spaces were made into theaters by means of the work that transpired there. Amateur actors and directors in Moscow and Petrograd transformed cafeterias, storerooms, bars, and basements into performance spaces. They moved into areas formerly reserved for the privileged classes before the revolution. The Komsomol club of the First City District in Petrograd, for example, was based in a gathering spot for city nobles called Russkoe Sobranie. The building had not been designed for theatrical performances, so the new inhabitants fashioned their stage in what had once been a spacious reading room. They made a curtain from the draperies and held them up by hand before performances. One factory theater in Moscow created costumes and sets out of contributions foraged from participants' apartments.[41]

Observers from the theatrical avant-garde found these innovations exhilarating because such steps seemed to follow their own suggestions to move away from naturalistic forms of presentation. The symbolist director Alexander Mgebrov, active in amateur theater circles, asserted that improvised spaces were superior to standard stages: "Seek your own arenas, my friends, and not moldy, stuffy, dusty boxes. . . . Your arena is everywhere and anywhere that you are. . . . Your arena is the whole world."[42]

Revolutionary architects saw the expansion of clubs as a chance to design new kinds of spaces that would facilitate collective interaction. In

38. Gorzka, *Arbeiterkultur*, 152.

39. A. S. Bulgakov and S. S. Danilov, *Gosudarstvennyi agitatsionnyi teatr v Leningrade, 1918–1930* (Moscow: Academia, 1931), 19–20.

40. Richard Schechner, "Toward a Poetics of Performance," in *Performance Theory*, 166.

41. Pavel Marinchik, *Rozhdenie komsomol'skogo teatra* (Leningrad: Iskusstvo, 1963), 19–20; "Kul'turno-prosvetitel'naia rabota moskovskogo proletariata," 79.

42. A. Mgebrov, "Proletarskaia kul'tura," *Griadushchee* 2/3 (1919): 23.

1919 the Petrograd Department of Education launched an architectural competition for a "Workers' Palace" that would be a "completely new building, with no links to the past." The elaborate proposal included three different-sized performance spaces—a huge hall that could seat from two to three thousand, a smaller gathering spot for two to three hundred, and a room-sized stage "suitable for amateur performances."[43] Although this plan was one in a long line of unrealized Soviet architectural projects, it showed that urban planners realized the importance of expanding the store of physical structures to house proliferating theatrical performances.

Some architects went even further, envisioning spaces where theatrical activity would not be set apart from the rest of club work. One activist in extracurricular education, A. Petrov, wrote extensively on club architecture. He was bitingly critical of conventional spaces where the theater dominated everything else, crowding out other work. "Where the theater begins," he wrote, meaning a conventional raised stage, "there the club ends."[44] Instead, he advocated multipurpose rooms that would be suited for a variety of functions, including small improvisations and theatrical games. Petrov's proposals were the first in a long line of Soviet debates over how the size and shape of performance spaces would affect the life of the club.[45]

Problems of space were made even more daunting because no one could be sure just how many actors or viewers there would be. During the Civil War, amateur theater groups were plagued by constantly shifting memberships. Urban youth, especially young men, were the most common participants in club activities. One overview of club activities in Moscow determined that the most active participants were young men aged twenty to twenty-two.[46] Not tied down by family responsibilities, they had the most free time. But this segment of the population was also most likely to volunteer, or be drafted—to the Red Army. "Unfortunately a common problem has greatly affected the continuation of our work," complained one cultural organizer in Petrograd. "Namely, the flow of the most active workers from Petrograd to the front or the

43. "Konkurs na 'Dvorets rabochikh,' "; "Dvorets rabochikh," *Iskusstvo kommuny* 19 January 1919.

44. A. Petrov, *Narodnye kluby* (Moscow, 1919), 11, cited in V. Khazanova, *Klubnaia zhizn' i arkhitektura kluba*, v. 1 (Moscow: Rossiiskii institut iskusstvoznaniia, 1994), 18.

45. Ibid., v. 1, 23–25, 32.

46. P. Knyshov, "O rabote v proletarskikh klubakh," *Gorn* 2/3 (1919): 42. See also E. Ozovaia, "O raionnom moskovskom Proletkul'te," *Vestnik zhizni* 6/7 (1919): 141; V. Mitiushin, "Tesnyi kontakt," *Gudki* 6 (1919): 16.

provinces. The lack of workers can be felt most strongly in theater."[47] It was on such shifting ground—with limited resources, physical impediments, and unreliable memberships—that the first Soviet amateur theaters took shape.

Oversight Agencies

During the early years of the Soviet regime, the new government quickly moved to centralize theatrical work by nationalizing the most important Russian theaters. By 1919, it also began to pass legislation limiting the independence of private stages. Narkompros created a central theatrical administration that claimed control over the buildings and property of all theaters, state-owned or private. This new bureaucratic body also reserved the right to control repertoire.[48] This rapid intervention into theatrical life has caused many scholars to see the demise of local control over community-based stages already during the Civil War.[49]

It would be a mistake, however, to confuse the new government's ambition with its actual accomplishments. The burgeoning network of amateur theaters in Moscow and Petrograd encouraged a rapidly expanding web of local and national institutions that attempted to monitor their work. Since many different agencies claimed control over amateur theatrical activity, overlap and conflict between them were inevitable. Competition between government sponsors, known by the special term "parallelism," was a standard feature of early Soviet socialism. It was especially pronounced during the Civil War period, when the responsibilities of government agencies were not yet clearly defined and semi-independent groups like the Proletkult still had some range of independent action. Paradoxically, this competition proved advantageous for some groups. Savvy local circles learned to play state agencies against one another, gaining more funds, space, and staff in the process.

Until the formation of the Central Division for Political Education (Glavpolitprosvet) within Narkompros in late 1920, central state oversight for urban theaters was exercised through Extracurricular Education Divisions (*Vneshkol'nye otdely*). In the two capitals, these divisions provided a variety of services for amateur theaters, including training

47. N. Noskov, "Na putiakh kul'turnogo stroitel'stva," *Zhizn' iskusstva* 101, 21 March 1919.

48. Sheila Fitzpatrick, *The Commissariat of Enlightenment: Soviet Organization of Education and the Arts under Lunacharsky* (Cambridge: Cambridge University Press, 1970), 142–46.

49. See Robert Thurston, *The Popular Theatre Movement in Russia, 1862–1919* (Evanston, Ill.: Northwestern University Press, 1998), 279–80.

programs for club theater workers. The Petrograd division was particularly active. It intervened in struggles over space and also tried to set minimum quality standards for amateur stages. One pronouncement from the Petrograd division decreed that no group should be allowed to go in front of audiences with fewer than five rehearsals under its belt and that no club should sponsor more than two performances a week. These efforts at standardization yielded few results.[50]

The Red Army also wielded significant influence over amateur theaters. Its Political Section (PUR—*Politicheskoe upravlenie voennogo revoliutsionnogo soveta*) had a theater division that sent performing troupes to the front and also planned mass spectacles and agitational trials (see below). The head of PUR, Nikolai Podvoisky, was a close friend of the avant-garde director Vsevolod Meyerhold, who took a personal interest in the army's theatrical activities. In the course of the Civil War, the Red Army devoted considerable educational resources to clubs, which were seen as a way to fill soldiers' free time with edifying forms of relaxation. These clubs introduced new audiences to conventional theater and also encouraged amateur improvisation as a method of education. By 1920, Red Army sources claimed control over a thousand club theaters.[51] The army proved an important training ground for individuals who would come to advocate a special agitational role for amateur theaters in the 1920s. These advocates included Adrian Piotrovskii and Sergei Radlov in Petrograd, who both were influential in the world of workers' clubs. Moscow's most radical voice for a new approach to the amateur stage in the 1920s was Vitalii Zhemchuzhnyi, who also directed amateur theaters in the Red Army during the Civil War.[52]

In Petrograd, the army opened its own set of theatrical training courses in 1919, called the Red Army Studio, which integrated influential figures from the world of prerevolutionary people's theater, as well as recruiting new activists to amateur theater. This division staged mass

50. "Ob"edinenie rabochikh klubov," *Krasnaia gazeta* 2 September 1919.

51. A. A. Gvozdev and A. Piotrovskii, "Petrogradskie teatry i prazdnestva v epokhu voennogo kommunizma," in *Istoriia sovetskogo teatra*, v. 1 (Leningrad: Gosizdat, 1933), 225. On Red Army theatrical activity, see also "Teatral'naia samodeiatel'nost' v Krasnoi Armii," in A. Z. Iufit, ed., *Russkii sovetskii teatr, 1917–1921* (Leningrad: Iskusstvo, 1968), 314–23; Mark von Hagen, *Soldiers in the Proletarian Dictatorship* (Ithaca: Cornell University Press, 1990), 111–14; and Elizabeth Wood, *Performing Justice in Revolutionary Russia: Agitation Trials, Society, and the State* (Berkeley: University of California Press, forthcoming), ch. 1 and 2.

52. Von Geldern, *Bolshevik Festivals*, 131–32; Iufit, *Russkii sovetskii teatr*, 320–21; David Zolotnitskii, *Sergei Radlov: The Shakespearean Fate of a Soviet Director* (Luxembourg: Harwood Academic Publishers, 1995), 5.

events, the examples of *massovoe deistvo* discussed at the worker-peasant theater conference. Its first and most successful work was *The Overthrow of the Autocracy*, a celebration of the February revolution. The division also offered training courses for theater instructors. The Baltic Fleet had its own theatrical studio, the Baltflot Theater, which provided models of repertoire and performance styles for other amateur theaters.[53]

The Proletkult organizations in Moscow and Petrograd controlled their own network of theatrical circles. Numerous city clubs were affiliated with the organization, most operating amateur theatrical studios. When possible, the central city organizations sent staff to oversee the work of these affiliates.[54] In Petrograd, the Proletkult opened a central theater studio already in early 1918, which experimented with a variety of new works designed to inspire amateur stages. The Moscow Proletkult opened its central studio a few months later. Proletkult journals and affiliated publications were an important source of new theatrical works addressing the revolution and Civil War, as well as reviews covering the work of amateur stages. In addition, the Proletkult sponsored instructors' training courses and numerous seminars and classes on theater history and dramatic techniques.[55]

Trade unions also took a healthy interest in amateur stages. In early 1919, the national trade union organization founded a cultural division, which claimed oversight over union-affiliated workers' clubs and theaters. Each city had its own trade union cultural bureaucracy. Individual unions also opened cultural divisions in charge of educational and artistic activity, some already beginning work in 1917.[56] Funds for trade union cultural projects came through membership dues, providing a funding source that was not directly dependent on government subsidies. Unions used these resources to renovate buildings for club activities and to train instructors to guide club work. Although the first priority of trade unions was technical education, that many urban amateur theaters operated out of trade union clubs gave the unions a measure of control. In Petrograd, the Railroad Workers' Union sponsored its own

53. On the Red Army studio, see von Geldern, *Bolshevik Festivals*, 124–33. On the Baltic fleet studio, see Gvozdev, "Petrogradskie teatry," in *Istoriia sovetskogo teatra*, 227.

54. V. Smyshliaev, "O rabote teatral'nogo otdela moskovskogo Proletkul'ta," *Gorn* 1 (1918): 53.

55. "Kul'turno-prosvetitel'naia rabota moskovskogo proletariata," *Gorn* 5 (1920): 71; D. Zolotnitskii, *Zori teatral'nogo Oktiabria* (Leningrad: Iskusstvo, 1976), 296–344.

56. V. A. Razumov, "Rol' rabochego klassa v stroitel'stve sotsialisticheskoi kul'tury v nachale revoliutsii i v gody grazhdanskoi voiny," in *Rol' rabochego klassa v razvitii sotsialisticheskoi kul'tury* (Moscow: Izdatel'stvo "Mysl'," 1976), 20.

theater training courses and opened a union-sponsored theater workshop. The Moscow Railroad Workers' Union also sponsored training
classes for local instructors, which included lectures on art and culture.[57]

The list of local institutions engaged in amateur theatrical activities
hardly ends here. In Moscow, the city soviet took an active part in supervising amateur stages. Its theatrical-pedagogical section opened a variety of classes with the goal of improving the quality of instruction and
performances.[58] Cooperatives operated their own theaters, some with
prerevolutionary roots. In addition, local Komsomol and Communist
Party organizations also opened theaters. One Komsomol club in Petrograd, begun in 1919, eventually evolved into TRAM (Teatr rabochei
molodezhi), the most influential amateur theater of the NEP and First
Five-Year Plan eras.[59]

In late 1920, central state supervision of amateur theaters fell to the
newly formed division of political education (Glavpolitprosvet) within
Narkompros. At the local level, extracurricular education divisions were
replaced by Politprosvet sections. This reorganization was partly intended to eliminate "parallelism" in the cultural field. Glavpolitprosvet
tried to wrest control of cultural work away from the army and trade
unions.[60] It was also instrumental in implementing the Communist
Party's newly articulated assault against the Proletkult.

Although competing institutions offered similar basic services to amateur stages, they often promoted very different aesthetic agendas. It
would be a mistake to overemphasize their ability to shape local work,
since all of them were understaffed and underfunded. Nonetheless, by
hiring instructors and disseminating publications they could set the
tone for their dependent circles. Thus the aesthetic proclivities of Adrian
Piotrovskii, head of the Politprosvet division in Petrograd, influenced
the agenda of groups dependent upon the division. Piotrovskii hired instructors who agreed with his general program, which was to turn away
from conventional plays and toward improvisations and mass actions.[61]
Conversely, savvy groups learned to apply to many different agencies
for funding. Thus trade union clubs, which received support from their
local and national institutions, also petitioned the Proletkult bureau-

57. On the cultural policies of trade unions during the Civil War, see Gorzka, *Arbeiterkultur*, 84–94. On Petrograd and Moscow groups, see Bulgakov and Danilov, *Gosudarstvennyi agitatsionnyi teatr*, 19.

58. Filippov, *Puti samodeiatel'nogo teatra*, 16.

59. Marinchik, *Rozhdenie*, 16.

60. On fights between PUR and Narkompros over control of army clubs, see Wood, *Performing Justice*, ch. 1.

61. Gvozdev, "Petrogradskie teatry," in *Istoriia sovetskogo teatra*, 251–54.

cracy for staff, money, and supplies.[62] A trade union theater in Petrograd gained funding from the local Narkompros division to become a local touring troupe, mounting performances on club stages all over the city.[63]

The welter of state and local agencies provided employment opportunities for established theater activists with long prerevolutionary resumes. Venerable figures like Tikhonovich found a home in the upper echelons of Narkompros. Valentin Smyshliaev, trained at the First Studio of Moscow Art Theater, headed the central theater workshop of the Moscow Proletkult and was also employed in Narkompros' Division for Mass Spectacles.[64] Other important figures with long pedigrees in the field of popular theater included Pavel Gaideburov, whose Traveling Popular Theater, founded in 1903, proved an important training ground for teachers and organizers of Soviet amateur theater circles. Gaideburov's group had toured the provinces before the revolution, with work aimed primarily at the local intelligentsia. With the advent of the First World War, his circle began to address more humble audiences, touring the front lines with works designed to educate and entertain the fighting forces. Gaideburov's base remained the Ligovskii People's Home, one of the most important urban institutions devoted to the education of the working-class intelligentsia. Here he insisted on a "classical" repertoire and steadfastly refused to change the content of performances to reflect the Bolshevik seizure of power. He also found work as the organizer and prime instructor for theater classes organized by the Petrograd division of extracurricular education, which was influential in recruiting energetic young people to the cause of popular theater.[65]

A new generation of theater activists found a calling (and a salary) in the maze of new Soviet bureaucratic structures. These included Dmitrii Shcheglov and Vitalii Zhemchuzhnyi, both born just before the turn of the century. Zhemchuzhnyi got his start in the army and eventually made his way into the cultural bureaucracy of the central Moscow Trade Union organization. Shcheglov's checkered career showed that instructors who were dissatisfied with the aesthetic direction of one agency could easily find support elsewhere. This skilled director found his first job in Gaideburov's Traveling Popular Theater. From this post he moved to Petrograd's newly founded Red Army Studio, where he helped to de-

62. There are numerous such petitions in the Proletkult archive. See, for example, the deliberations of the Proletkult Central Committee on 15 February 1919, RGALI, f. 1230, op. 1, d. 3, l. 15.

63. Bulgakov and Danilov, *Gosudarstvennyi agitatsionnyi teatr*, 14–15.

64. Iufit, *Istoriia sovetskogo teatra*, 81, 341; Zolotnitskii, *Zori*, 331–56, passim.

65. Von Geldern, *Bolshevik Festivals*, 119–22.

velop mass spectacles. The Petrograd Proletkult lured him away from that spot in 1919 with a promise of his own theatrical studio. When aesthetic conflicts developed there, he was recruited for the city's new theater division under the auspices of the local Politprosvet division, at that point headed by Piotrovskii. However, the contentious Shcheglov had troubles there as well, and he eventually ended up working for the cultural division of the provincial trade union bureaucracy.[66] Thus the tangle of overlapping agencies helped to promote the aesthetic diversity—or perhaps one should say aesthetic chaos—of amateur stages.

The Debate on Repertoire: Old and New Plays

By far the most rancorous debates surrounding amateur theaters—both during and after the Civil War—were about repertoire. While circle participants themselves were perhaps most focused on the very fact that they were performing, those who oversaw the proliferation of club stages were vitally concerned with the content of performances. Through published government lists, instructors' training courses, and interventions at the level of club theaters, cultural activists tried to shape a distinctly "revolutionary face" for amateur stages.

Those theater circles with a prerevolutionary pedigree had an existing repertoire at hand. They chose the same plays that had been common in intellectual-sponsored people's theaters before the revolution, among them works by Alexander Ostrovsky, Leo Tolstoi, and Maxim Gorky. Trade union stages, most founded after 1905, also performed selected works from the Russian classics, along with foreign works that could claim a revolutionary imprimatur.[67] New theater circles also drew on a prerevolutionary repertoire. The Northwestern Railroad Workers' club in Petrograd started operations with a standard supply of Ostrovsky plays. A study conducted by the Worker-Peasant Theater Division in 1920 determined that more than a third of all plays performed in some two hundred and fifty amateur theater circles around the country came from the classical repertoire.[68]

---

66. See Dmitrii Shcheglov, "U istokov," in *U istokov: Sbornik statei* (Moscow: VTO, 1960), 11–179, esp. 11, 26, 59, 127.

67. On the repertoire in urban amateur theaters before the revolution, see E. Anthony Swift, "Workers' Theater and 'Proletarian Culture' in Pre-Revolutionary Russia," *Russian History* 23 (1996): 80–82.

68. Bulgakov and Danilov, *Gosudarstvennyi agitatsionnyi teatr*, 15–18; "Samodeiatel'nye teatral'nye kruzhki v 1919 i 1920 godakh," GARF, f. 2313, op. 1, d. 134, ll. 3–3 ob. See also Tikhonovich, *Samodeiatel'nyi teatr*, 37–38.

Government agencies encouraged the use of the prerevolutionary repertoire by assembling lists of suitable plays. These compendiums included some of the most popular works on factory and club stages before the revolution, including Ostrovsky's dramas. They also indicated, however, that some officials of the new regime wanted to redefine what the classics meant. While Anton Chekhov's were plays often performed before and after the revolution, they were missing from a list of suitable works put out by the Moscow soviet. The compilers might have held the view, common in the early Soviet period, that Chekhov expressed the alien vision of the dying upper class. This agency also hoped to add some new names to the common amateur repertoire, including Greek classics, William Shakespeare, and a variety of contemporary Western European authors, including the revolutionary Belgian playwright Emile Verhaeren.[69]

Individual theater activists were also important in drawing up lists of appropriate prerevolutionary works. Piotrovskii put together an ambitious list of works for military stages that drew heavily on the theatrical classics, including Shakespeare, Molière, and prerevolutionary works focusing on social themes. He also suggested prerevolutionary plays that might be used as the basis for improvisations, including Nikolai Gogol's *Inspector General*, a work that satirized prerevolutionary officials.[70] In his influential volume *Creative Theater*, Platon Kerzhentsev also provided many suggestions for suitable prerevolutionary plays. Many of his suggestions had obvious political connotations, such as his endorsement of Gerhart Hauptmann's drama on a worker uprising, *The Weavers*, or Romain Rolland's heroic account of the French Revolution, *Taking the Bastille*.[71]

Those who agreed to stage the classics did not agree on the reasons. For some, they were simply a stopgap measure necessary until a new "revolutionary" repertoire could be developed.[72] For others, a mastery of the classics would prove that the proletariat had laid claim to the cultural riches of the past. The head of Narkompros, Anatolii Lunacharskii, was an unwavering advocate of the latter view, one he insisted also rep-

---

69. "Spisok p'es, redomendovannykh moskovskoi repertuarnoi komissiei," GARF, f. 2306 (Narkompros), op. 2, d. 357, ll. 38–38 ob.

70. Piotrovskii, *Krasnoarmeiskii teatr*, 14–16.

71. Kerzhentsev, *Tvorcheskii teatr*, 70–71.

72. This was a common position in the Proletkult. See V. I. Lebedev-Polianskii, ed., *Protokoly pervoi Vserossiiskoi konferentsii proletarskikh kul'turno-prosvetitel'nykh organizatsii* (Moscow: Proletarskaia kul'tura, 1918), 46.

resented the desires of most proletarian audiences.[73] These opposing positions would be rehearsed again and again in the next decade and a half until the classics were finally permanently enshrined in the amateur repertoire in the 1930s.

Almost all cultural leaders despised the work of second-rate popular authors, whose plays had circulated before the revolution. One of the prime examples of this supposedly shoddy material were the plays of Sofia Belaia, whose melodramatic potboilers had already outraged the cultural intelligentsia before the revolution. Her prolific output of plays, almost all extolling the moral superiority of poverty over wealth, were favorites on amateur stages. Only the Communist critic Piotr Kogan had kind words for Belaia's work, remarking that she revealed the heartlessness of the exploiting classes.[74] Ignoring the critical opinion against her, amateur stages turned to Belaia with enthusiasm. A 1920 study of amateur stages in Soviet-held territory listed her as the third most popular playwright, coming after Ostrovsky and Chekhov but before Gogol.[75] Red Army and trade union clubs even used her most popular play, *The Unemployed*, to mark important festivals.[76]

One disgruntled observer believed that the most popular works were the most frivolous, including outdated melodramas like *Two Orphans* and *The Fall of Pompeii*. Such plays served mainly to keep viewers' minds off their troubles. Contemporaries attributed the popularity of this "hackwork" to the fact that many provincial actors, suddenly put out of work by the revolution, passed themselves off as directors for new theater circles and then foisted inferior plays upon them.[77] Platon Kerzhentsev, the self-appointed doyen of worker amateur stages during the Civil War, bemoaned how amateur stages were performing the worst kinds of "bourgeois claptrap" in the most dilettantish fashion and lacked a serious approach to the task of building a new theatrical culture.[78]

While some government leaders were content to find an acceptable repertoire from prerevolutionary works, others were deeply troubled by

73. Fitzpatrick, *The Commissariat of Enlightenment*, 146–47.

74. P. Kogan, "Sotsialisticheskii teatr v gody revoliutsii," VT 40 (1919).

75. "Samodeiatel'nye teatral'nye kruzhki v 1919 i 1920 godakh," GARF f. 2313, op. 1, d. 134, l. 3 ob. On Belaia, see *Dictionary of Russian Women Writers* (Westport, Conn.: Greenwood Press, 1994), 72–73.

76. Kerzhentsev, *Tvorcheskii teatr*, 68. For an example of the play's staging, see "Teatry i kinematografy," *Krasnaia gazeta* 1 May 1918.

77. Sergei Orlovsky, "Moscow Theaters, 1917–1941," in Martha Bradshaw, ed., *Soviet Theaters, 1917–1941* (New York: Research Program on the USSR, 1954), 13; Z. G. Dal'tsev, "Moskva 1917–1923: Iz vospominanii," in *U istokov*, 185–88.

78. Platon Kerzhentsev, *Revoliutsiia i teatr* (Moscow: Dennitsa, 1918), 48.

this position. The longtime theater activist Nikolai L'vov believed that the revolution had made very little impact on the theater by 1920. Amateur circles were still largely copying the repertoire of professional stages, which had hardly changed in the preceding ten years. What evidence did theater offer to show that a revolution had taken place? Where were the new plays that could reflect the new reality, he queried.[79] L'vov was not alone in his distress. For many advocates of a revolutionary theater, old plays could not meet the needs of the new society that was supposed to be taking shape.

To encourage new works, cultural bureaucrats proposed a variety of innovative methods. One of the most common was the playwriting competition, sponsored by many different institutions. Already in early 1918, the Proletkult announced prizes for the best dramatic work of a "new, original [*samobytnyi*], revolutionary proletarian character." The Narkompros division in Petrograd soon followed suit, opening a competition for a revolutionary melodrama, a form that both Lunacharskii and Maxim Gorky deemed particularly inspiring in the revolutionary age. Individual trade unions and Red Army divisions also sponsored playwriting contests.[80]

Competitions, however, were a cumbersome method to invent a new repertoire. They were not only time consuming—someone had to sort through the many entries—but they also posed formal restrictions on works. Many authors circumvented this process and came up with their own short works that were directly focused on the current crises of Civil War and social transformation. Called *agitki* (singular *agitka*—an abbreviation for *agitatsionnaia p'esa* or agitation play), these works addressed immediate social problems and attempted to sway audiences to support the Red cause. Often one-issue works with easily identifiable themes, they aimed to stem desertion, win peasant support, and even sketch out a hazy but optimistic future that would come with Bolshevik victory. They were very common on Red Army stages and in areas that were directly affected by fighting during the Civil War.

Agitki were usually very short, commonly with one act and only rarely more than two. They aimed to bring across a single point and to inspire political action. Thus detailed character development was not required. Characters were most often distinct and sharply juxtaposed social types—Red Army soldiers versus White Army soldiers, capitalists

79. N. L'vov, "P'esa ili stsenarii," *Vestnik rabotnikov iskusstv*, 2/3 (1920): 53–54.

80. Iufit, *Russkii sovetskii teatr*, 358–60; Daniel Gerould, "Gorky, Melodrama, and the Development of Early Soviet Theatre," *Theatre Journal* 7 (Winter 1976): 33–44; L. Tamashin, *Sovetskaia dramaturgiia v gody grazhdanskoi voiny* (Moscow: Iskusstvo, 1961), 271–80.

versus workers.[81] Indeed, there is something very similar between a dominant style of Civil War posters, those portraying a world sharply differentiated between the good characteristics of the Bolsheviks and the evil characteristics of their opponents, and agitation plays. "The emphasis in this type of poster is on the caricatures themselves rather than on the narrative," notes Victoria Bonnell in her study of Soviet poster art.[82] One could say the same for *agitki*. Like the posters, with their easily identifiable figures of the strong soldier in his peaked Red Army cap juxtaposed to the fat capitalist in his top hat, *agitki* used stereotypes to make their points. Perhaps these similarities should not be surprising, since *agitki* and many of the posters had similar goals—to inform often illiterate audiences quickly and inspire them to action. Later critics would criticize *agitki* for their *plakatnost'*, or their poster-like quality.

With their clear delineation between good and evil, most *agitki* can be characterized as melodramas. Peter Brooks' influential work has shown the complex structure of melodramatic literature, belying the genre's reputation as overly simplistic. These mini-melodramas of the Russian Civil War reveal key elements of the genre, including a world polarized into moral absolutes. However, *agitki* characters do not give voice to deep feelings or reveal their innermost thoughts, a key element of bourgeois melodrama. Instead, they work out guidelines for proper political behavior in the new world created by the revolution. For Brooks, melodramas are the expression of a highly personalized sense of good and evil.[83] *Agitki*, by contrast, attempted to formulate collective standards applicable to all.

Most of these short plays were written for the moment and thus did not gain wide viewerships. One exception was *For the Red Soviets* (*Za krasnye sovety*), by the Proletkult member Pavel Arskii. It is set in the home village of a peasant who had become a Red commander. White forces had seized the village and killed his wife and children. When the village is finally liberated by the Reds, the aggrieved commander issues a fiery appeal to join the Bolshevik cause in order to defeat the enemy. It

81. On *agitki* in general see Tamashin, *Sovetskaia dramaturgiia*, 104–33; Robert Russell, *Russian Drama of the Revolutionary Period* (London: Macmillan, 1988), 34–36; idem, "The First Soviet Plays," in Robert Russell and Andrew Barratt, eds., *Russian Theatre in the Age of Modernism* (London: Macmillan, 1990), 152–54.

82. Victoria Bonnell, *Iconography of Power: Soviet Political Posters under Lenin and Stalin* (Berkeley: University of California Press, 1997), 200.

83. Peter Brooks, *The Melodramatic Imagination: Balzac, Henry James, Melodrama, and the Mode of Excess* (New Haven: Yale University Press, 1976), 11–12, 16.

was widely staged by the Red Army as a method to discourage desertion, a common theme in agitational plays.[84] Other *agitki* sought to illus-
trate the kind of world the revolution was meant to create. An example
would be a work by another Proletkult author, Pavel Bessal'ko, who
wrote an allegorical play about a bricklayer who wanted to be an architect. The hero uses his skills to build a revolutionary tower of Babel that
would end national divisions and inspire an international language.[85]
The play was popular both in club theaters and in theater studios of the
Red Army. As was common for many of these short works, participants
changed them to suit their tastes. In one Red Army version, led by the
cultural activist Zhemchuzhnyi, performers added a scene after the
completion of the tower, where representatives from all the nations of
the earth bring presents to thank the builder for his efforts. This version
ended with the singing of the *Internationale*.[86]

Writers also made use of Russia's folk heritage, instilling new content
into old forms. The best example is the radical transformation of the traditional folk drama *The Boat* (*Lodka*). This loosely structured work can be
traced back to the late eighteenth century. It began as a celebration of
boatmen who worked on the Volga. By the nineteenth century, it came
to feature fiery Cossack outlaw leaders who confronted rich landlords
on their journey down the river. Soviet improvisations turned *The Boat*
into a celebration of historic uprisings against the tsars, praising such
Cossack rebels as Stenka Razin and Ataman Ermak.[87] The traditional
bad boy of the Russian puppet theater, Petrushka, was also enlisted during the early Soviet period for satirical *agitki*. In the process, he was
transformed from a disrupter of social order into an advocate for the
Red cause.[88]

When original scripts were not at hand, theater circles adapted non-
dramatic material for their purposes, creating a hybrid form known as

84. For Pavel Arskii's play, see V. F. Pimenov, ed., *Pervye sovetskie p'esy* (Moscow:
Iskusstvo, 1958), 489–99.

85. P. Bessal'ko, "Kamenshchik," *Plamia* 33 (1919): 2–7.

86. Iufit, *Russkii sovetskii teatr*, 320–21.

87. On *Lodka* before the revolution, see V. I. Vsevolodskii-Gerngross, *Russkaia ustnaia
narodnaia drama* (Moscow: Izdatel'stvo Akademii Nauk SSSR, 1959), 38–79 and Elizabeth
Warner, *The Russian Folk Theatre* (The Hague: Mouton, 1977), 127–40; for its use in the Red
Army, see Piotrovskii, *Krasnaia armiia*, 7; and von Geldern, *Bolshevik Festivals*, 124–25.

88. On Petrushka's long history and many transformations, see Catriona Kelly,
Petrushka: The Russian Carnival Puppet Theatre (Cambridge: Cambridge University Press,
1990), esp. 179–211. On *agitki* with Petrushka themes, see Tamashin, *Sovetskaia dramaturgiia*,
124.

the *instsenirovka*. Through this process, short stories, poetry, and even political speeches were transformed into staged performances. The most straightforward kind of *instsenirovka* was the adaptation of a single work of literature into dramatic form. Competition announcements often included lists of stories and novels that were deemed suitable for theatrical renditions. One call from the Moscow Proletkult, for example, proposed stories by Victor Hugo, Anatole France, and Jack London.[89] *Instsenirovki* also wove together many works by a single author into a cohesive performance, a technique frequently used with poetry. The poems of Walt Whitman, Vladimir Maiakovskii, and Aleksei Gastev were all used as the basis for dramatic events during the Civil War. *Instsenirovki* were also shaped out of collections of different works, sometimes tied together by a narrator or individuals given specific parts. "Dawn of the Proletkult," composed by Vasilii Ignatov, was a compendium of different works by a number of proletarian poets. It introduced figures like "capital" and "the Russian Soviet Republic," who acted as narrators to give a common structure to the poems.[90]

Social Dramas

Despite their hasty composition, most new works written for performance during the Civil War still bore a strong resemblance to conventional plays. They presented actors with a list of characters; they offered a story with a clear beginning, middle, and end that had been predetermined by the author; and they clearly differentiated between the performers and the audience. As such, they still functioned within the world of aesthetic drama, taking their formal inspiration (if not their political messages) from standard performance practices. However, some works composed during the Civil War began to question standard notions of authorship and audience involvement. They gave performers a more central role in shaping the content of the work and integrated the audience in a more direct way. In the process, they blurred the lines between aesthetic and social drama.

Improvisations were one such method, a common practice in the theater studios of the Red Army and the Proletkult. Usually, with the help of an instructor, participants would choose a theme, like a mother's attempts to dissuade her son from joining the army or a wife's resistance

---

89. "Konkurs Proletkul'ta," VT 70 (1920): 19.

90. "Vecher Uolta Uitmena," *Krasnaia gazeta* 24 July 1918; Iufit, *Russkii sovetskii teatr*, 320; Tamashin, *Sovetskaia dramaturgiia*, 44, 52.

to her husband's departure. From this base they would devise a rudimentary plot structure. According to one club leader, participants were eager to provide themes for improvisations. Some clubs even solicited suggestions from the audience and determined what they would perform by drawing lots at random out of a bag.[91] The many pressures and divisions that the Civil War caused within families were a common topic of these sketches. One improvised story involved two brothers, one White and one Red, who both loved the same woman. In the end, the woman chose to link her future to the Bolshevik.[92] Although the plot exaggerated the dilemmas most individuals faced in the Civil War, it illuminated the wrenching, life-altering choices demanded in a revolutionary period.

Another innovation was the living newspaper (*zhivaia gazeta*), a form that would come to have considerable influence in the Soviet Union and beyond in the next decade. This improvised genre grew out of efforts to present the news to audiences in an easily understandable form. Public readings to audiences without the ability to read or without easy access to newspapers or books had a long tradition in Russia. During the Civil War, when paper was a scarce commodity, the Soviet news agency, ROSTA, encouraged open readings of newspapers, with special times and places set aside for this activity. The readings were often augmented with music, scenery, and poetry. It was but a short step for agitational drama circles to act out the main characters in the feature stories.[93] While the performance texts often had very clever writing, the broad topics they addressed were not determined by the authors. The inspiration for the content lay in current events, such as the current status of the Red Army, the international situation, or the food supply. Living newspapers aimed not simply to inform viewers but also to inspire action—to get audience members to fight harder, or turn in food speculators, or join the Bolshevik Party.

During the Civil War, the professional satirical troupe of the Red Army, the Theater of Revolutionary Satire, or Terevsat, did much to help popularize the methods of living newspapers. Terevsat considered its job to be providing humorous commentary on current political events and used newspaper reports to structure improvisations. Their

91. Iufit, *Russkii sovetskii teatr*, 318–20; "Khronika Proletkul'ta," *Proletarskaia kul'tura* 15/16 (1920): 79.

92. N. Karzhanskii, *Kollektivnaia dramaturgiia* (Moscow: Gosizdat, 1922), 56–57, 73.

93. M. Slukhovskii, *Ustnaia gazeta kak vid politiko-prosvetitel'noi raboty* (Moscow: Krasnaia zvezda, 1924), 14, 22–27, 35.

performances followed a format similar to that of a newspaper—first commentary on the international situation, then on national events, and then satirical works based on local affairs. The Moscow Terevsat performed in clubs and factories, familiarizing audiences with its satirical style of improvised performance.[94] With these examples before them, amateur circles had models to begin their own living newspapers.

Yet another revolutionary innovation were the agitational trials, or *agitsudy*. They first emerged as a widespread method of educational entertainment during the Civil War. Agit-trials, which put controversial issues to viewers for their judgment, also had prerevolutionary roots. Mock trials of matchmakers were a routine part of peasant courting rituals. The legal reforms of the nineteenth century encouraged the use of moot courts to instill an understanding of courtroom procedures. Peasant forms of rough justice, or *samosud*, through which rural communities devised their own form of punishment for offenders of shared values, also had some parallels to agit-trials.[95]

The Red Army was the major propagator of agitational trials during the Civil War. Soldiers stationed near Kharkov in late 1919 put the main character of the play *The Vengeance of Fate (Mest' Sud'by)* on trial, a wife who had killed her brutal husband. The participants were drawn by lots and the entire audience took part in the proceedings, which ended in an acquittal. Historical figures were also put on trial, including Rasputin and in one case even Lenin. Some of these events were massive affairs. In 1920 the Southern Army staged its first large-scale agitational court, "The Trial of Wrangel," before an audience of some ten thousand spectators. In this case, the outcome was preordained; Wrangel, the White general, was condemned to extinction by scripted witnesses who did not solicit the audience's response.

By late 1920 the Red Army political education workers focused much of their attention on agitational trials. These were staged in areas of heightened political tension and offered a way to articulate and resolve some of the problems of the unstable new regime. Any number of politi-

94. See the memoirs of Terevsat leader M. Ia. Pustynin in Iufit, *Russkii sovetskii teatr*, 185–87; Zolotnitskii, *Zori*, 195; and J. A. E. Curtiss, "Down with the Foxtrot! Concepts of Satire in the Soviet Theatre of the 1920s," in *Russian Theatre in the Age of Modernism*, 221. For the evolution of this form in the 1920s, see ch. 2.

95. On the prerevolutionary origins of agit-trials, see Julie Cassaday, "The Theater of the World and the Theater of the State: Drama and the Show Trial in Early Soviet Russia," (Ph.D. dissertation, Stanford University, 1995), 51–53; on its roots in folk drama, see Warner, *The Russian Folk Theatre*, 51.

cal enemies were brought to trial—among them the anti-Bolshevik Ukrainian nationalist, Simon Petliura, and the leader of Polish opposition, Josef Pilsudski. As "The Trial of Lenin" shows, the heroes of the moment were also brought to trial—and given a forum to dispute charges brought against them.[96] Trials were expanded from cases against concrete individuals—something that could conceivably bear some similarities to a real courtroom trial—to broader spheres of activity. Unnamed enemies, such as the bearers of syphilis, army deserters, and global capital, were also called into the agitational courtroom.

Agit-trials within the army could be massive affairs, involving casts of thousands. The method was also employed in the more intimate context of club theaters, however. One club workshop staged its own trial of enemies, putting Pilsudski on trial in 1920. Club members in the Bauman district of Moscow decided to put the year 1920 on trial at the beginning of 1921. Audience members accused the old year of bringing them war and hardship. In the end, the year 1920 was able to acquit itself eloquently, insisting that it had paved the way to a more optimistic period.[97] The broad range of subjects addressed in agit-trials during the Civil War prepared the way for their widespread use during the next decade, when they became an important genre of club performances.

The Red Army was also influential in staging and encouraging large mass spectacles, which emerged as an important venue for the new Bolshevik government to articulate its aims to the population at large. These events aimed to present a coherent history of the revolution from the Bolshevik point of view. Modeled in part on tsarist festivals and engaging the talents of some of the finest theatrical professionals in Russia, these elaborate events engaged literally a cast of thousands.[98] Amateur theater groups from workers' clubs and the Red Army were integrated into mass scenes, working together with theater professionals. In Petro-

96. On agit-trials in the army, see Wood, *Performing Justice*, ch. 1; Tamashin, *Sovetskaia dramaturgiia* 57–60; and von Geldern, *Bolshevik Festivals* 110, 172, 181.

97. Karzhanskii, *Kollektivnaia dramaturgiia*, 66–69; Wood, *Performing Justice*, ch. 1.

98. There is a large literature on these festivals. See A. I. Mazaev, *Prazdnik kak sotsial'no-khudozhestvennoe iavlenie* (Moscow: Nauka, 1978), esp. 277–300; V. P. Tolstoi, ed., *Agitatsionno-massovoe iskusstvo: Oformlenie prazdnestv*, 2 v. (Moscow: Iskusstvo, 1984); von Geldern, *Bolshevik Festivals*; Christel Lane, *The Rites of Rulers* (Cambridge: Cambridge University Press, 1981), 153–73; Rosalinda Sartorti, "Stalinism and Carnival"; Richard Stites, *Revolutionary Dreams: Utopian Vision and Experimental Life in the Russian Revolution* (New York: Oxford, 1989), 79–100. For a contemporary assessment, see Gvozdev, "Petrogradskie teatry," in *Istoriia sovetskogo teatra*, 264–90.

grad on May Day 1920, for example, army and navy amateur groups performed together with theater students and professionals in a mass event entitled "The Spartacus Rebellion."[99]

In a fashion similar to the large public displays, clubs staged festivities that aimed to fix a prehistory of the revolution. One Petrograd Proletkult studio, under the leadership of Dmitrii Shcheglov, focused its entire theatrical activity on dramatizing turning points in the Russian revolutionary movement, including peasant rebellions, the Decembrist uprising, and the revolution of 1905.[100] May Day and November 7, the anniversary of the revolution, emerged as the two most important Soviet holidays. Festivities were held all over the two capitals and included worker districts. Factory workers joined festive processions in their districts, and humble local clubs were decorated with posters and slogans to mark the holiday. Celebrated with musical concerts, plays, and agitational works on the street, these pivotal holidays gave club members an opportunity to celebrate within their own neighborhoods, claiming local spaces as their own.[101]

⁂

If revolution loves the theater, what happens when the revolution ends? This question was posed by many observers and activists in amateur theaters as the Civil War was coming to an close. The very proliferation of stages, so astonishing to all observers, was in part a product of the upheaval. Not only were actors trying on new social roles, but impoverished neighborhoods were attempting to fashion some sort of entertainment with the meager resources at their disposal. The innovative staging methods devised during the Civil War made a virtue of necessity. They were flexible, allowed adjustment to local conditions, and could provide "educational" entertainment for the audience. They required neither long rehearsal time nor elaborate costumes to be effective.

Just as some political theorists saw the deprivations of the Civil War as a shortcut to real Communism, some cultural activists saw these emergency measures as the roots of a new revolutionary theater. But for

99. Tolstoi, ed., *Agitatsionno-massovoe iskusstvo*, v. 1, 108–9.

100. Tamashin, *Sovetskaia dramaturgiia*, 30.

101. Tolstoi, ed., *Agitatsionno-massovoe iskusstvo*, v. 1, 49–50, 71, 95, 115; "Teatral'nye studii," *Gudki* 2 (1919): 26; Gorzka, *Arbeiterkultur*, 143–45.

others, the end of the Civil War meant that cultural work could return to "normal." Trade unions and factories could begin to build clubhouses with well-appointed stages. Theater circle members could devote themselves to classes and rehearsals. The result would be an amateur theater of higher quality, devoted to aesthetic drama.

A debate on the future of amateur theaters was aired in Petrograd's main cultural journal, *Zhizn' iskusstva (The Life of Art)* in March 1921, just as the Tenth Party Congress was meeting to announce the measures known as the New Economic Policy. The literary critic and social commentator Viktor Shklovskii published an article assessing the remarkable proliferation of theater circles. He suggested that their continued existence and expansion was not a sign of cultural creativity but rather a symptom of a serious social malaise. The rush to the theater was a kind of psychosis, an attempt to avoid the real difficulties of life. "These millions of circles should not be closed—one cannot forbid people their ravings. As a sign of sickness, they should be studied by sociologists. But we cannot use them to construct a new life."[102]

This passionate condemnation of amateur theaters in their current form drew a heated response from the Petrograd cultural activist Adrian Piotrovskii, who had emerged as one of the most important advocates of improvisational theater during the Civil War. Piotrovskii drew precisely the opposite conclusion from the proliferation of theater groups. They came from the best and strongest sources of Soviet life, from Red Army soldiers and Communist youth. They did not turn from life but rather embraced it, staging trials, mysteries, and improvisations. In addition, they had a fundamentally different aim than amateur theater groups of old; their purpose was not to imitate life but rather to transform it. "Now let one thing be clear," intoned Piotrovskii. "The thousands of theater circles spread across the republic are militant signs of how daily life is being revolutionized [*revoliutsionizirovanie byta*]."[103]

This exchange marked a controversy over the cultural legacy of the Civil War. To what extent would the innovations of the revolutionary period live on in a transformed social and political climate? Where

102. Viktor Shklovskii, "Drama i massovye predstavleniia," *Zhizn' iskusstva*, 9–11 March, 1921. This oft-cited article is reprinted in Viktor Shklovskii, *Khod konia: Sbornik statei* (Moscow: Gelikon, 1923), 59–63.

103. A. Piotrovskii, "Ne k teatry, a k prazdnestvu," *Zhizn' iskusstva* 19–22 March, 1921. This article is also republished in an excerpted form in Adrian Piotrovskii, *Za sovetskii teatr! Sbornik statei* (Leningrad: Academia, 1925), 25–26.

would the nation look to find a path toward "new life"? While Shklovskii searched for some return to "normal," to a world not infested with innumerable theater circles, Piotrovskii and others like him hoped to continue and advance Civil War cultural strategies into an era of social compromise.

2

Small Forms on Small Stages

THE CONCLUSION of the Russian Civil War brought new challenges to all those engaged in constructing a Soviet culture. Efforts to rebuild the shattered economic base of the country, begun in 1921, meant that there were substantially fewer state funds available for cultural projects. Optimistic plans to construct new club buildings and new stages for amateur theaters were put off for several years. In addition, in order to infuse life into the economy, the Soviet government allowed limited capitalist enterprise to start up again in the form of the New Economic Policy (NEP). This program was not only an economic threat to those who hoped for the rapid victory of socialism, but it also posed significant cultural dangers in the minds of many affiliated with amateur theater. Urban commercial life quickly revived, offering entertainment opportunities ranging from imported films to boulevard literature. Many Bolsheviks, as well as their allies from the prerevolutionary people's theater movement, saw these aspects of urban life as a threat to the creation of a healthy and edifying culture for the masses.

Even though funds were tight, state agencies at both the national and the local level realized the importance of launching cultural campaigns to win the population over to the Soviet cause. The Soviet state of the 1920s might be best called an "enlightenment state," in the words of Michael David-Fox, so focused was it on transforming the consciousness of its citizens. "By the early 1920s," writes David-Fox, "Bolshevik leaders across factional lines came to portray cultural transformation, educational work, and the creation of a Bolshevik intelligentsia as pivotal to the fate of regime and revolution."[1] Non-professional theatrical groups, which had proven themselves effective propagandists during the Civil War, emerged as an important arena in the struggle to educate the broad population to become enthusiastic Soviet citizens.

While sponsoring agencies had high expectations for amateur stages, they rarely provided new funds or resources. How, under these circumstances, could amateur stages best fulfill their pedagogical tasks? In this chapter I investigate one answer put forward initially by a select group of cultural activists in Petrograd and Moscow. They proposed abandoning conventional repertoires for club stages altogether, replacing them with the improvisational methods that had already gained ground during the Russian Civil War. These methods were called "small forms" (*malye formy*), yet another redefinition of a prerevolutionary term. Before the Bolsheviks came to power, the theater of small forms referred to music halls and vaudeville theaters.[2] Now small forms meant agit-trials, satirical sketches, and living newspapers.

The agitational theater of small forms satirized Soviet enemies and praised Soviet heroes. It was used to impart lessons on how Soviet citizens should live—what books they should read, what their hygienic habits should be, and how they should relate to the Soviet regime. These methods were in part a response to the new cultural offerings of the NEP era. Sponsors envisioned the healthy entertainments of Soviet clubs, among them amateur theatrical works, as an alternative to "decadent" forms of commercial culture made possible by NEP's restricted capitalism. The theater of small forms was intended to be engaging; many skits used humor and buffoonery. Some groups consciously employed elements of NEP culture in order to interest viewers, giving them what they hoped was a healthy socialist twist. Thus this didactic theater was intended both to educate and entertain.

Limited cultural funding facilitated the turn to small forms. These improvisational methods were for the most part not dependent on well-appointed stages and expensive production techniques. Performers often played characters very much like themselves and therefore did not require expensive costumes or make-up. Because small forms were conceived as a method to bring performers closer to audiences, the humble performance spaces of clubs, with their small or non-existent stages, were not the impediment that they would have been for more conven-

1. Michael David-Fox, *Revolution of the Mind: Higher Learning among the Bolsheviks, 1918–1929* (Ithaca: Cornell University Press, 1997), 4–5, quotation 5.

2. Laurence Senelick, "Theatre," in Nicholas Rzhevsky, ed., *The Cambridge Companion to Modern Russian Culture* (Cambridge: Cambridge University Press, 1998), 273.

tional productions. Some groups, like the Moscow Blue Blouse theater, commanded its followers to eschew complex costumes and sets, turning necessities into virtues. "Blue Blouse rejects all beautiful, realistic sets and decorations," read one manifesto. "There will be absolutely no birch trees or little rivers."[3]

Yet even while small forms gained ground, there were heated debates surrounding the eventual direction of amateur theater. Were these improvisational forms an end in themselves? Did they point toward the development of new kinds of "big" theater—new plays and operas with a revolutionary thematic and presentational style? Or were they temporary, stop-gap measures for poorly equipped club stages and poorly trained amateur actors, measures that could be phased out as conditions improved? These questions were debated within state agencies and trade union bureaucracies, among theatrical professionals interested in amateur work, and inside club theatrical groups themselves. Certainly, some club stage advocates believed that if a new, distinctive style of Soviet theater ever was going to take shape it would emerge from the shabby environs of workers' clubs and not from the glittering stages of the old theaters.

The Turn to Small Forms

The promotion of small forms on local stages came initially from local agencies in Petrograd/Leningrad and Moscow at the onset of the New Economic Policy. Their advocacy of a unique, politicized repertoire for amateur theaters found favor among select local groups. By 1923, the Communist Party endorsed the idea that club cultural work should be directly relevant to political and economic campaigns, a pronouncement interpreted as an endorsement of this direction on the amateur stage. The national trade union leadership soon followed suit. Although not all amateur theater groups abandoned prerevolutionary works and full-length Soviet plays in the early years of NEP, there was a definite swing to small forms. Local living newspaper groups were an especially popular manifestation of this aesthetic turn.

The first efforts to formulate a unique form of amateur performance took shape in Petrograd at the end of the Civil War. Petrograd Politprosvet activists devised a special organizational framework within clubs to structure cultural work, a model they called the "united artistic circle" (*edinyi khudozhestvennyi kruzhok*—often called by its acronym,

---

3. "Prostye sovety uchastnikam sinebluznoi gazety," *Siniaia bluza* (henceforth cited as SB) 18 (1925): 4.

 EKhK). The goal was to make the life of the club revolve around Soviet festivals. Adrian Piotrovskii, the head of the Petrograd Politprosvet division, envisioned the united artistic circle as a way to continue and expand the agitational, propagandistic direction of club theatrical work begun during the Civil War. He believed that many amateur theater circles had already made theatrical festivals a central focus of their work.[4] In Piotrovskii's view, the united artistic circle simply described and clarified the direction that theatrical work had already taken in factory and neighborhood clubs.[5] The central idea was to make all club artistic and educational circles work together toward the same goal. Music groups, physical education circles, and literary circles would all participate in the creation of a mass theatrical "happening" (*deistvo*). The newly emerging festival days of the revolution were the perfect occasion for these events. All would contribute to a celebration of Bloody Sunday, May Day, and the October Revolution. This new direction emerged from popular tastes, wrote Piotrovskii in 1921: "There is no pull toward the 'spectacle' [*zrelishche*] of professional theater; instead, popular theatrical events, popular performances have burst forth into light."[6]

In Piotrovskii's description, local theatrical activity was spontaneously moving toward club festivals; the united artistic circle was a method to better coordinate that activity. Piotrovskii's focus was on spontaneity, local creativity, and (although he did not say so directly) local resources. As Katerina Clark has noted, the united artistic circle displayed in striking clarity the newly constrained economic circumstances of NEP.[7] What was proposed was in essence a bargain-basement festival, removed from the main squares of the city to the humble confines of club stages and their immediate neighborhoods.

In addition to these fiscal attractions, the united artistic circle marked a significant turn toward greater uniformity and control. What was pro-

4. *Petrogradskaia obshchegorodskaia konferentsiia rabochikh klubov* (Petrograd: Petrogradskii otdel narodnogo obrazovaniia, 1920), 116–17. See James von Geldern, "Nietzschean Leaders and Followers in Soviet Mass Theater, 1917–1927," in Bernice Glatzer Rosenthal, ed., *Nietzsche and Soviet Culture* (Cambridge: Cambridge University Press, 1994), 127–48, for the broad intellectual context that encouraged Piotrovskii's ideas.

5. Adrian Piotrovskii, "Rabota Nekrasovtsev," in *Sbornik instsenirovok: Opyty kollektivnoi dramaturgii* (Leningrad: Izdatel'stvo knizhnogo sektora Gubono, 1924), 3–4.

6. A. I. Piotrovskii, "Edinyi khudozhestvennyi kruzhok," in *Za sovetskii teatr! Sbornik statei* (Leningrad: Academia, 1925), 7–9, quotation 7.

7. Katerina Clark, *Petersburg: Crucible of Cultural Revolution* (Cambridge: Harvard University Press, 1995), 146–47. See also James von Geldern, *Bolshevik Festivals, 1917–1920* (Berkeley: University of California Press, 1993), 216–19.

posed was nothing less than a complete transformation of amateur the-atricals. No longer would clubs devote themselves to performing classic or contemporary plays. Rather, they would focus their work on a festive calendar of revolutionary celebrations. Moreover, some descriptions of the united artistic circle significantly curtailed the element of spontane-ity. It was the club's political circle that gained the responsibility for drawing up the guidelines and taking control of artistic work.[8] Grigorii Avlov, part of the cultural division of the Petrograd Politprosvet and ed-itor of the most widely distributed book on united artistic circles, made the central role of the political group even more pronounced. The model he chose was that of a factory, where all sectors cooperated in the cre-ation of a final product. The function of central planner was given to the political circle.[9]

It is not hard to understand the appeal of the united artistic circle for government and trade union organizations. In its ideal form, all club cultural activity would propagate the principles and goals of the revolu-tion, supervised by political organs within the club. Petrograd Polit-prosvet workers enthusiastically embraced this new direction. By 1921, the political education division had opened a "Central Agitational Stu-dio" that experimented with forms of collective improvisation. Headed by a former member of Gaideburov's theater, V. V. Shimanovskii, this studio grew out of the agitational work of railroad unions during the Civil War.[10] The following year Shimanovskii's studio served as the ba-sis for a special provincial Politprosvet division in charge of amateur theater. It sent trained workers out to monitor and direct the work of city clubs and tried to coordinate their activities. Soon the city's educa-tion division formed a special Home of Amateur Theater (Dom samod-eiatel'nogo teatra), again under Shimanovskii's guidance, which pro-vided a central performance stage where local clubs could show their work.[11]

Politprosvet institutions in Petrograd served as a focal point for the new agenda of amateur theaters. They provided a training ground for

8. See M. Danilevskii, "K provedeniiu prazdnika v klube," in *Oktiabr' v rabochikh klubakh* (Moscow: Krasnaia nov', 1923), 4–5.

9. G. Avlov, "Samodeiatel'nyi teatr i rabota edinogo khudozhestvennogo kruzhka," in G. Avlov, ed., *Edinyi khudozhestvennyi kruzhok: Metody klubno-khudozhestvennoi raboty* (Leningrad: Izdatel'stvo knizhnogo sektora Gubono, 1925), 11–23. See the graphic depic-tion of the united artistic circle, a pyramid with the political circle at the apex, 40–41.

10. A. A. Gvozdev and A. Piotrovskii, "Rabochii i krasnoarmeiskii teatr," in *Istoriia sovetskogo teatra*, v. 1 (Leningrad: Leningradskoe otdelenie Gosizdata, 1933), 252.

11. G-n, "Gosudarstvennyi dom samodeiatel'nogo teatra," ZI 22 (1923): 22.

the methods of the united artistic circle and designed repertoire for amateur stages. To take just one example, two participants in the Shimanovskii studio, Iakov Zadykhin and Vladimir Severnyi, composed scripts of *instsenirovki* to mark the 1923 May Day festival.[12] The Home of Amateur Theater helped to coordinate festival celebrations, noting which dates of the Red Calendar deserved commemoration and drawing up lists of suitable repertoire.[13]

In Moscow, it was the Proletkult organization that initially called for a more focused agitational approach in club theaters. At the end of 1921, the city's main Proletkult studio adopted a plan that rejected the plays of Ostrovsky in favor of "improvisations, living newspapers, and agitational work."[14] In a long overview of the city's club activities, the leader of the Proletkult club division, Raisa Ginzburg, called for an end to standard repertoire on club stages in favor of a more didactic direction.[15] By late 1922, the Proletkult began to advance these ideas in terms very similar to cultural workers in Petrograd. They called for the creation of a "united studio of the arts" (*edinaia studiia iskusstv*). All sections of the club would serve a common purpose, focusing on the harmonious interaction of club members to achieve the improvement of proletarian life.[16] As a consequence, "theater work inevitably will turn to *instsenirovki* focused on the burning issues of the day, on *agitki*, evenings of scenarios, revolutionary cabarets, living newspapers, theatricized courts, etc."[17] The Proletkult plan included a long list of classes in art and political education.

The turn to small forms got a real boost in April 1923, when the Twelfth Communist Party Congress determined that clubs should become active centers of mass propaganda designed to encourage the creative abilities of the working class.[18] While the resolution also addressed

12. "Po rabochim klubam," ZI 15 (1923): 18. Both writers would have long histories as authors of agitational works.

13. "K prazdnikam revoliutsii," ZI 10 (1923): 12.

14. "Zhizn' Proletkul'ta," *Gorn* 6 (1922): 151.

15. R. Ginzburg, "Rabochie kluby pri novoi ekonomicheskoi politike," *Gorn* 6 (1922): 101–2.

16. See the records of a November 1922 Proletkult plenum, "Vserossiiskii Proletkul't," *Gorn* 8 (1923): 237, and Raisa Ginzburg, "Moskovskii Proletkul't v klubakh profsoiuzov," ibid., 260.

17. *Iskusstvo v rabochem klube* (Moscow: Vserossiiskii Proletkul't, 1924), 12. See also V. Pletnev, *Rabochii klub* (Moscow: Vserossiiskii Proletkul't, 1925), 52–54.

18. *Kommunisticheskaia partiia Sovetskogo Soiuza v rezoliutsiiakh i resheniiakh s''ezdov, konferentsii i plenumov TsK*, v. 2:1917–24 (Moscow: Izdatel'stvo politicheskoi literatury, 1970), 456–57.

the necessity of leisure-time activities in clubs, many national and local institutions interpreted it as a call for better-coordinated agitational work from club cultural circles. Accordingly, they began to formulate programs for club activity that followed the general direction set by the Politprosvet division in Petrograd: they embraced agitational, educational work as the main focus of club activities. Although there were differences in emphasis, all these programs shared basic assumptions for amateur theaters. No longer would their primary task be to practice and disseminate conventional theatrical skills and repertoire. Rather, their main goal was to serve the club community as a whole and to provide highly politicized and topical activities.

The national trade union bureaucracy gave a resounding endorsement to agitational methods in club artistic circles.[19] The cultural division determined that all artistic groups, including theater circles, would no longer be cut off from the general activities of the club. Instead, they should direct their efforts toward agitation and education. Evoking the words of the Party congress, the national trade union convention on club work meeting in the spring of 1924 voted to tie the work of all club circles to political education aimed at the broad masses. All club activity was to be unified into a single complex plan, embracing politics, professional life, and culture.[20]

The most radical proposal for small forms was devised by a group of Moscow Politprosvet workers in the summer of 1923.[21] They rejected any form of theatrical work that was set off from general club activity. They even rejected common nomenclature like "theatrical studio" or "theatrical circle," proposing instead the new name of "action circles" (*deistvennye kruzhki*) or "action cells" (*deistvennye iacheiki*) that would initiate mass activities in clubs.[22] The supporters of this position, including the long-time theater activist Nikolai L'vov and club instructors M. V. Danilevskii and Vitalii Zhemchuzhnyi, formed the Association of Action Circle Instructors, which sought a radical transformation (some would say annihilation) of theatrical work in clubs. The motto of the action circle was: "Stop play acting and start organizing life."[23] To show

19. "Rabochii klub i ego zadachi," *Prizyv* 5 (1924): 174.
20. "Formy i metody klubnoi raboty," *Prizyv* 5 (1924): 175.
21. See Nikolai L'vov's personal archive, GTSTM, f. 150, notebook 1, ll. 25–29.
22. S. Lugovskoi, "Teatral'naia studiia, kruzhok ili deistvennaia iacheika?" *Rabochii klub* (henceforth cited as RK) 1 (1924): 12–14.
23. "Za chto my boremsia," RK 3/4 (1924): 18–22, quotation 22. According to L'vov's archive, he was the author of this manifesto.

how this method marked a break from past approaches, the Moscow proponents suggested that the words "spectacle" (*spektakl'*), "actor" (*akter*), and "play" (*igra*) no longer be used. Instead, they would be replaced by "presentation" (*vystuplenie*), "performer" (*ispolnitel'*), and "action" (*deistvie*).[24] This linguistic shift was meant to show that artistic work in clubs would be fundamentally different from professional artistic work. Clubs should never aim to imbue professional artistic techniques among their students. According to a manifesto written by Zhemchuzhnyi, "In its organization and methodology, artistic work in clubs should not be different from other club work. For this reason, the goals and methods of club artistic work is *fundamentally* different than the professional arts. The goal of clubs should never be to establish a professional artistic studio."[25]

Agencies that supported the turn to small forms created courses to train instructors in the new techniques. The Home of Amateur Theater in Leningrad offered classes for theatrical workers.[26] The Moscow Proletkult designed a number of short training sessions, some with the collaboration of the Association of Action Circles.[27] In 1924 the central Moscow trade union organization opened the Theatrical-Artistic Bureau, which approved a suitable repertoire for club stages and also attempted to provide technical assistance and coordinate the work of local groups.[28]

The shift to small forms brought fresh resources to club theaters. Instructors trained in the new methods put themselves at the disposal of amateur theaters. Government agencies began to publish collections of short plays and sketches that could be performed by local theaters. In addition, a number of new journals devoted at least in part to amateur stages and their repertoire made their appearance, including *The Worker Viewer* (*Rabochii zritel'*) and *The New Viewer* (*Novyi zritel'*), both located in Moscow, and *Worker and Theater* (*Rabochii i teatr*) from Leningrad. These publications, along with the older *Life of Art* (*Zhizn' iskusstva*), gave extensive space to performances on club stages. Two other impor-

24. "Resoliutsiia priniataia na sobranii deistvennogo kruzhka," 15 May, 1924, GTSTM, f. 150, no. 17, l. 10.

25. V. Zhemchuzhnyi, "Printsipy khudozhestvennoi raboty v klubakh," n.d., RGALI, f. 963 (Gosudarstvennyi teatr im. Meierkhol'da), op. 1, d. 1120, l. 23, emphasis in the original.

26. "Gosudarstvennyi dom samodeiatel'nogo teatra," ZI 22 (1923): 22.

27. "Moskovskii Proletkul't," *Gorn* 8 (1923): 242; "Vechernie teatral'no-instruktorskie kursy Proletkul'ta," *Rabochii zritel'* (henceforth cited as RZ) 32/33 (1924): 16.

28. See, for example, A. Iudin, "Teatral'naia rabota v raionakh," RZ 18 (1924): 9; Sukhanov, "Kak MGSPS budet obsluzhivat' teatrom rabochie massy," RZ 19 (1924): 6.

tant journals with coverage of amateur stages began in 1924: *Workers'
Club* (*Rabochii klub*) and *Blue Blouse* (*Siniaia bluza*), both of which published sample works that local groups were encouraged to alter for their
own purposes.

These publications are filled with what one might call "conversion
stories," illustrating the switch from conventional repertoire to small
forms within individual clubs. The tales have a similar structure: a club
theater labored away with heroic prerevolutionary plays or silly melodramas, accomplishing very little. Performances were rare and inade-
quate. They had nothing to do with other events in the life of the club.
Then suddenly the direction changed. From this point on the theater circle began to produce works for club events and festivals, becoming hap-
pily integrated into the life of the club. The impetus for change was not
uniform in these tales; sometimes they came from the trade union sponsoring club work, sometimes club leaders intervened, and sometimes
amateur actors themselves took credit for the reorganization. The
Moscow Transit Workers' Union decided to alter the methods of a regional club, inviting a director trained in small forms to take charge. Almost overnight, the repertoire changed from Ostrovsky plays to celebrations honoring International Women's Day. At the Northern Railroad
Club, the chief administrator dispensed with the old expert in charge of
theater. Members of a club at a Moscow metal-working factory decided
to adopt the new methods on their own, since they could not afford to
pay an instructor.[29]

Not all amateur theater circles embraced small forms. One instructor
who had been to a training course in Moscow and altered his club's
work according to the "new course" met resistance from viewers. They
did not like the *instsenirovka Bourgeois in Hell* (*Burzhui v adu*) and asked
for a play from the prerevolutionary repertoire.[30] Some groups produced
mixed repertoires. The Nekrasov People's Home in Leningrad performed a homemade *instsenirovka* together with two acts of Denis Fon-
vizin's *The Infant*, a standard of the prerevolutionary Russian repertoire.
According to one worker correspondent attending the event, the Fon-
vizin play did not compare well with the improvised work.[31] The
Moscow Perfume Factory "Freedom" ended up with two theater

29. "Raionnyi klub rabochikh transportnogo soiuza," RK 5 (1924): 64; "U zheleznodorozhnikov," RK 6 (1924): 60; "K svetlomu budushchemu," RK 8 (1924): 43.
30. E. Beskin, "Na novykh putiakh," *Prizyv* 5 (1924): 55–56.
31. Rabkor Chustov, "V dome prosveshcheniia im. Nekrasova," ZI 27 (1924): 18. See also
"Klub Krasnyi lechebnik," ZI 29 (1924): 17.

groups, one that followed an old repertoire and another determined to devise new works. Those who had chosen the new direction called themselves "conscious workers" (*soznatel'nye*) as opposed to their "dilettantish" (*liubitel'skie*) former colleagues. The supporters of plays were still harboring hurt feelings at the Red October Club a year after theater members switched to small forms.[32] The changes sometimes caused considerable bad blood. Members who resisted small forms were pronounced guilty of "dramatism" (*teatral'shchina*).[33] Old-style drama circles had "crippled the worker from the bench," in the opinion of an activist from a Moscow metalworkers' club, "evoking from him either the most mundane dilettantism or turning him into a bad actor."[34]

Not surprisingly, the rift between those embracing small forms and those who preferred a more conventional repertoire was often interpreted as a split between the young and old in clubs. In early NEP, as during the Civil War, young people were the main users of clubs and the primary participants in theater workshops. A 1924 survey of large clubs in Moscow determined that the approximately ninety percent of those in artistic circles were young people. "Workers clubs are becoming youth clubs," the author concluded.[35] Both advocates and foes of small forms saw the marked transformation of club theater as a reflection of its youthful composition. For those in favor of the shift, it was a sign of the radical and experimental nature of young people. "Youth instinctively turns away from old forms," wrote the trade union cultural leader, Emil Beskin, "believing them to be a vessel for old feelings and thoughts."[36] Critics saw things differently. They felt that the disjointed, iconoclastic repertoire was a sign of youthful inexperience and maintained that older workers were not interested at all.[37] These radically juxtaposed positions lent an aggressive undertone to discussions about club performances. Small forms were not simply an aesthetic direction; they im-

32. "Dramkruzhok parfiumernoi fabriki 'Svoboda,' " RK 6 (1924): 61; O. Liubomirskii, "Klub 'Krasnyi Oktiabr',' " NZ 6 (1925): 2. Shcheglov mentions similar splits in Leningrad; see *U istokov: Sbornik statei* (Moscow: VTO, 1960), 102.

33. E. Beskin, "Na novykh putiakh," *Prizyv* 5 (1924): 53.

34. Petr Sibartsev, "Na perelome," RZ 22 (1924): 20.

35. S. R-ch, "Molodezh' i vzroslye v klube," RK 2 (1924): 50. See also John Hatch, "The Formation of Working Class Cultural Institutions during NEP," *Carl Beck Papers*, no. 806 (1990): 11–12; and Diane Koenker, "Class and Consciousness in Socialist Society," in Sheila Fitzpatrick et al., eds., *Russia in the Era of NEP* (Bloomington: Indiana University Press, 1991), 49–50.

36. E. Beskin, "Teatral'noe segodnia," *Prizyv* 1 (1924): 96.

37. V. Bogoliubov, "O klubnoi p'ese," RK 23 (1925): 73.

plied political choices as well. For those in favor of the shift, their opponents were guilty of holding suspect beliefs. "We have noticed that the
drama circle used to suffer from 'petty bourgeois theater,' " observed
worker correspondents in the journal *New Viewer*. "But it has made a
good recovery from that illness."[38]

Festivals and Celebrations

Small forms tied the work of theater groups to the dates of the "Red
Calendar," a fluid list of celebrations designed to supplant Russian religious festivals and transmit the values of the new regime.[39] The two
most central dates were May Day and the anniversary of the revolution.
Other celebrations might include January 9, to mark the revolution of
1905; January 15, the death date of German revolutionary leaders Rosa
Luxemburg and Karl Liebknecht; January 21, the anniversary of Lenin's
death; February 23, Red Army Day; March 8, International Women's
Day; March 12, the anniversary of the fall of tsarism; March 18, the day
of the Paris Commune; and the anti-religious festivals of Komsomol
Easter and Komsomol Christmas.[40] New celebrations and special occasions were added to the list at the local level. Amateur theaters also participated in efforts to publicize local election campaigns, to celebrate the
founding dates of clubs, and to entertain at their sponsoring trade
union's annual convention. Participants and club leaders frequently
complained that this extensive list of festivities made performance
groups struggle from campaign to campaign, without time for adequate
preparation or rehearsal.[41]

Festivals were designed as participatory events, allowing as many
people as possible a chance to perform—resulting in mixed-media
events that could last all through the night. Many clubs opened the festivities with "An Evening of Remembrances." Workers with a personal
link to the holiday being celebrated, such as the revolution of 1905 or a
May Day celebration before the revolution, got a chance to tell their sto-

38. "Krasnyi luch," NZ 8 (1924): 12.

39. For assessments of the Red Calendar, see A. I. Mazaev, *Prazdnik kak sotsial'no-khudozhestvennoe iavlenie* (Moscow: Nauka, 1978), 349–56; E. A. Ermolin, *Materializatsiia prizraka: Totalitarnyi teatr sovetskikh massovykh aktsii 1920–1930kh godov* (Iaroslavl: Iaroslavskii
gosudarstvennyi pedagogicheskii universitet, 1996); Daniel Peris, *Storming the Heavens: The
Soviet League of the Militant Godless* (Ithaca, NY: Cornell University Press, 1998), 86–90.

40. See M. Veprinskii, *Khudozhestvennye kruzhki i krasnyi kalendar'* (Moscow: Gosizdat,
1926), 40–47.

41. O. Liubomirskii, "Bedy dramkruzhkov," NZ 30 (1924): 11.

ries.[42] The entertainments could include recitations of favorite poems, along with musical interludes by the club choir and orchestra. Art circles were active making banners, posters, and decorations. Sometimes physical education groups got involved, presenting feats of skill for the audience.[43] The British writer Huntley Carter, who visited Moscow in the early 1920s, offered this account of a May Day celebration:

> The performance and room decorations and inscriptions were clearly designed to usher in May Day, just as a certain church service is designed to usher in New Year's Day in England.... The club room, which was crowded to suffocation, was festooned with evergreens, draped with red and hung with portraits of Lenin, Trotsky, and Marx, and with inscriptions.... The exhibition was an improvised revue designed to emphasize the importance of May Day and its implications. One might call it a family affair in honour of the October communistic revolution.[44]

The festive family spirit was also noticed by Soviet observers. One witness to a Petrograd May Day celebration determined that "there were no spectators—everyone was a performer, a participant."[45]

Leaving the cramped spaces of clubs behind, some theater groups took their performances out into the streets, mounting trucks and platforms or using nearby squares as their performance space. The 1925 May Day celebration on Vasileostrovskii Island in Leningrad was a three-day affair, with club circles taking part in outdoor festivities the first day and returning to their club stages for the second and third.[46] Festival performances were sometimes very elaborate, staged like small versions of the huge events of the Civil War years. The Trekhgornyi Factory in Moscow acted out scenes from John Reed's book *Ten Days That Shook the World* for the 1924 October celebration. Divided into fifteen different parts, the dramatization involved some two hundred participants.[47] The Lenin Workers' Palace in Moscow staged an *instsenirovka* for the 1924 October celebration that portrayed the history of the revolution

42. "Klubnye postanovki k Oktiabr'skoi godovshchine," ZI 44 (1923): 25–26.

43. "Svedeniia," March 1925, GARF f. 7952 (Istoriia fabrik i zavodov), op. 3, d. 228, l. 29.

44. Huntley Carter, *The New Theatre and Cinema of Soviet Russia* (London: Chapman and Dodd, 1924), 101–2.

45. Vl. S., "Ne slovo, a delo," ZI 18 (1923): 19.

46. N. P. Izvekov, "1 maia 1925 g.," in *Massovye prazdnestva* (Leningrad: Academia, 1926), 107.

47. Utkes, "Gotovimsia k Oktiabriu," RZ 21 (1924): 23; Andrei Shibaev, "Na puti k samodeiatel'nomu teatru," RZ 28 (1924): 6.

from the start of the First World War to the Bolshevik takeover. The cast included three hundred civilians and one hundred soldiers.[48]

Annual trade union conferences were a popular venue for agitational performances. Meeting in large halls, the conferences provided a forum where theaters from several clubs could collaborate and perform for a captive audience of trade union delegates. The Red Woodworkers' Club of Moscow decided to act out their union's charter at the annual union convention in 1924. Their goal, according to one viewer, was "to give the rank-and-file trade union member a chance to familiarize himself with the dry language of the union charter by artistic means." This observer was especially impressed by the scene in which the membership rules were enacted. Doors on stage opened wide to include all workers, regardless of sex or nationality. The doors closed quickly, however, when former members of the tsarist police, capitalists, or priests tried to enter. These undesirable elements, dressed up as "wolves in sheep's clothing," were excluded from the union's ranks.[49]

With the emergence of journals and publications aimed at amateur stages, it was not necessary for club stages to devise their own texts. If they found the work appealing, club circles could use published scripts for a variety of celebrations. One example of this new material is a 1924 work, *Hands off China* (*Ruki proch' ot Kitaia*), published in the journal *Blue Blouse*. Using rhymed couplets, this text depicts the victimization of the Chinese peasantry by Western and Japanese imperialists. Only the Soviet Union intervenes to help the people of China assert their independence. "China, squeeze imperialism with your claws!" intones the character representing the Soviet Union. "Hands off China! Let's have a [Chinese] October!"[50] This short play, which offered a Soviet interpretation of international events and celebrated the October revolution simultaneously, was a popular choice for October festivities in Moscow in 1924. Five different club theaters used it to mark the holiday.[51]

Groups that embraced small forms judged instructors by their ability to stage successful festival performances. The Timiriazev Club in Moscow underwent a long search for an instructor who could meet the rigorous schedule of Soviet celebrations. After unsuccessful experiences with two instructors from the Moscow Art Theater and one from the

48. V. I. O., "Instsenirovka 'Oktiabr'," RZ 29 (1924): 19.

49. Derevoobdelochnik no. 5994, "Instsenirovka ustava derevoobdelochnikov," RZ 25/26 (1924): 32.

50. "Ruki proch' ot Kitaia," SB 4 (1924): 4–10, quotation 10.

51. RK 10/11 (1924): 78–79; "Khronika klubov," RZ 25/26 (1924): 35.

"Hands off China" (*Ruki proch' ot Kitaia*). A Blue Blouse performance. Harvard Theatre Collection, The Houghton Library. Reproduced with permission.

Meyerhold Theater, members finally turned to the Moscow Politprosvet
department for help. It sent the action circle advocate, Nikolai L'vov,
who in short order turned the group toward agitational productions.
Shortly after L'vov was hired, the circle staged a self-created work for
the 1924 May Day celebrations, *In Honor of May Day* (*K vstreche pervogo
maia*).[52]

The use of improvisational methods allowed club theaters to prepare
performances in a hurry—one of the chief advantages of small forms.
Participants in the Ivan Fedorov Printers' Club in Moscow decided just
two days before Christmas that they would like to stage an anti-religious event. They brainstormed together and came up with a plot tracing how a worker convinced his wife to use icons as fuel for the
samovar. Forty-eight hours later, an *instsenirovka* entitled "A Purpose
for Icons" was staged for the club community. Introduced by a lecture
on the scientific creation of the world and a short performance by the

52. "Kak dobilis' uspekha," RZ 27 (1924): 8.

club's living newspaper group, the improvised text was presented to a largely sympathetic young audience.[53]

These efforts at creation from below and broad participation gave a new spin to the word *samodeiatel'nost'*, which for many club participants came to mean "homemade." Those who enthusiastically supported the turn to small forms claimed that it empowered the participants to try their own hands at cultural creation. Surveying the preparations for the 1923 October festival in Leningrad, Grigorii Avlov praised the level of independent work. Some groups were using prepared texts, which they altered to suit their purposes. Others had works that were written by individual group members or group leaders. The most impressive circles were those who created their works collectively, revealing the creative potential of the theater of small forms.[54]

Investigations of Daily Life: Agit-Trials and Living Newspapers

Festivals by their very nature were special occasions, separate from the quotidian world. In addition, most early Soviet festivals had an overt political meaning; they honored turning points in the revolutionary struggle and marked important moments for the new state. As such, they did not have a direct influence on workers' daily lives. For many advocates of small forms, marking festivals was not enough. They believed that daily habits and social interactions (in Russian *byt*) could be analyzed and transformed through performance. Two styles of agitational theater were particularly suited to topics of daily life: the *agitsud*, or agit-trial, and the living newspaper.

Agit-trials emerged as an important form of amateur performance during the Civil War, when they were used to praise the heroes and excoriate the enemies of the revolution.[55] In the 1920s, their subject matter was broadened significantly. Workers who would not join a union were put on trial to demonstrate proper behavior at the factory. Social problems were acted out in trials of alcoholics and prostitutes. A wide range of trials also examined historical issues, like "The Trial of Those Responsible for the First World War."[56] Some agit-trials were easily integrated

---

53. P. R., "Rozhdestvo v klube," *Prizyv* 1 (1925): 97–98.
54. G. Avlov, "Oktiabr' v klubakh," ZI 43 (1923): 15.
55. See ch. 1.
56. This taxonomy of agit-trials comes from Grigorii Avlov, *Klubnyi samodeiatel'nyi teatr* (Leningrad: Teakinopechat', 1930), 93–94.

into festival celebrations; "The Trial of Father Gapon," for example, was often staged during the events marking the anniversary of 1905.[57]

One kind of agit-trial aimed for verisimilitude, attempting to follow the structure and atmosphere of a real trial as much as possible. These events enumerated the violated paragraphs of the legal code. Both prosecuting and defense attorneys took part, as well as witnesses for both sides. The Leningrad club activist Grigorii Avlov insisted that the more realistic the trial, the more effective it would be. It was better to try the hooligan than hooliganism. His own "Trial of Hooligans" was a case in point. The two young men on trial for misbehavior, Pavel Iudin and Ivan Karnauchov, were introduced with detailed information about their character and appearance. In the course of the trial, viewers learned about the social circumstances and political beliefs of the accused.[58]

But not all trials followed these guidelines. Some, such as "The Trial of Bourgeois Marriage," put abstract concepts on the witness stand. Even inanimate objects could win their day in court. In "The Political Trial of the Bible," the good book itself had a speaking role. In the course of questioning, the Bible was forced to admit to many inconsistencies about its authorship and contents. Unnamed worker witnesses asked tough questions that the Bible had difficulty answering: If people were made of clay, then how could they burn? How could two of all animals in the world fit on Noah's Ark with enough food for forty days? The Bible's one defender, an illiterate peasant girl, could say only that she believed the Bible was the word of God. She could not defend its contents in detail because she had never read them.[59] While the basic structure of the event bore some resemblance to a trial—with a prosecutor, a defendant, and witnesses—clearly this scenario was intended more to make the Bible look foolish than to give the audience a sense of life in the courtroom.

Trials also varied according to their predetermined nature. Many texts for agit-trials were published as elaborate scripts, with the speeches of witnesses and attorneys set down and the verdict preordained. Although the printed speeches (some quite detailed) were presented as a base for improvisation, and although the texts sometimes

57. See, for example, "Sud nad gaponovshchinoi," RK 2 (1924): 61.

58. Avlov, *Klubnyi samodeiatel'nyi teatr*, 94; idem, *Sud nad khuliganami* (Moscow: Doloi negramotnost', 1927), 10.

59. "Politsud nad Bibliei," *Komsomol'skaia paskha* (Moscow: Novaia Moskva, 1924), 111–28. It was performed at the Tsindel' textile factory in Moscow in 1924 (RK 7 [1924]: 38).

offered a variety of possible verdicts, the general outcome was unmistakable. In the many agit-trials of hooligans, for example, the young offenders were never allowed to escape without punishment. Here the drama of the event was in the performance, not the outcome.

However, other trials were impromptu events, sometimes written by local participants and casting members of the audience as witnesses and jurors with the power to come to their own conclusions. This kind of trial could sometimes bring surprising results. A factory circle from Petrograd playing in the countryside in the summer of 1923 had a very difficult time convincing village audiences to convict the character of a corrupt priest.[60] Isaac Babel's controversial collection of stories, *Red Cavalry*, was put on trial in a Moscow club in 1926. Although the speeches against the book were passionate, Babel himself made an appearance to argue in his defense. The assembled crowd not only acquitted Babel, but also judged his work to be a real service to the revolution.[61]

Agit-trials in the 1920s aimed to stamp out old habits and inculcate new ones. This purpose is strikingly evident in one trial written by the Moscow advocate of action circles, Vitalii Zhemchuzhnyi, called "An Evening of Books" (*Vecher knig*). This humorous work lampooned popular reading tastes, which tended toward religious works, detective novels, romantic potboilers, and Tarzan adventures. The judge in the trial, the American socialist author Upton Sinclair sent the work of the prerevolutionary romantic writer Anastasia Verbitskaia to the archive; he allowed God, a character in the drama, to go free since no one paid attention to him anymore; and he determined that all of Nat Pinkerton's books should be burned "to the last letter." Only Tarzan managed to escape judgment, since he escaped from the courtroom during a brawl. By the end, the audience was presented with a new, wholesome reading library, including Soviet adventure stories and, of course, the works of Upton Sinclair himself.[62]

Agit-trials also attempted to teach audiences new standards of public health. "The Trial of a Midwife Who Performed an Illegal Abortion" showed the risks of the abortion and the content of the Soviet abortion law.[63] Venereal disease was a very common theme. In a Moscow typog-

60. P. P., "Vpechatleniia teatral'nogo instruktora," ZI 22 (1923): 21–22.

61. V. Zhurina, "Diskussiia o khudozhestvennoi rabote," RK 29 (1926): 56.

62. This humorous trial is translated in James von Geldern and Richard Stites, eds., *Mass Culture in Soviet Russia* (Bloomington: Indiana University Press, 1995), 74–84, quotation 84. For evidence of its performance, see "Rabochii klub na Volkhovstroe," ZI 35 (1924): 20.

63. "V Tsentral'nom klube pechatnikov," ZI 8 (1924): 16.

"An Evening of Books" (*Vecher knigi*). The photograph depicts Komsomol members fighting with the representatives of bad literature, including God, Anastasia Verbit-skaia, and Nat Pinkerton. Bakhrushin State Central Theatrical Museum. Reproduced with permission.

raphers' club, a hypothetical case was brought for a hearing; a man had infected his wife and children with syphilis. The court had a magnani-mous verdict in this case. Because of his ignorance, the man should be cured and educated, not punished.[64] The traditional Russian scourge of alcoholism was another common theme. In one work, "The Trial of the Old Life" (*Sud nad starym bytom*), a frequently drunk worker was put on trial for beating his wife and keeping her from political work. Not only was he condemned to jail at the end of the trial, but so were the small shop owner and tavern keeper, who kept him supplied with alcohol.[65]

While many works for amateur theaters lacked major parts for women, agit-trials offered them starring roles, frequently as the chief ob-stacles to the new life. Agit-trial titles, which read like the names of bad

64. K. Glubinskaia, "Sud nad sifilitikom," RZ 19 (1924): 17–18.
65. Boris Andreev, *Sud nad starym bytom* (Moscow: Deloi negramotnost', 1926).

mysteries, give a sense of women's "crimes": "The Trial of the Woman Who Did Not Take Advantage of the October Revolution," "The Trial of the Illiterate Woman Worker," and "The Trial of the Mother Who Deserted Her Child."[66] One script, "The Woman Worker Who Did Not Attend General Meetings," examined six offending women who avoided trade union gatherings. Although the women had very different reasons for their truancy, ranging from fear to boredom, they were all charged with cultural and political backwardness.[67]

Club life itself was a theme for agit-trials, as activists considered ways to draw more workers to club activities. "The Trial of the Old Club" featured a surprising list of witnesses. One by one the library, the piano, and the drama studio came forward to accuse the club of poor organization, poor equipment, and lack of space. In the end, the old club broke down in tears because its members were preparing to leave for a new building.[68]

By claiming the small conflicts of everyday life as a proper subject matter, agit-trials could potentially turn nasty, singling out members of the audience for shame and censure. "The Trial of Six Workers at the Red October Factory" focused on actual factory workers who were deemed to have undermined cultural work. Their specific "crimes"—spreading rumors about the club and preferring an evening at a pub to wholesome entertainment—were presented in some detail in the proceedings. Although the accused were allowed to defend themselves, their comments were limited to lengthy admissions of guilt and promises of reform.[69] This use of agit-trials as a form of urban *charivari*, or *samosud*, would become much more common during the First Five-Year Plan, when many forms of agitational theater took an aggressive stance toward the audience.

Even more common than agit-trials were living newspapers, which began to appear in great numbers on amateur stages after the phenomenal success of a professional living newspaper circle from Moscow, Blue Blouse (*Siniaia bluza*).[70] The unusual name stemmed from the group's ba-

66. "Sittsenabivnaia fabrika byvsh. Tsindel'," RK 7 (1924): 38; ZI 24 (1925): 21.
67. "Rabotnitsa ne poseshchaiushchaia obshchikh sobranii," RK 20/21 (1925): 20–28.
68. A. Abramov, "Kak my 'sdelali' sud," RZ 22 (1924): 22.
69. "Sud nad klubom," RK 2 (1924): 30–32.
70. On Blue Blouse, see Claudine Amiard-Chevral, "La Blouse bleue," in Le Théâtre d'agit-prop de 1917 à 1932, v. 1, L'URSS (Lausanne: La Cité—L'Age d'Homme, 1977), 99–109; František Deak, "Blue Blouse, 1923–1928," Drama Review 17: no. 1 (1973): 35–46; and E. Uvarova, Estradnyi teatr: miniatiury, obozreniia, miuzik-kholly, 1917–1945 (Moscow: Iskusstvo, 1983), 95–96, 100–104.

sic costume element, a blue work shirt, which is called a *bluza* in Russian. Begun at the Moscow School of Journalism in 1923, Blue Blouse was headed by the energetic Boris Iuzhanin, who had prepared living newspapers for the Red Army during the Civil War. The group attracted the writing skills of some of the country's finest satirical authors, including Sergei Tretiakov, Argo (Abram Markovich Gol'denberg), and Vladimir Maiakovskii. According to theater historian František Deak, Blue Blouse was "the largest movement in the history of theatre in which the avant-garde participated."[71]

Presenting the news of the day in a vibrant mix of satirical songs, lively posters, dances, and pantomime, the Blue Blouse living newspaper soon won an enthusiastic audience in Moscow. A performance typically opened with a parade of the "headlines," followed by from eight to fifteen short vignettes on topics ranging from international affairs to local complaints about factory management.[72] The actors amended their simple work clothes with exaggerated props to identify the role they were performing, such as a top hat for a capitalist or a large red pencil for a bureaucrat. Since the troupe did not need sophisticated stages or lighting, it could perform almost anywhere. In the early 1920s Blue Blouse played in clubs, cafeterias, and factory floors throughout Moscow and Moscow province.[73]

In 1924, Blue Blouse was incorporated into the Moscow Trade Union cultural division. With this increased financial backing, it was able to start its well-known journal, *Blue Blouse*, which stayed in publication until 1928. The journal published scripts for living newspapers, offered advice on costumes and staging, and printed scores for Blue Blouse songs. It served as an inspiration for local groups wanting to stage their own performances. They either adopted the printed material whole cloth or used it as a model for their own creations. After a popular Blue Blouse presentation at the Moscow Elektrozavod factory in 1924, drama club members voted to start their own living newspaper. "In the future the living newspaper 'Electrical Current' (*Elektrotok*) will direct its work toward the productive life of the factory and will only make limited use of the material in Blue Blouse," the club members determined.[74] It was only one of many living newspapers formed from below, including the "Red

71. Deak, "Blue Blouse," 46.
72. See the Blue Blouse's instructions on the structure of a successful living newspaper, "Eshche raz—kak stroit' zhivuiu gazetu na mestakh," SB 13 (1925): 60.
73. See, for example, Andrei Shibaev, "Sinebluzniki," RZ 19 (1924): 15–16.
74. "Zhivaia gazeta 'Elektrotok,' " RZ 20 (1924): 16.

A Blue Blouse troupe. Harvard Theatre Collection, The Houghton Library. Reproduced with permission.

Tie" (*Krasnyi galstuk*), the "Red Sting" (*Krasnoe zhalo*), "Red Coil" (*Krasnaia katushka*), and the "Red Scourge" (*Krasnyi bich*).[75]

The success of Moscow's Blue Blouse sparked emulation in Leningrad. In early 1924, the Leningrad Trade Union Organization founded its own professional living newspaper group, Work Bench (*Stanok*). The agitational theatrical studio of the city's Politprosvet organization began a living newspaper as well.[76] Both of these professional circles served a similar function to Blue Blouse in Moscow; their perfor-

75. F. Troshin, "Nashi gazety," RZ 25/26 (1924): 33; Rabkor Svoi, " 'Krasnoe Zhalo' klub imeni Libknekhta," RZ 28 (1924): 20.

76. "Khronika," *Rabochii i teatr* (henceforth cited as RiT) 7 (1924): 19; V. Shimanovskii, "Zadachi tsentral'noi agitstudii," RiT 2 (1924): 15.

mances encouraged the creation of living newspapers at the club and
factory level, with colorful names like "Our Pencil," and "Factory
Whistle."[77]

By the summer of 1924, living newspapers gained national backing as
a potent agitational form. The national convention of club workers,
sponsored by the trade union organization and Glavpolitprosvet, endorsed living newspapers as a "method of agitation and propaganda,
serving the political, productive, and domestic [*bytovye*] tasks of the proletariat."[78] By the following year, living newspapers were widespread on
amateur stages in both capitals. The Leningrad journal *Worker and Theater* printed a separate page devoted to local groups, and one observer
determined that "some people are talking about the 'triumphant proces-
sion' of living newspaper through factories and plants."[79] In a survey of
one hundred city clubs, the Moscow-based journal *Worker's Club* revealed that living newspapers were the most popular form of performance, drawing in larger audiences than any other theatrical events.[80]

Advocates gave living newspapers an almost magical power to attract
and educate audiences. One viewer was supposedly so taken by a lively
Blue Blouse performance that he forgot to leave the club as usual for the
local bar. His wife was astonished when he came home sober.[81] An enthusiastic supporter from the Moscow Construction Workers' Union
claimed that Blue Blouse performances always generated lively discussions in workers' barracks and even inspired some workers to find out
more about the event portrayed on stage. "When a worker sees [the
British politician] Curzon or some other important political figure, he is
very interested in this guy who has played such a funny role on stage.
And afterwards, even if he hasn't understood everything, he begins to
look around to find out more."[82]

It is not hard to see living newspapers' attraction for cultural activists
and for many viewers. Their agitational and didactic function was self-
evident, because they always included information about contemporary
national and international politics. They were often humorous, offering
comic relief to viewers used to much drier political fare. Posters, slides,

77. " 'Nash karandash' No. 2," RiT 12 (1925): 14; "Klub im. tov. Volodarskogo," RiT 16
(1925): 15.

78. "Zhivaia i stennaia gazeta v rabochem klube," *Prizyv* 5 (1924): 182.

79. B. Fedorovskii, "Vyvod," RiT 11 (1925): 14; see also Sergei Spasskii, "Pis'mo iz
Leningrada," NZ 11 (1925): 7.

80. E. K., "Khudozhestvennaia rabota v klube," RK 24 (1924): 20–21.

81. Sh. Ia., "Pochashche by," RZ 19 (1924): 17.

82. "Zhivye gazety v klube," *Prizyv* 6 (1924): 110; see also 112.

A Blue Blouse demonstration at the Club of Foreign Office Employees. Harvard Theatre Collection, The Houghton Library. Reproduced with permission.

and sometimes even film clips were included, providing information and visual stimulation. They also were easily changed and amended to meet local conditions; a section for "letters to the editor" could contain complaints and commentary about concrete problems at the club or work site.

Those who wrote the texts for living newspapers attempted to put the traditions of folk theater to use in a new way, thus providing a familiar entree for urban audiences. A director from the Moscow Blue Blouse theater called his group a *balagan*, a Russian folk theater, and claimed that for precisely this reason Blue Blouse was comprehensible to worker audiences.[83] Parts of the performance were called a *"raek,"* or peepshow verse, an important element of fairground theater. Many living newspapers included a role for a carnival-like barker, called a *rupor* or *raeshnik*, who introduced the action and tied the various small skits together.

83. "Zhivaia gazeta v klube," *Prizyv* 6 (1924): 103.

Works included humorous four-lined rhymed ditties, or *chastushki*, an integral part of Russian urban and rural folk culture since the nineteenth century. The naughty star of Russian puppet theater, Petrushka, sometimes made an appearance.[84] The living newspaper script "Give us a New Life" (*Daesh' Novyi Byt*), published in 1924 and performed by several groups in 1924 and 1925, contained a part for a *ryzhii*, the traditional red-haired Russian clown.[85]

Not only did living newspapers attempt to transform folk culture for agitational use, they also drew on familiar forms of urban popular culture as well. In one programmatic statement, the editors of *Blue Blouse* insisted that a living newspaper should be performed at a fast pace and look like a film to the audience.[86] Music was a crucial part of a Blue Blouse performance, and participants drew on melodies popular in cafés and nightclubs. The opening march for all Blue Blouse performances, "We Are the Blue Blousists," was set to the tune of the popular song "We Are the Blacksmiths."[87] Organizers made no excuses for this eclectic approach; they maintained that their task was to reach out to unsophisticated viewers, appealing to their emotions as well as to their intellect.

The rapid expansion of Blue Blouse influence won it enemies as well as fans. Some critics resented the group's professional standing, saying it was a theater for workers, not by workers. They charged that professional groups had influenced the creation of local living newspapers from the top down. "Where was the self-activation [*samodeiatel'nost'*] in this?" wondered one Leningrad union activist.[88] Other viewers did not believe that satire was an effective educational tool. "Does anything remain in workers' heads but laughter after a Blue Blouse performance?" asked a trade union leader.[89]

In contrast to Blue Blouse and other professional troupes, local living newspapers were located close to their audience and could address issues of direct relevance to the life of the club and the community. Partic-

84. On the *chastushki*, see Steven Frank, " 'Simple Folk, Savage Customs?': Youth, Sociability, and the Dynamics of Culture in Rural Russia, 1856–1914," *Journal of Social History* 25, no. 4 (1992), 723–24. On Petrushka in the Soviet context, see Catriona Kelly, *Petrushka: The Russian Carnival Puppet Theatre* (Cambridge: Cambridge University Press, 1990), 179–211.

85. "Daesh' novyi byt!" *Iskusstvo v rabochem klube*, 72–95.

86. "Kak rabotaet 'Siniaia bluza,' " SB 7 (1925): 4; "Na sinebluzom fronte," SB 23/24 (1925): 85.

87. "Marsh sinei bluzy," SB 2 (1924): 94–95.

88. "Zhivaia gazeta," RiT 12 (1924): 6. For the response of Blue Blouse advocates, see "Teatralizovannaia gazeta—profakterskaia i klubnaia," SB 13 (1925): 3–4.

89. *Prizyv* 6 (1924):106–7, 111.

An amateur performance at the Moscow Sales Workers' Club. Bakhrushin State Central Theatrical Museum. Reproduced with permission.

ipants included concrete details about problems in their union or work place and could shape their repertoire to fit any special event. Local groups could also aim their performances toward particular audiences. Komsomol-based newspapers addressed the problems of youth; a living newspaper sponsored by educational workers included a section called "Teachers during NEP."[90] It was the thrill of immediacy that supposedly won audiences over to living newspapers, with the most contemporary material drawing the most interest. At an anniversary celebration for the Central Sales Workers' Club in Moscow, a living newspaper addressed the accomplishments and failures of different club circles, much to the delight of the audience. Such methods brought about a strong bond between the performers and the viewers, insisted one advocate.[91]

However, homebred living newspapers often faced complaints for following the patterns designed by professionals too closely. The vast

90. F. M., "U prosveshchentsev," ZI 14 (1925): 16; "Zhivaia gazeta Mossel'prom," NZ 2 (1925): 17.

91. G., "Godovshchina kluba," RK 5 (1924): 49; K., "Zhivaia gazeta v klube Pervoi obraztsovoi tipografii," RK 3/4 (1924): 71.

majority of local groups imitated Blue Blouse models, claimed the passionate advocate of action circles, Vitalii Zhemchuzhnyi. They did not involve the entire club in their preparation and drew their performers from drama circles alone. Because participants did not write their own work, performances did not address the specific needs and interests of the audience.[92]

Because they attempted to educate and entertain simultaneously, both amateur and professional living newspaper groups found themselves caught up in what Denise Youngblood has called the "entertainment or enlightenment debate" that dominated the Soviet film industry in the 1920s. One faction of Soviet filmmakers looked to foreign films for their inspiration, trying to use popular elements—suspense, slapstick humor, happy endings—to draw in viewers while imbuing their films with a Soviet message. They were opposed by those who argued that such concessions to capitalist methods undermined the films' socialist content. Instead, directors should concentrate on edifying and didactic topics that could not be mistaken for bourgeois products.[93]

In their efforts to integrate elements of urban commercial culture, living newspaper groups found themselves in a similar situation to filmmakers who sought to make their movies entertaining. In the words of one advocate, living newspapers were "a political genre, but a light and cheerful kind that is good for workers who want to relax and have a good time."[94] Sanctimonious critics complained that this was precisely the problem. Their work looked too much like bourgeois cabaret. "The performance has a theatrical character, along the lines of 'Crooked Jimmy' [a prerevolutionary cabaret], but the copy is worse than the original," complained a representative from the Central Art Workers' Union.[95] One worker correspondent claimed that the living newspaper "Red Scourge" offered an inauthentic analysis of hooliganism among Soviet youth—the hooligans looked more like Parisians than "our own." He also did not like the dances, the many jokes, and the frivolous portrayal of the Komsomol girl. The entire performance was "sloppy, superficial, and thoughtless."[96] "If this is theater," wrote two worker critics

92. V. Zhemchuzhnyi, "Klubnaia zhivaia gazeta," RK 15 (1925): 26–27.

93. Denise Youngblood, *Movies for the Masses* (Cambridge: Cambridge University Press, 1992), esp. chs. 2 and 3.

94. "Zhivaia gazeta v klube," *Prizyv* 6 (1924): 105.

95. Ibid. For similar comments, see R. G., "Siniaia Bluza v mestnom prelomlenii," RK 15 (1925): 31–33, where she complains about the "café-chantant" musical style of Blue Blouse performances.

96. Rabkov F. Lev, "Zhivaia gazeta 'Krasnyi bich,' " RZ 31 (1924): 19.

in response to a Blue Blouse performance, "then it is an unhealthy kind. . . . Put an end to bourgeois elements in workers' theater."[97]

Living newspapers, both professional and amateur, attempted a difficult balancing act. They tried to merge political information of national and local relevance, presenting it in a witty and engaging style. Complaints focused on their inability to meet all of these requirements—their approach to politics was too frivolous, their coverage of local problems too superficial, and they made too many concessions to commercial popular culture in their efforts to engage audiences. Eventually, these charges would coalesce into a blanket condemnation of "Blue Blouse-ism," a term of approbation that criticized living newspapers' satirical approach to serious issues and their episodic presentational style. It was a critique that attacked the central premise of most living newspapers— that elements of urban popular culture were appropriate conduits for political education.

Small Forms and the Avant-Garde

With their episodic structure and non-naturalistic staging, amateur productions employing small forms bore a distinct similarity to the theatrical experiments of the avant-garde. This similarity was hardly surprising, since avant-gardists were deeply involved in what they saw as an exciting attempt to create a utilitarian theater that would not simply observe life but also change it.[98] Students of Vsevolod Meyerhold, the doyen of avant-garde theater, took positions in amateur theater groups. Writers from the Left Front of the Arts (LEF) wrote scripts for Blue Blouse and amateur living newspaper circles.[99] The involvement of these artists brought precious resources to struggling amateur stages; in addition, it linked the fate of small forms to the avant-garde.

Meyerhold was a significant supporter of the club theater of small forms. In early 1924 he opened a "Club Methodological Laboratory" as part of his training courses in Moscow. It prepared directors for club theaters, reviewed manuscripts for club performances, devised plans for mass spectacles, and debated the aesthetic principles of club theatrical work.[100] The workshop endorsed a variety of small forms, including *inst-*

97. M. Piatnitskaia and Gavrikov, "Ob oshibkakh 'Sinei bluzy,' " RZ 20 (1924): 12.

98. B. Arvatov, "Zhivaia gazeta, kak teatral'naia forma," ZI 44 (1925): 2.

99. O. Liubomirskii, "1919—Sovrabotnik—1924," NZ 43 (1924): 10.

100. Archival holdings for the studio are in RGALI, f. 963, op. 1, dd. 1088–1141. For contemporary accounts of its work, see Ligov, "Kruzhkovody, organizuites'!" RiT 13 (1924): 17; L-ai, "Na pomoshch' klubam," RZ 30 (1924): 7; "Klubnaia rabota meierkhol'dtsev," RK 12 (1924): 47; Nesterov (a participant), "God raboty," ZI 2 (1925): 12–13.

senirovki and living newspapers. Improvisations took precedence over ready-made works. "Only when there is no material and no time to prepare any should the circle turn to plays," read one instruction.[101]

Training club instructors was the studio's most important task. Meyerhold enrolled students with a wide range of experience. Some, like Olga Galaktionova, came with modest credentials, having worked only briefly in the provinces before arriving at the studio. Others had considerable experience and would go on to make big names for themselves in the world of Soviet culture. These included Nikolai Ekk, who was simultaneously a student in Meyerhold's directors' studio and the Meyerhold Theater. He eventually turned from theater to movies and directed the first Soviet sound film, *The Road to Life (Putevka v zhizn')* in 1931. Another studio participant with a similar trajectory was Ivan Pyr'ev, who began in the Proletkult and also studied acting and directing with Meyerhold. He turned to film already in the middle of the 1920s and by the next decade began to build a reputation as a director of filmed musical comedies. His biggest hits included *Tractor Drivers (Traktoristy)* and *Kuban Cossacks (Kubanskie kazaki)*, which gained a reputation as one of the worst examples of Stalinist culture during the Khrushchev era.[102]

Meyerhold's laboratory acted as an employment facilitator, fielding requests from local clubs for experienced instructors. "We have almost no money," read one query from a local chemical factory. "However, we do have a good group of young workers who are interested in the theater."[103] Instructors were sent to clubs that were willing to pay their salaries. By late 1925, the club laboratory had provided instructors for more than forty different Moscow clubs. The sponsors included trade unions, the Komsomol, the Red Army, and five clubs under the control of the GPU, the Soviet secret police.[104] Most students worked in the capital, but some received placements in the provinces. Pyr'ev ended up in Ekaterinburg in 1924.[105]

Wherever they went, these instructors encouraged the turn to small

101. "Klubno-metodologicheskaia laboratoriia pri teatre i masterskikh im. Vs. Meierkhol'da," RGALI, f. 963, op. 1, d. 1058, l. 3.

102. "Klubno-metodologicheskaia laboratoriia—anketa [1926]," RGALI, f. 963, op. 1, d. 1103, ll. 59, 66.

103. RGALI, f. 963, op. 1, d. 1094, l. 5.

104. "Klubno-metodologicheskaia laboratoriia pri teatre i masterskikh im. Vs. Meierkhol'da," 5. XI 1925, RGALI, f. 963, op. 1, d. 1058, ll. 2–3; L-ai, "Na pomoshch' klubam," RZ 30 (1924): 7.

105. O. L., "Ekaterinburg," NZ 38 (1924): 13.

forms. One Moscow club, which had been performing Ostrovsky plays, changed entirely with the arrival of Goltsov, a Meyerhold student. Participants began to use different kinds of material, like satirical stories from the journal *The Godless* (*Bezbozhnik*) as the basis for their improvised work. Ispolnev, another Meyerhold student, took charge of the club at the large Trekhgornyi textile mill in Moscow, where he concentrated his efforts on staging club festivals.[106]

The Meyerhold laboratory encouraged instructors to write their own material. In a 1926 questionnaire, Nikolai Ekk boasted that only five percent of the work he staged in his four years of club activity was written by others; the rest he devised himself, together with his students. Two of his works, *The Red Eagles* (*Krasnye orliata*) and *Ky sy my* were published and performed in numerous clubs. Boris Ivanter, a leader of several Moscow clubs, composed *The Earth in Flames* (*Zemlia zazhglas'*) in 1924 together with his wife Vera. It tells the story of the Bolsheviks' rise to power and subsequent efforts by the bourgeoisie to subvert the revolution. This work played on numerous factory stages in 1924, including the Triangle Rubber Plant in Moscow and the Putilov factory in Leningrad.[107] Nikolai Mologin devised a humorous work making fun of bureaucratic language and the Soviets' new-found love of acronyms. Entitled "Upruiaz" (an acronym for "*Uproshennyi russkii iazyk*"—Simplified Russian Language), it proposed that individuals should start using abbreviations and acronyms in their daily speech. In addition, Mologin's witty script suggested that people should leave off Russian's complicated grammatical endings and communicate only with word roots, a change that might have been welcomed by non-Russians struggling with the language. It was staged at several clubs, including the Central Printers' Club, where Mologin was in charge.[108]

Studio members also organized large-scale festivals that drew in a number of amateur theater groups. The laboratory worked together with the Red Army to prepare plans for a "Red Stadium." Although the structure was never built, a number of large outdoor events using amateur participants were staged at its proposed site at the Lenin Hills in

106. "Raionnyi klub rabochikh transportnogo soiuza," RK 5 (1924): 64; O. L., "Klub Trekhgornoi manufaktury," NZ 10 (1924): 8.

107. B. and V. Ivanter, *Zemlia zazhglas'. P'esa v trekh chastiakh* (Moscow: Molodaia gvardiia, 1924). For evidence of its performance, see *Pravda*, 12 November 1924, and RiT 6 (1924): 15.

108. Nikolai Mologin, "Upruiaz," RGALI f. 963, op. 1, d. 118, ll. 3–7; "Po rabochim klubam," *Pravda* 12 January 1924.

Moscow.[109] In addition, studio participants planned and executed elaborate neighborhood festivals. One such event in Moscow celebrated the history of the Sokol district Communist Party. Using masses of raw material sent by the Communist Party Committee, two studio members devised a scenario that examined significant events from the revolution until 1925, incorporating data and statistics about the Sokol region. It was staged by Nikolai Ekk to mark the 1925 anniversary of the revolution.[110]

Through their efforts, Meyerhold students believed they were bringing sophisticated professional techniques to a broad audience. For them, the Meyerhold Theater was the main inspiration for small forms on amateur stages. One statement from the Meyerhold laboratory determined that those wishing to compose compelling living newspapers should look to Meyerhold's production of *The Trust D.E.* for inspiration.[111] This play, based on a novel by Ilia Ehrenburg, caused a sensation in the world of professional theater with its use of jazz, stylish dance numbers, and physical education routines. Theoretical statements issued by the laboratory charged that other groups supporting small forms, particularly the action circles led by Zhemchuzhnyi, were making use of Meyerhold's methods without giving him credit.[112]

Artists from Moscow's action circles and the Politprosvet division in Leningrad, however, believed that Meyerhold had gotten his inspiration from amateur theaters, and not the other way around. "In the struggle against naturalistic and psychological tendencies, professional theaters have produced their conventions of heroism and buffoonery, their synthetic methods integrating music, song, and dance, under the influence (*pod znakom*) of amateur theaters," declared Adrian Piotrovskii.[113] Stefan Mokulskii, from Leningrad's State Institute of the History of Art, con-

109. O. L., "Klubnaia rabota na Krasnom stadione," NZ 21 (1924): 14; on the project in general, see Susan Corbesero, "If We Build It, They Will Come: The International Red Stadium Society," unpublished manuscript.

110. "Tekst instsenirovannogo otcheta Sokol'n. raikom VKP," RGALI, f. 963, op. 1, d. 1104, ll. 1–12; "Klubno-metodologicheskaia laboratoriia pri teatre i masterskikh im. Vs. Meierkhol'da," 5 November 1925, RGALI, f. 963, op. 1, d. 1088, l. 17; "Oktiabr' v klubakh," *Pravda* 11 November 1925.

111. "Proekt tezisov o 'zhivoi gazete,' " 1 December 1925, RGALI, f. 963. op. 1, d. 1089, l. 80. On the impact of *The Trust D.E.*, see S. Frederick Starr, *Red and Hot: The Fate of Jazz in the Soviet Union* (New York: Limelight Editions, 1985), 50–52.

112. "Osnovnye polozheniia doklada tt. Zhemchuzhnogo i L'vova," RGALI, f. 963, op. 1, d. 1120, l. 25 ob.

113. A. Piotrovskii, "Samodeiatel'nyi teatr i sovetskaia teatral'naia kul'tura: Vmesto predisloviia," in Avlov, *Klubnyi samodeiatel'nyi teatr,* 9; see also S. Mokul'skii, "Pobegi novogo iskusstva," ZI 21 (1925): 13.

curred. Professional theater is challenged in each historical epoch by amateur theatrical forms—and this was precisely what was happening in Soviet Russia. The proletariat was creating its own forms of art, daily life, and knowledge within workers' clubs and Komsomol circles, he determined.[114]

Given the affinities between the theater of small forms and the avant-garde, is it possible to find a constituency among urban youth and working people for experimental theater? Until now, scholars have routinely rejected the idea that the avant-garde had much of a following outside the educated population, a conclusion we can find echoed in one school of 1920s criticism.[115] But at least some club participants appreciated Meyerhold's methods enough to imitate them. The Kalinin Club in Leningrad put on a self-generated work called "Path to Victory" (*Put' k pobede*) that was obviously influenced by Meyerhold, according to one critic. The Sapronov Club in Moscow copied Meyerhold's controversial interpretation of Ostrovsky's play *The Forest* (*Les*), performing it for club members and other groups.[116]

In addition, worker viewers frequented the Meyerhold Theater. A number of worker correspondents (*rabkory*) attending a discussion about *The Trust D.E.* found it stimulating and insisted that it offered a very critical look at the bourgeoisie. "I talked to the workers at my factory," said one reporter. "There were some who found deficiencies but in general they praised it."[117] The *rabkor* Iurii Kobrin was an enthusiastic supporter of Meyerhold's methods. In his short pamphlet *The Meyerhold Theater and the Worker Viewer*, he insisted that this innovative stage had a large and enthusiastic proletarian audience. Evidence from the Moscow agency that distributed tickets to trade unions provides some verification for this claim. The most popular tickets were those for the Meyerhold Theater, which were "snatched up and never returned."[118] Evidently, not all worker viewers were averse to theatrical experimentation.

114. S. Mokul'skii, "O samodeiatel'nom teatre," ZI 29 (1924): 6.
115. Dobrenko, *The Making of the State Reader*, 120–21; Régine Robin, "Popular Literature of the 1920s," in *Russia in the Era of NEP*, 253–67, esp. 261. For a small sample of contemporary views, see V. Vsevolodskii, " 'Levyi' teatr sego dnia," ZI 6 (1924): 6; S. Prokof'ev, "Tozhe 'revoliutsionery,' " RZ 10 (1924): 1.
116. M. N-n, "Klub imeni tov. Kalinina," ZI 20 (1925): 19; "V klube imeni Sapronova," NZ 33 (1924): 15, and NZ 30 (1924): 6.
117. L. Leonov, "Rabkory o D.E.," RZ 24 (1924): 12.
118. Iurii Kobrin, *Teatr im. Vs. Meierkhol'da i rabochii zritel'* (Moscow: Moskovskoe teatral'noe izdatel'stvo, 1926), esp. 23; A. Tsenovskii, "Chto liubit rabochii?" RiT 25 (1925): 7.

Eventually the ties between amateur stages and the avant-garde would work against small forms. Critics who opposed this direction in clubs used the same terms to denounce amateur performances as those reserved for the avant-garde, namely, that the approach was alien to proletarian taste and "bourgeois" in inspiration. "The worker is a realist down to his bones," wrote one observer. "He doesn't like phrases. He cannot stand abstractions. And by the way, for him the symbolic, entertaining concoctions of a closed off clique of educators, such as talking factory whistles or cake-walking money, are just so much red tape."[119]

Spontaneity and Consciousness

After watching an exhibition of amateur theaters in Leningrad in 1925, the distinguished theater historian, Alexei Gvozdev, announced, "There now can be no doubt that a new theater will be created not from above but rather from below."[120] Debates about who was responsible for the making of Soviet culture—the broad population, the intelligentsia, or the state—began with the revolution and continue on in scholarship to this day. For amateur theaters of the early 1920s, it was clearly a combination. Piotrovskii was inspired by the methods he observed on the club stages of revolutionary Petrograd. He then used his considerable influence as head of the city's Politprosvet division to ensure that these methods were refined and spread to as many amateur stages as possible. Small forms were appealing to at least a segment of actors and audiences because they were inclusive, opening up the stage to a large number of people. They also held the promise of conveying "local knowledge," with spaces to insert the small victories and heartfelt needs of those creating and viewing them. Their structure, comprised of many small skits and vignettes, made the process of creation easier, opening it up to untrained club members. Thus they appeared to offer proof of the spontaneous, self-generated creativity of the masses. "Self-activity—that is the most distinctive feature of workers' theater. This is its most important difference from professional theater. Here the workers are simultaneously the carpenters, actors, and authors," effused one observer of a performance at Leningrad's Nekrasov People's Home.[121]

Advocates of small forms believed that they undercut the power of "bourgeois" professionals, who still dominated the world of established

---

119. Aleksei Gotfrid, "Nuzhna-li p'esa rabochemu klubu," RiT 11 (1924): 15.
120. A. A. Gvozdev, "Samodeiatel'nyi teatr," *Molodaia gvardiia* 8 (1925): 197.
121. Sergei Tomskii, "V rabochem klube," ZI 37 (1923): 23.

theater. Soviet club theater was the negation of bourgeois theater in all of its forms, insisted Grigorii Avlov of the Leningrad Politprosvet organization.[122] It was called into life because professional theaters were not addressing the needs of workers and peasants to reflect upon their political situation and engage in the construction of a new political order. Because professional theaters had refused that role, a new kind of theater needed to take shape with a politicized, openly utilitarian purpose.[123]

Many participants in the theater of small forms went a step further and rejected the idea of professionalization altogether. They denied that club theatrical circles should try to find talented individuals who could be prepared for and promoted to the professional stage. Trade union leader S. Levman believed that the task of amateur theater was to serve the club community as a whole and to engage members in mass work, not to prepare well-trained actors.[124] One union activist endorsed the unified artistic circle because this method supposedly limited the influence of specialists.[125] Because small forms allowed participants to use speeches, newspaper articles, and other commonly available materials for theatrical work, it allowed energetic circles to work on their own without professional intermediaries.

Yet despite these broad claims for self-determination, the amateur theater of small forms was also created by club instructors (some with impressive theatrical credentials) and sponsoring agencies. Even when amateurs wrote their own material, they were influenced by printed scripts from a variety of official sources. Reports of festival repertoire show considerable uniformity, a uniformity that was encouraged by state organizations overseeing cultural work. The Petrograd section of autonomous theater collected information on fifty-seven clubs performing works for the 1923 May Day celebrations; thirty-three used works prepared by the city's Politprosvet division.[126] A circular drawn up by the Moscow branch of the Communist Party, Komsomol, the trade union organization, and the Politprosvet division for the first anniversary of Lenin's death in 1925 offered this advice: "Prepared texts should be used only in extreme circumstances. All work should be built around the autonomous activity of club members." At the same time, though,

---

122. G. Avlov, "Samodeiatel'nost' ili bezdeiatel'nost'," ZI 24 (1923): 9.
123. G. Avlov, Klubnyi samodeiatel'nyi teatr, 22–24.
124. S. Levman, "Khudozhestvennaia rabota v klube," Prizyv 3 (1924): 29.
125. E. Beskin, "O dramaticheskikh klubnykh kruzhkakh," Prizyv 2 (1924): 57–58.
126. "Podgotovka k prazdnovaniiu 1-go maia po sektsii Samodeiatel'nogo teatra," ZI 17 (1923): 19.

the brochure included a list of acceptable repertoire and also determined the official slogans for the celebration.[127]

The sponsoring agencies for clubs, particularly local trade union divisions, were important supporters of the turn to small forms. They interceded to reorganize club management and to find instructors sympathetic to new modes of theatrical presentation. Many club training programs, from the Meyerhold laboratory to the Petrograd/Leningrad Politprosvet division, turned out instructors who wanted to stage holiday celebrations and living newspapers rather than Ostrovsky plays. Regardless of claims to the contrary by the most passionate defenders of small forms, the guidance of these instructors was a significant factor in changing local repertoires.

The amateur theater of small forms offered a vehicle for self-expression for participants, but one that was heavily supervised. The spontaneity of participants was guided and directed by a number of agencies whose job it was to ensure that the final product was imbued with "consciousness," with slogans and programs endorsed by the Communist Party and trade union and political agencies. Its overt messages were almost always politically correct; performances directed viewers to mark the holidays of the new state, sober up, and avoid boulevard literature left over from the old regime. Thus, "do-it-yourself" theater was not entirely the creation of its actors or audience. As one advocate argued, *samodeiatel'nost'* did not mean doing whatever one wanted. Without any sense of irony he continued, "It is most correct to speak about organized and directed self-activity."[128]

Despite the transparent didacticism, supporters of this style of performance worked with their audience in mind. They tried to engage and interest viewers. It was precisely this attempt to mix education with pleasure that angered many critics of small forms. They argued that club works were too amateurish, too disjointed, and too close to commercial culture to be effective aesthetic or political tools. Perhaps most important, they insisted that club forms were simply too small to articulate the grand dreams and accomplishments of the victorious Soviet revolution.

127. "Plan provedeniia kampanii po godovshchine smerti V. I. Lenina i '9 ianvaria' v klubakh i krasnykh ugolkakh," RGALI, f. 963, op. 1, d. 1096, ll. 1–5, quotation l.4.
128. E. Beskin, "Khudozhestvennaia rabota v klube," *Prizyv* 6 (1924): 34.

3

From "Club Plays" to the Classics

A 1926 editorial in the Moscow journal *The New Viewer* asserted that Soviet theater was undergoing a fundamental transformation. During the first period of revolutionary upheaval, amateur stages had been an important force in destroying old forms and challenging professional stages. That period, however, was over. Now the battle had begun for higher quality and a new kind of professionalism, a battle that all theaters could engage in together.[1] These statements in a journal aimed at a working-class audience and covering amateur stages would have been inconceivable only a few years earlier. They showed that the radical anti-professionalism of the early NEP period was on the wane.

Katerina Clark has called NEP a period of "quiet revolution in intellectual life," when some of the most distinctive elements of Soviet culture began to take shape. Particularly during the second half of NEP, the period investigated in this chapter, intellectuals began to group themselves into ever broader and ideologically more diverse organizations that bore some similarity to the professional unions formed in the 1930s. At the same time, the Communist Party and Komsomol established an important place as the sponsors of critical journals devoted to politics and culture. The result was a radical simplification of cultural debate.[2]

1. "Litsom k novomu tea-professionalizmu," NZ 47 (1926): 3–4.
2. On realignments among professionals, see Katerina Clark, "The 'Quiet Revolution' in Soviet Intellectual Life," in Sheila Fitzpatrick et al., eds., *Russia in the Era of NEP* (Bloomington: Indiana University Press, 1991), 210–30.

On the surface, at least, there was no such simplification process in the world of amateur theater. Instead, the offerings on club stages became more diverse in the second half of the 1920s. Small forms, which predominated in Moscow and Leningrad a few years earlier, began to share stage time with special plays written for club theaters as well as works intended for the professional stage. Yet even while the offerings expanded, the discussions about the significance of amateur theater narrowed. Two large camps took shape, one supporting the innovations of small forms and the other advocating a larger, grander style. The journals devoted to amateur stages were filled with vituperative attacks on rival directions: some denounced the incomprehensible and unsatisfying "leftism" of small forms whereas others saved their venom for the reactionary "naturalism" of those who were copying the works they saw on the professional stage.

The economic recovery of the second half of NEP changed the social context of amateur performance. After several years of hardship, state resources began flowing to factories and trade unions again. These modest increases gave them a chance to consider building or renovating spaces for performance. Paradoxically, new resources infused more animosity into the struggle between small and large forms. The shape and placement of the stage in new structures indicated what kind of performances the builders expected to see. Economic recovery brought anxieties as well, since it was achieved through the semi-capitalist mechanisms of the New Economic Policy. For some groups, this very fact made prosperity dubious. They felt it was no time to relax their revolutionary vigilance, nor to give up the agitational tactics that reminded actors and audiences of their political duties.

There was a clear (if temporary) winner in this struggle over the form and content of amateur performance. At the 1927 conference on theater sponsored by the Communist Party's Agitprop division, the organizational principles of the theater of small forms, especially the united artistic circle, came in for heavy criticism. Small forms had become too predictable to interest broad audiences, conference organizers determined. Moreover, significant changes in the repertoire of professional theaters, which had begun staging plays addressed to the revolution, made their work more appealing. Agitprop and trade union leaders recommended a new spirit of cooperation between amateurs and professionals. At the same time, however, they articulated their views in such a way as to show that amateurs would be the junior partners in this collaboration. In the words of final conference resolutions, the "theories thought up in isolated offices" that opposed amateur and professional methods had nothing to do with Marxism.[3]

Small Forms Besieged

The heyday of small forms began to wane by the middle of the 1920s. Living newspapers and improvisations faced criticism from cultural consumers, who claimed that they had become too monotonous; from club activists, who worried that they were driving older workers from clubs; and from political organizers, who were concerned about their spontaneous and uncontrolled nature. Some supporters of small forms themselves argued that they led organically to a search for more complex works that would still convey an agitational message but do so in a more compelling fashion.

Criticisms of small forms came in part from the audience. The most influential viewers were worker correspondents (*rabkory*), self-taught critics from the lower classes who gained positions in journals and newspapers during NEP.[4] While most of their attention was addressed to the professional stage, they also evaluated amateur performances. Although they did not always agree, many worker correspondents were skeptical of the improvisational theater of small forms, believing that it was not really designed with workers in mind. One *rabkor* sent to review a living newspaper performance at the Volodarskii Railroad Workers' Club in Leningrad had to admit that the audience loved the show. Viewers applauded wildly and even demanded encores. The critic made short work of their enthusiasm, however. "There were almost no workers in the crowd. Perhaps that explains the success of these completely trashy numbers [*chisto khalturnykh nomerov*]." Another *rabkor* insisted that clubs filled up for festival performances only because they were free: "It is true that sometimes the viewers applaud, but their applause is not meant for the work. Rather [it is meant for] the actors and for the revolutionary content of the *instsenirovka*."[5] It was not enough to be proud of a performance just because workers had done it themselves,

3. S. M. Krylov, ed., *Puti razvitiia teatra: Stenograficheskii otchet i resheniia partiinogo soveshchaniia po voprosam teatra pri Agitprope TsK VKP (b) v mae 1927 g.* (Moscow: Kinopechat', 1927), 498.

4. On worker correspondents and professional theaters, see L. A. Pinegina, *Sovetskii rabochii klass i khudozhestvennaia kul'tura* (Moscow: Izdatel'stvo Moskovskogo universiteta, 1984), 176–79.

5. Rabkor A. Stepkoi, "Zhivaia gazeta TPO," ZI 1 (1925): 15; Rabkor I. Iankelevich, "Vspomnite ob iskusstve," RiT 17 (1925): 20.

determined one critic in *The New Viewer*. Opinions like these showed little faith in the creative abilities of the working class.[6]

Worker correspondents were not the only ones to complain. The well-worn stereotypes and predictability of small forms irritated many others. One trade union leader argued that audiences were fed up with standardized depictions of cruel bureaucrats, honest workers, and brainless secretaries powdering their noses.[7] Moreover, the villains of small forms did not really have a contemporary ring. Such predictable stereotypes simplified social reality, insisted the club instructor Dmitrii Shcheglov. "Not all Mensheviks are bastards and not all generals blood suckers. . . . Finally, the working class does not always function as a collective (or rather as a mass). It has its own distinctive figures (heroes)."[8]

Even those who found agitational works compelling maintained that a constant diet of small forms was more than they could stomach. In scattered accounts, reporters complained that viewers found living newspapers poorly executed, mundane, and uninspiring. "They are not interesting," one audience member at the Red October Club in Moscow claimed. "We can read newspapers ourselves."[9] Other small forms met similar reactions, with at least some audience members finding them disorganized and episodic. One reviewer of an *instsenirovka* performed in honor of Bloody Sunday in a central Moscow club called it an "arsenal of effects and buffoonery" that in no way evoked the historical drama of the march on the tsar.[10]

The perceived link to bad economic times was also a mark against small forms. By 1925, key economic factors began to swing sharply upward, finally reaching prewar levels by the following year. The draconian measures of early NEP that had meant harsh budget cuts for cultural institutions slowly were rescinded, bringing funds for club construction and expansion. The improvisational theater of the Civil War and early NEP had made the most of scarce resources. Many club theaters were still making do with small spaces, at the same time that club memberships were growing. A Moscow study of more than one hundred clubs conducted in late 1924 discovered that only a few could accommodate performances for more than five hundred people. Large festival events

6. A. Sh., "Boliachki klubnogo spektaklia," NZ 7 (1926): 10.

7. I. Isaev, *Osnovnye voprosy klubnoi stseny* (Moscow: VTSSPS, 1928), 11, 29.

8. D. Shcheglov, *Teatral'no-khudozhestvennaia rabota v klubakh: Metodika i praktika* (Leningrad: Gubprofsovet, 1926), 7.

9. O. Liubomirskii, "Klub 'Krasnyi Oktiabr'," NZ 6 (1925): 12. See also "Pochemu vzroslyi rabochii ne idet v klub?" RK 12 (1925): 57.

10. V. Nikulin, "V tsentral'nom klube kommunal'nikov," NZ 5 (1925): 12.

sometimes needed to be held in shifts.[11] With the improving economy, trade unions and factories began to discuss new space allocations. A club building boom began in the second half of NEP, although many new structures were not completed until the First Five-Year Plan.[12] First on many lists was the construction of a large auditorium with a foyer, a stage, and dressing rooms, all of which would facilitate larger and more elaborate events.[13]

Some of the most innovative club designs were begun in this period, including the Moscow buildings of Konstantin Mel'nikov, which remain the among most famous examples of constructivist architecture. Mel'nikov's clubs featured a stark geometric exterior design and innovative interior spaces. His Rusakov Municipal Workers' Club in Moscow, begun in 1927, made all kinds of performances possible. Large doors opened from the street into the club, so that demonstrations could move easily from inside to outside. The auditorium featured moveable walls, allowing the interior space to be divided into six separate meeting rooms to accommodate both large and small productions.[14]

The building boom renewed the debate about interior space that had already begun during the Civil War. How elaborate should new clubs be? What kinds of stages should they feature? Advocates of small forms wanted theater work to be completely integrated into club activities. Thus, they objected to making large auditoriums with raised stages the focal point of club structures, since this would physically separate club performances and encourage a passive audience. Architects began with elaborate stages when they made their designs, remarked one commentator in the journal *Workers' Club*, a strong supporter of small forms. He insisted that special theatrical spaces were not necessary for a successful club structure. Instead, it was essential to make rooms designed for meeting and discussion the focal point of new buildings.[15] One important leader of the Blue Blouse living newspaper troupe, Sergei Iutkevich, advocated a style of theater that would require no stage at all.[16] However, neither architects nor club users were very sympathetic to this plea for a small-scale architecture. The new structures being planned, with

11. E. K., "O byte rabochego kluba," RK 2 (1925), 27.

12. For overviews of club construction in late NEP, see Gabriele Gorzka, *Arbeiterkultur in der Sowjetunion* (Berlin: Arno Spitz, 1990), 246–64; V. Khazanova, *Klubnaia zhizn' i arkhitektura kluba*, v. 1 (Moscow: Rossiiskii institut iskusstvoznaniia, 1994), 44–74.

13. N. Vorontyneva, "Stroitel'stvo rabochikh klubov," RK 24 (1925): 14.

14. Gorzka, *Arbeiterkultur*, 258–61; S. Frederick Starr, *Melnikov: Solo Architect in a Mass Society* (Princeton: Princeton University Press, 1978), 134–40.

15. R. Begak, "Litso kluba," RK 30/31 (1926): 71–74.

16. Khazanova, *Klubnaia zhizn'*, v. 1, 77.

space for costumes and scenery, undermined the minimalist aesthetics of small forms.

A more important challenge to small forms was the question of their political reliability. The open-ended nature of improvised performance put control of the final product in local hands. The ultimate decisions about content were left to the actors and directors, some of whom, in the words of one observer, were "politically illiterate."[17] More often than not, shoddy preparations were the result of haste; overburdened theater circles did not have time to give their works the care that they deserved and performed them before political circles had time to monitor their content. The end result was low-quality work, which could easily be seen as a sign of disrespect for the very institutions that theaters intended to celebrate. One critic was particularly offended by a club's poor performance at a celebration of the October Revolution in 1925.[18] Although charges of intentional political subversion were rare (that would come later), political overseers objected to performances that departed from goals set by the Communist Party and trade unions. For the *rabkor* Alexander Shibaev, the solution was more oversight, including the use of prepared texts that had been closely examined by political authorities.[19]

Because small forms were linked to youth, their standing in clubs was further threatened when the political reliability of Soviet young people came under increasing scrutiny. Young people, especially students, were the most vocal backers of Leon Trotsky when Joseph Stalin began to consolidate his political power base in 1923–24. Trotsky had addressed himself directly to young people in widely distributed periodicals such as *Pravda* and the Komsomol's *Young Guard*, encouraging them to see themselves as the nation's most important political and cultural constituency. He had also been a vocal advocate of workers' clubs as a place where youth could gather and discuss their experiences. When Trotsky came under fire, young people who supported him began to face political difficulties.[20] The Leningrad Komsomol was censured and

17. Arnold Gal', "O rabochikh iumoristakh," RZ 32/33 (1924): 31.
18. Liubomirskii, "Klub 'Krasnyi Oktiabr'," " 12. See similar complaints about a May Day performance in I.D., "Pervomaiskaia instsenirovka v klube Gosznaka," RK 41 (1927): 58.
19. A. Sh., "Boliachki klubnogo spektaklia," NZ 7 (1926): 10.
20. On the links between Trotsky and Soviet youth, see Sheila Fitzpatrick, *Education and Social Mobility in the Soviet Union, 1921–1934* (Cambridge: Cambridge University Press, 1979), 94–97; Michael David-Fox, *Revolution of the Mind* (Ithaca: Cornell University Press, 1997), 151–60; and Anne Gorsuch, *Enthusiasts, Bohemians, and Delinquents Soviet Youth Culture, 1921–1928* (Bloomington: Indiana University Press, forthcoming). For Trotsky's views on youth and clubs, see Leon Trotsky, "Leninism and Workers' Clubs,"

reorganized because of the support it gave to Zinoviev and Kamenev, two other opponents of Stalin, in 1925. In late NEP, young people emerged as the most articulate supporters of the United Opposition, the brief alliance of Trotsky, Zinoviev, and Kamenev against the party secretary.[21]

While one segment of Soviet youth expressed suspect political loyalties, other groups seemed more interested in having a good time. Urban youth were also the most enthusiastic consumers of Western styles in clothing, film, music, and dance. Young people formed the largest single constituency for imported movies, sometimes sneaking into upscale theaters to see their favorites over and over again. A very visible youth subculture copied the hairstyles and clothing they saw depicted in films, appearing as "flappers" and "dandies." Urban clubs and houses of culture were a cheap gathering spot where they could practice the fox-trot and other dances linked to the decadent West.[22]

Because young people had a reputation for disruptive behavior, their continued dominance of club life began to be seen as a serious problem. Study after study conducted in the late 1920s revealed that young people were the leading constituency in almost all areas of club work, including artistic circles. The Sickle and Hammer factory in Moscow reported that seventy percent of club participants were young. The Red Putilov Club in Leningrad had the same high number.[23] "It is true," stated the central trade union leader F. Seniushkin in 1925, "that the club lives and bustles with worker youth and pioneers. But this just goes to show that the club is not yet drawing in adult workers. Instead, it attracts the Komsomol, which of course is not bad. . . . *But in addition to youth we have a huge layer of middle-level workers for whom we have to show some concern.*"[24]

The question "Why doesn't the adult worker go to clubs?" appeared almost simultaneously in many cultural journals. The issue was impor-

[1924] in his *Problems of Everyday Life* (New York: Monad Press, 1973), 288–322, esp. 289–91.

21. On the Leningrad Komsomol, see Eric Naiman, *Sex in Public* (Princeton: Princeton University Press, 1997), 266–70, and Ralph Fisher, *Pattern for Soviet Youth* (New York: Columbia University Press, 1955), 116–18.

22. On young people and Western culture, see Gorsuch, *Enthusiasts* chs. 5 and 6. See also Denise Youngblood, *Movies for the Masses* (Cambridge: Cambridge University Press, 1992), 27, 52–54, and Christopher Gilman, "The Fox-trot and the New Economic Policy," *Experiment* 2 (1996): 443–75.

23. *Kluby Moskvy i gubernii* (Moscow: Trud i kniga, 1926), 29; V. Bliumenfel'd, "Melochi klubnogo byta," RK 3 (1926): 42–45.

24. F. Seniushkin, "Zadachi klubnoi raboty," *Prizyv* 1 (1925): 5, emphasis in the original.

tant to cultural organizers because it meant that the club could not really serve as a new kind of public space that could replace the isolated world of the home. Young people were singled out as the root of the problem. Club leaders charged young people with drunkenness, disruptive behavior, and the defacement of club property, all of which drove more respectable elements from club events. Some clubs even formed volunteer militia groups (*druzhinniki*) to keep young people in line.[25] As Joan Neuberger's innovative work on prerevolutionary St. Petersburg has shown, anxieties about cultural cohesion and loosening public control easily translated into charges of "hooliganism."[26] Even before the gang rape of a peasant woman by young Leningrad workers turned hooliganism into a national obsession in the fall of 1926, fears of young people's disruptive influence in clubs filled the writings of low-level bureaucrats.[27] These fears affected the discussion about small forms because young people were considered to be the most enthusiastic supporters. Older workers did not go to clubs because there was nothing for them to do there, complained one union leader. There was no quiet place for them to relax, the corridors were filled with noise and fistfights, and living newspapers did not interest them. "Bearded" viewers yearned for more serious content and complexity.[28]

The rhetoric of social progress also worked against small forms. The years since the revolution had brought real improvements in the lives of average workers, insisted many club activists. These positive changes included a measurable growth in the sophistication of working-class tastes. The 1925 Communist Party decree on literature addressed the "huge rise in the masses' cultural demands."[29] Echoing this language, theater critics insisted that the revolution had refined the tastes of the broad masses. According to one worker correspondent, "The worker viewer has increased his theatrical and cultural level and expects a more

25. M. Zel'manov, "U trekhgortsev," *Prizyv* 3 (1925): 123; R. Ginzburg, "Bor'ba s khuliganstvom," RK 27 (1926): 11–15; A. Krutov, "Bor'ba s khuliganstvom v rabochikh klubakh," RK 36 (1926): 30–33.

26. Joan Neuberger, *Hooliganism: Crime, Culture, and Power in St. Petersburg, 1900–1914* (Berkeley: University of California Press, 1993), esp. 275–79.

27. On the national anti-hooliganism campaign, which even at the time was interpreted as a fear of young people's potential oppositional power, see Naiman, *Sex in Public*, 250–88, and Gorsuch, *Enthusiasts*, ch. 8.

28. Giberman-Vostokov, "K voprosu o privlechenii vzroslykh v kluby," RK 27 (1926): 66.

29. "O politike partii v oblasti khudozhestvennoi literatury," in *Voprosy kul'tury pri diktature proletariata* (Moscow: Gosudarstvennoe izdatel'stvo, 1925), 215.

serious and complete performance from the theater and the club."[30] Following this logic, small forms were equated with small minds. Small forms were much lower on the artistic scale than large ones, insisted one Leningrad cultural worker: "The push toward 'higher' scenic forms by worker artists is completely understandable. Only such forms can convey the emotional experiences of the working class."[31]

With the sources at hand, it is very difficult to verify the claim that audiences in general were becoming more sophisticated and thus turning away from the simple agitational style of improvised theater. Audience studies of amateur stages were rare in the 1920s. Certainly, the most vilified genre of agitational theater, living newspapers, continued to prosper; more than thirty-five local groups performed at a Leningrad competition in 1927.[32] The journal *Blue Blouse* provided ample evidence of the proliferation of such groups throughout the nation. In his work on Moscow clubs in late NEP, John Hatch argues that political theater lost significant ground to films as a popular form of entertainment. Nonetheless, some of the records he uses for the Sickle and Hammer factory in Moscow reveal that events featuring living newspapers, especially when they were free, continued to draw sizeable crowds.[33]

What one can say with more certainty is that the turn to more diverse repertoires came from within amateur theater circles themselves. At least at the outset it was not imposed by trade union, Komsomol, or Narkompros organs. It was only at the end of 1925—well after heated debates were already underway in the journals devoted to amateur theater—that the head of the art division of Glavpolitprosvet, Robert Pel'she, announced that agitational forms were beginning to play themselves out and that amateur theaters needed to search for more complex modes of performance.[34] And it was not until 1927 that this view received official codification at the Agitprop conference on theater. By that

30. Rabkor Aleksandrov, "P'esa, a ne instsenirovka," RiT 26 (1925): 13.

31. M. Bystryi, "O malykh (nizkikh) i bol'shikh (vysokikh) teatral'nykh formakh," ZI 13 (1926): 4.

32. B. Filippov, "Klubno-khudozhestvennye konkursy," in Z. A. Edel'son and B. M. Filippov, eds., *Profsoiuzy i iskusstvo: Sbornik statei s prilozheniem rezoliutsii Pervoi leningradskoi mezhsoiuznoi konferentsii po voprosam khudozhestvennoi raboty* (Leningrad: Izdatel'stvo Leningradskogo gubprofsoveta, 1927), 46.

33. See John Hatch, "Hangouts and Hangovers: State, Class and Culture in Moscow's Workers' Club Movement, 1925–1928," *Russian Review* 53, no. 1 (1994): 107–13; and the Sickle and Hammer factory records for March 1925, GARF f. 7952 (*Istoriia fabrik i zavodov*), op. 3, d. 228, l. 29, and for July–September 1927, d. 233, l. 29.

34. "Itogi Vsesoiuznogo soveshchaniia pri Glavpolitprosvete," ZI 1 (1926): 2.

time, a number of amateur circles in Moscow and Leningrad had moved away from a repertoire limited to small forms alone.

Club Plays

The mounting criticism of small forms led club participants to consider different kinds of works that might engage a broader segment of viewers. The first steps away from small forms were themselves quite small, however. Club advocates began to call for a special form of "club play" that would take its inspiration from *instsenirovki*, agit-trials, and living newspapers. Similar to small forms, these would ideally be created from within the united artistic circle; they would also address themselves to the issues of contemporary life.[35] Club plays would differ from agitational forms by adding complex characters and following a unified story line. Such works needed to have an agitational content without being overbearing, determined one Leningrad critic. They should use simple, clear language and convey a logically constructed narrative. Such an approach would result in richer and more satisfying works that could speak to a broad working-class audience.[36]

The club play was a hybrid genre. Not only did advocates insist that their inspiration and roots should remain in the agitational theater of small forms, but they were also intended to be tailored to suit the specific difficulties and limitations of amateur stages. They had fewer characters, props, and technical challenges than did plays written for professional theaters. Because most clubs wanted new works at regular intervals to interest their audiences and mark Soviet festivals, they were also supposed to be fairly easy to prepare. This blurred the line dividing club plays from small forms. One advocate insisted that club plays reject the principles of psychological realism, which he believed formed the foundation of most professional theater. Like small forms, club plays would still be based on the principle of "massism" (*massovost'*), which meant they would be addressed to the broad masses in the most inclusive way possible.[37] In an overview of different types of Soviet plays, another author defined what he believed were the essential elements of a club play: it had to have a unified story while maintaining modest staging requirements and a contemporary theme. These works should not

35. A. Borisov, "Put' k p'ese," RiT 10 (1925): 19; Rabkor A. Zharikov, "Nuzhna p'esa," RiT 11 (1925): 16.
36. Rabkor Nikolaev, "Kakoi dolzhna byt' klubnaia p'esa," RiT 27 (1925): 8.
37. Boris Andreev, "Kollektivnaia dramaturgiia," RiT 34 (1925): 13.

attempt naturalistic, psychologically complex portrayals of characters, but they should move beyond the simple stereotypes, or "masks," of living newspapers.[38]

Advocates of club plays stressed repeatedly that they should emerge through the united artistic circle and not be appropriated ready made from available printed works. These points were made most forcefully by the Leningrad Proletkult leader, Valerii Bliumenfel'd, who wrote a number of articles on club plays for Leningrad journals and the Moscow publication *Workers' Club*. He envisioned a club play emerging from collective efforts, thus remaining true to the structure embraced by the advocates of small forms. These works "would maintain the basic forms of *instsenirovki* and living newspapers, but at the same time possess a unified and satisfying subject." Purely agitational works presented slogans, not life; club plays could come closer to the portrayal of life and move from agitation (a simple message for the masses) to propaganda (a more complex message for the more sophisticated). In the process, clubs would be better able to combat the rush of viewers to films and prerevolutionary melodramas.[39] I. Ispolnev, a founding member of the Moscow action circle who had initially rejected any kind of play, went even further than Bliumenfel'd. He used the dialectic to describe the cultural process underway. Initially, amateur theaters had copied the work of professional stages. Then they had rejected this position and insisted on their own original works, such as living newspapers. But now he suggested that there must be a synthesis of these two extremes. "We have arrived at a unique and original form of theater performance, at the 'club spectacle' which contains all new forms, but united into a single unified action, and even sometimes into a single intrigue."[40] For both of these authors, club plays were a necessary, discrete evolutionary step beyond small forms.

This supposed synthesis of small and large forms met opposition from both the artistic left and right. Even these modest proposals were a threat to those who wanted to continue improvisation and collective work. For such individuals, club plays posed a danger because they marked a move toward more conventional repertoires. Once an amateur

---

38. A. Borodin, "Tekhnika klubnoi dramaturgii," RK 48 (1927): 29.

39. V. Bliumenfel'd, "O klubnoi p'ese," RK 22 (1925): 48–52, quotation 48. See also idem, "Massovaia dramaturgiia: Na puti k klubnoi p'ese," ZI 42 (1925): 7–8, and "Klubnaia dramaturgiia," RK 30/31 (1926): 11–17.

40. I. Ispolnev, "Teatral'naia deistvennaia rabota v klube," RK 22 (1925): 53–54, quotation 54.

circle had turned to plays, advocates of small forms feared that further steps toward prerevolutionary works and pieces designed for professional theaters would necessarily follow. That raised the danger that frivolous hackwork and apolitical entertainment might come to dominate amateur stages. These objections were raised most forcefully by Vitalii Zhemchuzhnyi, the most outspoken member of the Moscow action circle. He insisted that it was impossible to meld the two modes together because they were based on different principles: "Let us not study from centuries-old dramatic work and absorb the stagnant and alien dramatic canon. Rather let us create new rules for performance art."[41]

But another faction of critics believed that club plays should distance themselves much further from the impromptu methods of small forms. "Workers have longed for a deeper approach to questions of production and daily life in all their living dialectic," determined one Moscow club leader. "And this has not taken place, and cannot take place, in improvisations and living newspapers."[42] A group letter signed by the staff of two large Moscow centers, the Sverdlov and Sapronov Clubs, stated that the united artistic circle itself should be tossed out because it was removed from life and gave too much power to the drama and literature groups within the club. They endorsed club plays and also insisted that more attention be given to providing participants better training in acting.[43]

A number of short plays were generated from within club circles. *Our Daily Life (Nash byt)*, written and performed by the Moscow Electrical Light Factory Club, depicted a member of the German Communist Party working incognito at the Moscow plant. He went from division to division, trying to discover how the factory worked and what difference the revolution had made in people's lives. The protagonist "together with the viewers uncovered the good and bad aspects of the factory, the day care center, the club and the dormitory," one audience member observed. The focus on local themes reportedly drew an enthusiastic crowd: "Hearing that the factory intelligentsia didn't come off too well, the whole office came to watch. Many people recognized themselves in the play." Another homemade play, presented at the Moscow Artamonovskii Tram Park, showed how an older worker became convinced that the revolution was a good thing and explained his new convictions

41. V. Zhemchuzhnyi, "Po porucheniiu Assotsiatsii instruktorov deistvennykh iacheek," RK 23 (1925): 70–72, quotation 72.

42. V. Bogoliubov, "Nasha tribuna," RK 23 (1925): 73.

43. "Rabotniki klubov im. Ia. M. Sverdlova i im. V. Sapronova," RK 23 (1925): 69–70.

to doubting peasants.[44] Noting this turn to self-generated plays, a writer in the journal *Soviet Art (Sovetskoe iskusstvo)* pronounced that amateur art was entering a new and more sophisticated stage.[45]

But just as living newspaper circles faced problems creating their own texts, amateur theater groups did not always have the time or talent to devise successful club plays. One work, *Face the Countryside (Litsom k derevne)*, by a Leningrad worker who was studying in special classes at the university, received very bad reviews. It was not really a play at all, wrote one worker correspondent. Instead, it was a collection of scenes from city and country life without cohesion or a common thread. A serious, unified work required more preparation than the month and a half that the factory circle had spent on this production, the critic chided.[46] A play with the enticing title of *Factory Love (Fabrichnaia liubov')*, written by a Komsomol member and addressing the sexual mores of young people, was panned for its weak dramatic structure and poor language.[47]

To alleviate the problem of repertoire, a specialized class of professional writers began to compose plays designed specifically for clubs. Widely published club authors included Boris Iurtsev, G. Bronikovskii, Vladimir Severnyi, Dmitrii Shcheglov, and Iakov Zadykhin. Very few of their works were ever performed by professional theaters. Most of these authors had begun their careers composing short agitational works and later turned to plays. Only Dmitrii Shcheglov had insisted on the play form from the beginning, making his mark as the leading opponent of the united artistic circle in Leningrad.

Iakov Zadykhin was involved with the Agitational Theater in Leningrad and also took part in the central Komsomol club theater that would eventually evolve into the youth theater TRAM.[48] A successful play written for the club stage was Zadykhin's *Hooligan*, which examined a popular theme of club plays in the mid-1920s—the transformation of rowdy youth into upright Soviet citizens. The play, published in 1925, depicts the change of a drunken, unemployed young man into a

44. Zbytko, "Sami pishem p'esy," RZ 24 (1924): 23; M., "Po Oktiabriu ravniaisia!" RZ 28 (1924): 20.

45. V. Rudin, "Na poroge novogo samodeiatel'nogo iskusstva," *Sovetskoe iskusstvo* 1 (1925): 15–16.

46. On the creation of this work, see El'f, "Po nemnogu, no uporno!" RiT 24 (1925): 5; for the critique, see Rabkor Shevalkov, "U tekstil'shchikov," RiT 47 (1925): 15.

47. D. Tolmachev, "Fabrichnaia liubov'," ZI 31 (1925): 16.

48. On Zadykhin's involvement in Leningrad theaters, see RiT 39 (1925) and A. S. Bulgakov and S. S. Danilov, *Gosudarstvennyi agitatsionnyi teatr v Leningrade* (Moscow: Academia, 1931), 156, 167.

model worker. There are many twists and turns along the way. One complication involves his former liaison with the daughter of a prosperous NEPman. Another has to do with a serious theft in the factory where he ends up working, a crime for which he is initially blamed. Nonetheless, with the help of his Komsomol girlfriend, a worker correspondent, he eventually enters the ranks of productive proletarians, even managing to save his factory from industrial sabotage.[49]

Hooligan is a cheerful play that offers a socialist-style happy ending. Not only does the hero announce his pending marriage to the exemplary worker correspondent, but he is also named a hero of labor for saving the factory. The hooligan villains, his former friends, are not particularly unsavory characters. Although they drink and swear, their main disruptive act is to throw rocks through the windows of the local House of Culture. The funniest parts of the play satirize elements of NEP popular culture through the figure of Katka, the daughter of the NEPman. Her main goal in life is to attain the kind of romance she has seen depicted in imported films. Against the wishes of her parents, she quickly transfers her affections from the main character to one of his hooligan friends. This young man, interested in her father's money, wins her affections by declaring, "You have stolen my heart like the daughter of the thief of Baghdad," alluding to the popular Douglas Fairbanks film that was one of the biggest box-office hits in the Soviet Union during the 1920s.[50] When the suitor delivers a flowery address while Katka is standing at her window, she exclaims, "It's just like in the movies."[51] In a Moscow performance by the Central Collective of Textile Workers, this star-struck shopkeeper's daughter stole the show.[52]

Zadykhin's work reveals the hybrid nature of club plays. Unlike most *instsenirovki* and living newspapers, it is not made up of many short segments; instead, it is divided into four discrete acts. The characters have personal names and the beginnings of developed personalities. It also tells a cohesive story. The advocate of psychological realism, Shcheglov, called it "a completely realistic play about daily life."[53] Nonetheless, the play still bears a strong resemblance to the agitational theater of small forms. The characters are easily recognizable social types, especially the

49. Ia. L. Zadykhin, *Khuligan* (Leningrad: MODPiK, 1925).

50. Ibid., 20. On the popularity of *The Thief of Baghdad*, see Youngblood, *Movies for the Masses*, 20.

51. Zadykhin, *Khuligan*, 22.

52. Nikolai L'vov, "Tsentral'nyi kollektiv tekstil'shchikov," NZ 23 (1927): 9.

53. Dmitrii Shcheglov, "U istokov," in *U istokov* (Moscow: VTO, 1960), 175.

family of NEPmen and the upright Komsomol heroine. Only the hero experiences any kind of transformation during the play; the rest are static figures. Zadykhin's effort to use elements of urban popular culture was typical of small forms. Moreover, this work was clearly written with an eye to the limited resources at the disposal of amateur stages. It had only ten speaking roles, with a few additional walk-on parts. Not much was demanded in the way of scenery, making it very easy to stage.

To aid club theaters in choosing suitable works, the national Politprosvet organization began to publish reference works that offered an overview of plays suitable for club stages. The *Repertory Guide (Repertuarnyi ukazatel')*, published in 1925, listed works according to their theme (class struggle, war and revolution, old and new life) and offered brief summaries. The *Repertory Bulletin (Repertuarnyi biulleten')*, a periodical beginning publication in 1926, was more elaborate. It not only had plot summaries but also noted the staging requirements, the number and gender of parts, and the price of publication.[54] In the following year, the national and Moscow trade union organizations began the publication of *Club Stage (Klubnaia stsena)*, the first Soviet journal devoted entirely to amateur theater. It gave an overview and critique of current practices and also published the texts of short plays. One of the first issues included a work by Vladimir Severnyi, *Rotten Thread (Gnilaia priazha)*, which examined a historic textile workers' strike.[55] With these resources at their disposal, club participants could choose works that matched their resources and abilities.

Reappraising Professionals

Small forms of the early 1920s were in part a negative response to professional theaters. Most had not changed their offerings significantly in the wake of the revolution. With the exception of the Meyerhold studio, prestigious, state-supported academic theaters had also not made any organized attempt to offer assistance to amateur stages. Thus, many club theaters proclaimed that they were the only ones interested in examining the great social changes the revolution had brought about; professional theaters had little to offer the average viewer.

54. *Repertuarnyi ukazatel': Sbornik otzyvov o p'esakh dlia professional'nogo i samodeiatel'nogo teatra* (Moscow: Glavpolitprosvet, 1925); *Repertuarnyi biulleten'* 1 (1926).

55. V. Severnyi, "Gnilaia priazha," *Klubnaia stsena* (henceforth cited as KS) 2 (1927): 49–69.

By the mid-1920s, however, some of the most important professional theaters began to perform new works that introduced revolutionary themes. Pressure from Narkompros and the installation of new directors brought significant changes to academic stages. After 1925, institutions like the Malyi Theater in Moscow, which until that point had concentrated on the classics, undertook new plays about the revolution and its aftermath.[56] For some amateurs, this shift meant that they no longer needed to justify their work in oppositional terms, which expanded their sphere of activity. Not only would they direct themselves to the pressing issues of the day, they would also try to prepare their audiences to view works in professional theaters. In addition, the spate of new works written on the theme of revolution made a more sophisticated repertoire available to amateurs. These changes minimized the difference between established and club stages—and raised the question of how club theaters would use the skills and repertoire of their professional colleagues.

Moreover, there was a marked shift in the discussion about the ultimate aims of the amateur stage. For those devoted to the agitational theater of small forms, amateur performance was an end in itself. Its tasks were to educate the viewing audience and build a new community centered on the club. But by the second half of NEP, some participants began to see amateur theater differently. It was a necessary but incipient building block toward a new kind of professional stage. This point of view was quite apparent in a heated discussion among worker correspondents in the Moscow journal *The Worker Viewer* in 1925 on the topic "What should a worker's theater be like?" Although one participant expressed doubts about any kind of cooperation with professionals, this was a minority view. Most insisted that amateur theater had to grow aesthetically to the point at which it could form the basis for a new professionalism. And for that to happen, amateurs needed to solicit the acting, directing, and writing skills of professionals. One participant insisted that amateurs could never hope to create a serious theater unless they reached out to include specialists.[57]

This idea that amateurism was something incomplete and rudimentary came even from factions of the artistic left, who had, by and large,

---

56. Richard Thorpe, "Academic Art in Revolutionary Russia: State, Society, and the Academic Stage, 1897–1929," unpublished manuscript, ch.7.

57. "Kakim dolzhen byt' rabochii teatr," RZ 7 (1925): 6–9. See also "Rabteatr iz dramkruzhka," RZ 1 (1925): 7–8.

been very sympathetic to the club stage. In a 1926 article in *Blue Blouse*, Osip Brik maintained that professional living newspapers groups were the only hope for a new, revolutionary theater in the Soviet Union. They alone had the flexibility and immediacy to interest a wide audience and make theater relevant to the broad population. By contrast, club theaters, even those staging small forms, served mainly an educational role. Brik asserted that it was impossible to build a new theater from amateurs alone. Blue Blouse needed to guide and inspire these stages, "to transform their chaotic self-activity [*stikhiinaia samodeiatel'nost'*] into productive methods." Blue Blouse "moved beyond dilettantish self-help [*liubitel'skaia samopomoshch'*] toward a new professionalism in acting."[58] By choosing derogatory words to describe amateur activity, such as *liubitel'skii* and *stikhiinyi*, Brik underscored the unpredictable nature of club theater. And although his aesthetic solutions were very different than those of most worker correspondents, he also felt that amateur stages were in great need of tutelage.

The new affinity between the professional and amateur stage was most apparent in club repertoire. As a new generation of Soviet playwrights began to create plays about the revolutionary struggle, amateurs started using their work. One example of these new authors was Vladimir Bill-Belotserkovskii, a former sailor whose prerevolutionary adventures had taken him to the United States. His plays, including *Echo, Port the Helm (Levo rulia)*, and *Storm*, examined the impact of the Russian revolution in the West and the tumultuous years of the Civil War. First performed at the Malyi Theater and the Moscow Trade Union Theater (Teatr MGSPS), they were quickly taken up by amateur stages. *Storm*, set in the Civil War, was a particular favorite in clubs. At the first Moscow competition of trade union club theaters in 1927, the metal workers' club, Aviakhim, won first prize for its rendition of this play.[59] Another new author was Alexander Afinogenov, who began his writing career for the Central Proletkult Theater in the 1920s. Several club stages, particularly in Moscow, staged his plays. One popular work was *Robert Tim*, which depicted a revolt of weavers in England in the nineteenth century. Konstantin Trenev's *Liubov' Iarovaia*, first performed at the Malyi Theater in 1926, traced the involvement of a rural school teacher on the Bolshevik side during the Civil War. This play was soon

58. O. M. Brik, "Segodnia i zavtra 'Sinei bluzy,' " SB 47/48 (1926): 1–15, quotations 7, 10.
59. Nikolai L'vov, "Mezhsoiuzhnye sorevnovaniia po zrelishchnoi rabote," NZ 24 (1927): 6.

taken up by amateur theaters as well, although its popularity did not peak until the 1930s.[60]

Following the satirical bent of many living newspapers and *inst-senirovki*, comic works written for the professional stage were also adopted by amateurs. One writer, Nikolai Erdman, whose plays were closely tied to the Meyerhold Theater in the 1920s, found a following in clubs. His biggest hit was the raucous satire *The Mandate (Mandat)*, which was both a critical and popular success. It told the story of an anti-Soviet family that attempted to achieve a "security warrant" by having the son join the Communist Party. This would not only protect them but make the daughter more attractive for marriage. After a number of twists and turns, which included the family cook being mistaken for the dead empress Alexandra, the social outcasts remained without the coveted document.[61] The play's biting treatment of NEPmen and a variety of hopeless prerevolutionary types made it a popular hit on club stages.

Another professional playwright who found a following on amateur stages was Boris Romashov. He wrote both serious dramas of the revolutionary struggle and comedies that were staged by the Malyi Theater and the Theater of Revolution. His depiction of the Civil War in South Russia, *Fedka Esaul*, was performed frequently in club theaters. His satire of NEP life, *The End of Krivoryl'sk (Konets Krivoryl'ska)*, was a popular if controversial work. It examined social change in a small Russian town, portraying a wide range of characters from counter-revolutionaries, to small tradesmen, to careerist officials. Unlike many NEP satires, it does not pit evil anti-regime elements against the brave representatives of the new state. Even the heroes of the piece, the Soviet officials and Komsomol members, have plenty of flaws. They drink too much, have numerous sexual liaisons, and forget their duties in order to rush off to Mary Pickford films.[62] Some *rabkor* critics objected to the play, saying that the portrayal of Soviet youth was much too negative.[63]

A limited number of classical plays also began to reappear on club stages in late NEP, after all but disappearing in the early 1920s. One critic in Leningrad noted an emerging specialization among amateur

60. For an overview of dramatic works popular in the late 1920s, see Harold B. Segal, *Twentieth-Century Russian Drama*, rev. ed. (Baltimore: The Johns Hopkins University Press, 1993), 147–81.

61. Nikolai Erdman, *The Mandate*, in *Two Plays*, trans. Marjorie Hoover (Ann Arbor: Ardis, 1975), 11–94.

62. Boris Sergeevich Romashov, *Konets Krivoryl'ska*, in his *P'esy* (Moscow: Khudozhestvennaia literatura, 1935), 143–245.

63. M. D-ov, S. Antonov, and S. Dubrovin, "Konets Krivoryl'ska," NZ 15 (1926): 12.

theaters there. Although most clubs performed works that reflected contemporary themes, a few staged primarily prerevolutionary classics, including Shakespeare, Lope de Vega, Molière, Carlo Goldoni, and Alexander Ostrovsky. *Hamlet* played to a packed house at the Leningrad Enlightenment Club. The Central Construction Workers' Union chose Gogol's *Inspector General*.[64] Select Moscow club theaters also turned to prerevolutionary plays. One stage, sponsored with the support of several city trade unions, included *The Lower Depths* by Gorky among its opening works. A competition of chemical trade union theaters in 1927 featured works by Gogol and Pushkin, along with contemporary plays.[65] Surveying this trend, Robert Pel'she of Narkompros concluded that it showed the growing sophistication of the average Soviet viewer, who now wanted a broader education in the arts.[66]

Those who looked to amateur theater for innovation, however, drew a different message from this shift to the classics and professional works. They felt that amateurs were moving backward, embracing prerevolutionary models of amateurism whereby groups simply copied what they saw on established stages. In the process, they tried to recreate the acting and staging techniques of professionals, which were usually beyond their abilities. In order to master complex works, they focused on one play for many months, or even years, which meant they performed very infrequently in the local club. As a result, amateur performance was once again isolated from the life of the club, undertaken with no consideration of the work going on in other circles. These pernicious trends would lead to an apolitical repertoire performed for the pure entertainment of viewers, warned Valerii Bliumenfel'd, who wanted club plays to emerge from amateur circles themselves.[67]

Nikolai L'vov saw the turn to classical plays as simply the latest stage in the battle between conservative and progressive forces that had begun at the Worker-Peasant Theater Conference in 1919. There, the conservatives from the popular theater movement had recommended Sophocles and Tolstoi; the progressive wing insisted that the masses create their own repertoire. While all those involved with amateur theater agreed that purely agitational works had grown tiresome, some were

---

64. Sergei Spasskii, "Pis'mo iz Leningrada," NZ 11 (1925): 7; "Teatr stroitelei," ZI 35 (1926): 24.

65. A. Zhuravlev, "Moskovskii rabochii teatr," NZ 41 (1926): 16; Am. Aks, "U khimikov," NZ 23 (1927): 9.

66. R. Pel'she, "Itogi sezona," *Repertuarnyi biulleten'* 4 (1927): 7.

67. V. Bliumenfel'd, "Samodeiatel'nost' ili professionalizm v klubnykh i khudozhestvennykh kruzhkakh," ZI 38 (1926): 9; see also idem, "Klubnaia dramaturgiia," RK 30/31 (1926): 12.

turning back the clock. Rather than attempt new works, they staged a repertoire common on amateur stages before the revolution. What L'vov saw as the progressive faction was building on what they had learned through agitational works, infusing their plays with more depth and complexity. "The struggle between these two directions has only just begun," he concluded.[68]

Although the struggle was for the future of amateur theater, both sides expressed their views with reference to the professional stage. Those who wanted a unique repertoire accused their opponents of following the strictures of the popular theater movement. Their ideas about acting and staging were derivative, guilty of a reactionary "naturalism" that exemplified the values and individualism of the bourgeoisie. The methods of Konstantin Stanislavsky, founder of the Moscow Art Theater, loomed large in this critique. His psychological approach to acting was unfit to capture the spirit of the collective. Clubs should never turn to naturalistic sets and try to imitate the psychological actor, argued one commentator in *The Life of Art*. Workers easily grasped the key elements of "leftist" theater, from its focus on the collective to its constructivist set designs."[69]

Those opposed to the theatrical left were ready with accusations of their own. They charged that their opponents were under the thrall of a segment of the bourgeois intelligentsia who had articulated their avant-garde ideas long before the revolution. Their work was a luxury for the very few but out of reach for the mass audience. Workers were baffled and offended by fragmented structure and strange staging of their performances.[70] Instead, these critics wanted more convincing characters, easily understandable plots, and a positive treatment of Soviet heroes. In short, they wanted what they called "realism." One outspoken *rabkor* insisted, "Workers' theater must be as realistic as possible. It should illuminate the life of the worker, satisfy his spiritual longings, and encourage his future growth. It should not include primitive folk forms [*ne dokhodit' do lubka*] but nonetheless be close and understandable to the working masses."[71] Two Moscow trade union leaders, put it this way: "[The

68. Nikolai L'vov, "Repertuar za desiat' let," NZ 41 (1927): 6.

69. B., "Klubnaia dramaturgiia," ZI 32 (1926): 7. See also Shagin, "O chem govorili na Pervoi leningradskoi mezhsoiuznoi khudozhestvennoi konferentsii," ZI 23 (1927): 4.

70. For the most extreme expression of these views, see *Rabochie o literature*, 45–52, 99–100. This work is a compilation of highly selective quotes from *The Worker Viewer*. For a searing critique of this book by a worker correspondent, see Turii Kobrin, *Teatr im Vs. Meierkhol'da i rabochii zritel'* (Moscow: Moskovskoe teatral'noe izdatel'stvo, 1926), 51.

71. Vdovin, cited in A. Sh., "Kakim dolzhen byt' rabochii teatr," NZ 11 (1926): 5.

worker viewer] wants to see life as it is. By this, he does not mean a naturalistic copy of life, but rather its most typical, realistic reproduction."[72] This quotation articulates in embryo some of the basic principles of socialist realism. As most established stages also moved toward realism, the aesthetic distance between amateur and professional diminished.

The "Smychka" in Theater

The idea of a *smychka*, or union, between the proletariat and the peasantry, two potentially hostile classes, was a central concept of the New Economic Policy. This bedrock principle was extended outside the sphere of economics and class relations to discuss fruitful interaction between other potentially opposing forces. In late 1925, Robert Pel'she broached the idea of a *smychka* in culture. "Now apparently a *smychka* between professional and amateur art is beginning to show itself," he asserted. "We must deepen this trend."[73]

Pel'she's comments indicate that the debate surrounding the repertoire of club theater, largely conducted in specialized journals in the early 1920s, began to emerge as a topic of national discussion. The Seventh National Trade Union Congress, meeting in late 1926, addressed the problem of club repertoire. Mikhail Tomskii, the head of the national trade union organization, endorsed greater cooperation between amateurs and professionals. He insisted that much of the literature made by workers themselves was of poor quality—vulgar in tone and ungrammatical. If appropriate new works could not be found, then it was better to perform old plays. The final resolutions indicated that trade unions were willing to look to professionals for aid: "It is imperative to attract the best artistic forces to create and rework good plays for club stages and to lead club circles."[74] At a special meeting devoted entirely to trade union cultural work in early 1927, the head of the national cultural division, Nikolai Evreinov (not to be confused with the famous theater director Nikolai Nikolaevich Evreinov, who had emigrated to France), made the message even clearer. He insisted that clubs attract professional groups to give model performances and strengthen ties with established stages in order to solicit better instructors.[75]

---

72. N. Volkonskii and A. Borodin, "Vliianie profteatra na klubnuiu stsenu," KS 2 (1927): 17.

73. "Itogi Vsesoiuznogo soveshchaniia pri Glavpolitprosvete," ZI 1 (1926): 2.

74. *Sed'moi s''ezd professional'nykh soiuzov* (Moscow: Profizdat, 1926), 67–69, 773, quotation 773.

75. "Za kachestvo klubnoi stseny," NZ 11 (1927): 8.

The gathering with the most significant impact on club stages was the national convention on theater sponsored by the Agitprop Division of the Communist Party in the spring of 1927. The main purpose of this meeting, designed to parallel the 1925 Party conference on literature, was to assess government policies for professional stages, reviewing their financial support, repertoire, and organization.[76] But because the conference was justified as a method to acknowledge the importance of theater to the laboring masses, amateur stages in urban centers and the countryside received considerable attention. At this congress, the notion that there should be a rapprochement (*sblizhenie*) between amateur and professionals received official codification. The conference determined that amateur theaters needed to learn artistic mastery from established stages. At the same time, professional theaters had to provide the mass viewer with a repertoire that reflected the problems and accomplishments of the contemporary era.

The assumption that audiences in amateur theaters were becoming more sophisticated and discriminating reached the level of truism at the conference, being repeated in every single speech and resolution. In his opening statements, the head of Agitprop, Vilis Knorin, linked workers' improving economic and political condition to their demands for better art.[77] He sounded a recurring theme at the proceedings—namely that amateur theaters had an important role to play as the transmitters of artistic values and the theatrical heritage: "Club and rural theaters at the present time must and should learn artistic mastery and the skills of directing and acting from professional theaters; they should transmit what they have learned to the broad masses."[78] The imbalance between amateur theaters, which were revolutionary but not artistic, and professional theaters, which were artistic but not revolutionary, had to come to an end.

The main speech on amateur theaters was presented by Evreinov from the central trade union bureaucracy. Such institutions were important, he began, because professional theaters could not begin to meet all the needs of the viewing public. By making reference to the several thousand amateur stages under trade union control, Evreinov argued

76. On the background for this conference, see Sheila Fitzpatrick, "The Emergence of Glaviskusstvo," *Soviet Studies* 32 (October, 1971): 238–41, and Thorpe, "Academic Art," ch. 7.

77. V. G. Knorin, "Teatr i sotsialisticheskoe stroitel'stvo," in S. M. Krylov, ed., *Puti razvitiia teatra*, 5.

78. Ibid., 12.

that amateur stages served a larger segment of the population than professional theaters. Because they were closer to their audiences, amateur
stages could more easily meet viewers' needs and could better serve as a
conduit for socialist education.[79]

But while he recognized the strategic importance of amateur theater,
Evreinov began with the assumption that these institutions were in a
deep state of crisis. Bitingly critical of current offerings, he denounced
the idea that performance works should only be generated from within
the club circle. He also attacked what he called the "false theories" of the
past, which had led club theaters astray. These included all of the ideas
that had formed the theoretical underpinnings for small forms. The unified artistic circle denied the importance of the artistic heritage and subordinated all creative work within the club to a single circle.[80] He was no
kinder to the principles behind action cells, which he referred to as "action art" (deistvennoe iskusstvo). This approach repudiated any specific
qualities for the art of the stage. Finally, in a rather confused coda, he denounced the concept of utilitarian art, a notion he traced to the Civil War
but which still had adherents in the trade union movement. All of these
ideas were cooked up in isolated offices by poorly qualified intellectuals
who wished to establish a monopoly on conceptions of proletarian culture.[81] They resulted in the worst possible kinds of agitational performances, works without any artistic value.

Evreinov believed that the movement away from small forms was
coming from below, from amateur theater groups themselves. The
worker viewer had begun to say, "Enough agitation, enough homemade concoctions [samodel'shchina]—give me theater." As a result, club
stages were beginning to choose large, important plays such as the
opera Rusalka, Bill-Belotserkovskii's Storm and the Dutch classic The
Good Hope. Protests against this shift in repertoire came not from viewers but rather from (unnamed) leaders who opposed artistic mastery
and the cultural heritage of the past.[82]

But rather than discard agitational work altogether, Evreinov proposed a mixed repertoire for clubs. Amateur stages should continue to
use small forms; they could have a positive political value and in general were easy to perform. However, these had to be combined with

79. N. N. Evreinov, "Stroitel'stvo samodeiatel'nogo teatra," ibid., 264–65.

80. Oddly, Evreinov attributes this idea to "Avilov" instead of Grigorii Avlov, who was
only one of its proponents in Leningrad (ibid., 267–68).

81. Ibid., 268–69, 498.

82. Ibid., 271–73, quotation 271–72.

plays written for club stages, works intended for professional theaters, and select representatives from the classics. The only way to achieve such a diverse repertoire, Evreinov suggested, was to strip club theaters of some of their agitational responsibilities. Such suggestions had been made by union leaders periodically during the 1920s to protect drama circles from their burdensome performance schedules. Evreinov articulated this position in uncompromising terms. "Finally," he proclaimed, "we must relieve circles of a whole variety of obligatory appearances for any number of campaigns. They now have to appear at all political campaigns and holidays—on March 8, the day of the Paris Commune, May Day, and others. For this reason drama circles cannot do serious work."[83] Evreinov's intention was to lighten the burden of drama circles so that they would have more time for serious preparation. Yet seen from another perspective, he actually heaped more responsibilities on them. In essence he charged them with two equally important but not necessarily complimentary tasks—political agitation (although in lesser amounts) and the artistic education of their audiences.

The wide-ranging discussion after Evreinov's speech rehashed the many controversies facing club theaters since the revolution. How were they supposed to attend to agitation and also create artistically satisfying work? queried one representative from Ivanovo-Voznesensk. Some club theaters had responded by creating two separate groups, one for agitation and one to tackle plays, but this put a further strain on scarce resources. Another delegate from the Urals commented that it was a good thing to lighten club theaters' heavy agitational load, which required them to perform for every festival and also for political campaigns of all kinds. Still, he questioned how appropriate an opera like *Rusalka* would be to mark the celebration of the October Revolution. Others insisted that if clubs were going to produce more effective artistic works, they needed significantly more resources. Most club stages were simply too small and poorly equipped to perform big plays. Thus, there remained no serious alternative to agitational works.[84]

Beneath these debates around repertoire, one can discern a real sense of anxiety about a production strategy that left significant control in local hands. Many speakers at the gathering complained about lack of vigilance over club stages, which resulted in the performance of prerevolutionary hack work and even works that had been officially banned by the government. But the most passionate exclamations of censure were

83. Ibid., 277.
84. Ibid., 278–79, 285–86, 296, 298.

reserved for living newspaper scripts, which some participants felt had become the purveyors of pornography. Evreinov quoted offensive lines from a work dedicated to International Women's Day, which he believed praised philandering and loose moral conduct. Other delegates had similar stories. According to one, living newspapers had become a forum for "salty and pornographic anecdotes."[85] The final resolutions at the conference called not only for tightened vigilance over the text of works performed, but also increased monitoring of the performances themselves—a recognition that improvised forms could vary considerably from one show to the next.[86]

Despite the considerable attention brought to amateur stages at the widely publicized national event, the conference served mainly to fix their junior status in any cultural partnership with professional stages. Many speakers found amateur theaters useful only to the degree that professional theaters could not meet all the needs of the population. "Professional theater cannot completely satisfy the interest of the broad proletarian masses in performance," read the final resolutions. "Because of this the club stage has become and will continue to be a significant tool to meet workers' cultural demands."[87] And although small forms were not abandoned entirely, the organizing methods that had supported their proliferation and their most widely used form, the living newspaper, were singled out for criticism. Evreinov denounced the theories of early NEP that claimed a special role for amateur theater in the creation of Soviet culture as so much radical nonsense.[88] Small forms were discussed primarily in terms of their inadequacies. The conference delegates did acknowledge why club stages might employ them; they were easy to perform, adapted easily to agitational goals, and allowed some local creativity. But these positive points were undercut by the premise that the most important task of club stages was to introduce a serious repertoire and show the masses the best examples of artistic work.

The Agitprop conference offered unambiguous advice to local amateur stages: call in the experts to improve your work. Certainly, delegates gathered at a trade union conference in Leningrad only a few weeks later got this message. Konstantin Tverskoi, head of the city-wide artistic section, insisted that trade unions must aim to "bring art closer to the masses" (iskusstvo—blizhe k massam). In local discussions on the-

85. For anxieties about "pornography," see ibid., 270–71, 301, quotation 293.
86. Ibid., 487.
87. Ibid., 490.
88. Ibid., 498.

ater, the most common demand he had heard was for higher quality work. The only way to achieve this was to bring in more professionals. He predicted that by the celebration of the tenth anniversary of the revolution, only a few months away, "the antagonism between professionals and amateurs will finally be eliminated."[89]

Tverskoi's prophesy was fulfilled through a joint project between trade union theaters and the Leningrad Bol'shoi Drama Theater, called "Ten Octobers" (*Desiat' Oktiabrei*). This mass spectacle, which included an estimated one thousand performers, celebrated ten years of Soviet power. Billed as a direct response to the Agitprop conference, the printed program even incorporated excerpts from the conference resolutions. The episodic script, with twenty-five separate sections, used literary works, songs, excerpts from plays, and political writings to tell the story of the revolution from Lenin's arrival at the Finland station until October 1927. It incorporated the performance and technical staff of the Bol'shoi Drama Theater, as well as thirty-five amateur theater groups, music circles, and living newspapers.[90]

It is worth stepping back for a moment to compare "Ten Octobers" to the mass festivals of the Civil War years, such as "The Storming of the Winter Palace" in 1920.[91] Those earlier events also included amateur performers, but only as part of the crowd scenes. In this celebration, amateurs had speaking and singing roles. They were given voice, and this reflected a positive change in the status of amateur creation in the Soviet artistic pantheon. According to one observer, however, "Ten Octobers" was structured so that the professional performers provided the narrative elements that moved the story forward. Amateur circles provided the local color, the background atmosphere; they were not integrated as equals.[92] This judgment was unintentionally confirmed by the main director of the spectacle, B. Andreev-Bashinskii from the Bol'shoi Drama Theater. He contended that the amateurs learned about professional discipline and mastery from the collaboration. For their part, the professionals were inspired by the immediacy of amateur theater and its direct political relevance to proletarian audiences.[93] While he surely meant his

89. Konstantin Tverskoi, "Teatral'naia rabota leningradskikh profsoiuzov," in *Profsoiuzy i iskusstvo*, 65.

90. *Desiat' Oktiabrei* (Leningrad: Bol'shoi dramaticheskii teatr, 1927).

91. See James von Geldern's detailed description of this event in *Bolshevik Festivals, 1917–1920* (Berkeley: University of California Press, 1990), 199–205.

92. V. B., "Spektakl' 'Desiat' Oktiabrei,' " KS 1 (1928): 74–75.

93. B. Andreev-Bashinskii, "Tekhnika massovoi postanovki: Kak my rabotali nad massovym predstavleniem," KS 1 (1928): 72.

comments to be appreciative of amateur performers, he nonetheless presented them as valuable raw materials that needed to be shaped and directed through professional intervention.

•⌒

The second half of the NEP period was a time of great diversity for amateur stages. Although sharply criticized by some viewers, living newspapers and other small forms remained popular. Plays designed specifically for clubs appeared in cheap editions and were also distributed in the new journal *Club Stage*. New dramas intended for professional stages, especially those dealing with the history of the revolution and contemporary life, also were common choices. Some circles turned to classic plays that had been common on club stages before the revolution.

This broad range of performances reflected a fundamental shift in ideas on the value and significance of professional stages. Once shunned as irrelevant or dangerous for amateur performers, many club theaters now looked to professionals for repertoire and assistance. They adapted work from major theaters and even collaborated on joint projects. Such a change in attitudes was hardly unique to amateur stages. By the middle of the 1920s, many utopian projects that envisioned a society less structured by hierarchies of skill and training had fallen by the wayside. The dream of an all-volunteer militia, put forward by a faction of the Red Army, evaporated. School curricula designed to nurture the whole person and avoid excessive specialization were revised as Soviet industry called for better training and students demanded programs that would offer better chances for advancement. Everywhere, the egalitarian currents of the Russian revolution were weakening.[94]

Nonetheless, we should not assume that calls for better training and skill meant the same thing to everyone who voiced them. Supervisory cultural institutions, such as trade union administrations and the Agitprop Division, hoped to limit the unpredictable nature of amateur performance; they wanted additional controls over poor production standards and poor choices in repertoire, which had allowed dangerous material to make its way on stage. Some professionals, like the director

94. See Mark von Hagen, *Soldiers in the Proletarian Dictatorship* (Ithaca: Cornell University Press, 1990), 206–8; Sheila Fitzpatrick, *Education and Social Mobility in the Soviet Union 1921–1934* (Cambridge: Cambridge University Press, 1979), 57, 63; and Richard Stites, *Revolutionary Dreams* (New York: Oxford University Press, 1989), 140–44.

of the Leningrad Bol'shoi Drama Theater, expressed the wish that amateur stages might help them gain better access to proletarian audiences.
As the program for "Ten Octobers" stated, amateurs could serve as a
bridge between professionals and the proletarian public.[95]

The motives of the participants and audiences of the amateur stage
were even more complex. A segment of the viewing audience hoped
that a more varied repertoire would make for more interesting viewing.
The financial improvements of late NEP, which meant expanded club
stages and more funds for props and costumes, allowed actors and directors to bring performance standards closer to those on the professional stage. For some advocates, this was evidence of the *smychka* in
culture; they were finally in a position to collaborate with their professional counterparts. But for others, this provided the basis for a new aggressive onslaught. Improvements by amateurs meant that select theaters, with intrinsic ties to lower-class audiences, might finally be able to
challenge the dominance of conventional stages.

95. *Desiat' Oktiabrei*, 7.

4

TRAM: The Vanguard of Amateur Art

THE LENINGRAD Theater of Working-Class Youth (Teatr rabochei molodezhi), called by its acronym TRAM, was the best-known amateur stage of the NEP period, eventually achieving a national reputation. Its far-reaching claims for the creative potential of amateurs and the special interests of Soviet youth sparked contentious discussions in the cultural press. Its original repertoire, a large part of which was published, was performed on club stages throughout the country. When its members abandoned their day jobs for full-time theatrical work in 1928, TRAM challenged conventional understandings of what it meant to be a professional. Because of the theater's notoriety and long record of controversy, TRAM participants have left behind a rich archival and published record of creative works and memoirs that make it possible to investigate its internal dynamics.[1] Thus, TRAM offers a unique opportunity to sketch out details about membership, creative decision making, and social interactions within the amateur theater movement.

During the years of the New Economic Policy, TRAM in many ways embodied the amateur art movement. Although it can hardly be consid-

1. On the TRAM movement, see N. Rabiniants, *Teatr iunosti: Ocherk istorii Leningradskogo gosudarstvennogo teatra imeni Leninskogo komsomola* (Leningrad: Gosudarstvennyi nauchno-issledovatel'skii institut teatra, muzyki i kinematografii, 1959); V. Mironova, TRAM: *Agitatsionnyi molodezhnyi teatr 1920–1930kh godov* (Leningrad: Iskusstvo, 1977); L. A. Pinegina, *Sovetskii rabochii klass i khudozhestvennaia kul'tura, 1917–1932* (Moscow: Izdatel'stvo Moskovskogo universiteta, 1984), 204–9; Lynn Mally, "The Rise and Fall of the Soviet Youth Theater TRAM," *Slavic Review* 51, no. 3 (Fall 1992): 411–30; Katerina Clark, *Petersburg, Crucible of Cultural Revolution* (Cambridge: Harvard University Press, 1996), 266–78.

ered typical, TRAM conformed to basic developmental patterns of amateur theaters. It began in a Komsomol club staging agitational works for a neighborhood clientele. By the mid-1920s, participants began to write their own plays. Their original creations touched on everyday problems and tackled a central dilemma for Soviet youth eager to find a place in the new society—the strained relationship between personal happiness and community responsibility. These works contained the fundamental elements of the club play. They had a clear didactic purpose but also vivid characters and compelling stories that were designed to spark discussion. The success of these plays turned the Leningrad TRAM into a model for factory and trade union stages. As new TRAM circles opened around the country, the Leningrad group presented itself as a vanguard organization for amateur club stages.

With its increasing success, the Leningrad TRAM turned professional in 1928, allowing its members to devote themselves entirely to acting and writing. This was a step open only to small number of amateur stages, which found support from political and trade union organizations. These newly minted specialists, fiercely loyal to their original audiences, proclaimed that they would be professionals of a new type who would not forget their social base. TRAM was most vociferous in these pronouncements, insisting that its aesthetic principles grew from the unique social and political position of club theater.

The grander TRAM's claims became, the more it exposed itself to criticism. Those who admired established professional theater felt that its work remained too amateurish; it offered no stable system of acting or directing that could inspire other groups. Amateur circles charged that it had distanced itself from its local constituency and no longer could generate a contemporary, relevant repertoire. This criticism became increasingly dominant during the years of the First Five-Year Plan, when a new kind of amateur circle took shape based directly in the factory workshop. For these aggressive small groups, TRAM had become the establishment, scarcely distinguishable from the nationally supported stages that it rejected.

TRAM *Takes Shape*

Like many Soviet amateur stages, TRAM could trace its roots to the Russian Civil War. Its inspired director was Mikhail Sokolovskii, a railroad worker born at the turn of the century who became a Komsomol organizer during the revolution. By 1919 Sokolovskii had taken charge of the literary studio for the Komsomol club in the First City District of

Petrograd. He used the studio to create texts for agitational performances, such as a Komsomol evening celebration in honor of the Paris Commune staged in March 1920.[2] Sokolovskii's penchant for agitation intensified when he was sent to Murmansk by the Komsomol to aid in efforts to defend the railroad against British attacks. While on assignment, he became involved in the railroad union's agitational studio, the Shimanovskii troupe. This proved an important contact, because Shimanovskii's group reshaped itself into the Petrograd Politprosvet's Central Agitational Studio after the war was over and provided resources and inspiration for Sokolovskii's own efforts.[3]

Not until 1922 did the Komsomol theater circle regroup, once again under Sokolovskii's leadership. Now located in the Gleron House, a Komsomol club named after a young Komsomol leader killed during the war, the theater embraced agitational tasks. The Gleron House club staged its first performance, an *instsenirovka* entitled "Five Years of the Komsomol," in June 1922. As was typical for the times, the script for the event was concocted in a mere three days.[4] With a mix of songs, poems, and mass scenes, the evening event's most stunning moment was when a young Red Army soldier rode a horse onto the stage.[5]

The theater studio at the Gleron House attracted a group of dedicated enthusiasts who would form the core of TRAM activists throughout the 1920s. At the center was a group of young writers who were in charge of generating scripts and living newspapers. This circle, which called itself "The Lever" (*Rychag*), included the Petrograd Komsomol and Politprosvet organizer Nikolai L'vov (not to be confused with the Moscow theater activist of the same name), Arkadii Gorbenko, Pavel Marinchik (the future memoirist of TRAM), Dmitrii Tolmachev, and Mura Kashevnik. They worked under the supervision of the writer A. V. Sventitskii, who earned the princely sum of thirty rubles a month for his role as the local "expert."[6] These young men, all of whom had been active in the Komsomol during the Civil War, gave the group its youthful, militant, masculine slant. Although young women participated in skits and per-

2. From Sokolovskii's account in "Vecher vospominanii rabotnikov TRAM'a ot 12 maia 1930g.," RGALI, f. 2723, op. 1, d. 534, l. 1; M. Sokolovksii, "U istokov tramovskogo dvizheniia," RiT 29/30 (1932): 11–12.

3. A. S. Bulgakov and S. S. Danilov, *Gosudarstvennyi agitatsionnyi teatr v Leningrade* (Moscow: Academia, 1931), 30–34.

4. Zograf, "Tvorcheskii put' Leningradskogo TRAM'a," RGALI, f. 2723, op. 1., d. 220, l. 17; N. L'vov cited in "Vtoroi vecher vospominanii," RGALI, f. 2723, op. 1, d. 534, l. 13 ob.

5. Pavel Marinchik, *Rozhdenie komsomol'skogo teatra* (Leningrad: Iskusstvo, 1963), 42–43.

6. Ibid., 61; "Vecher vospominanii," l. 5; Sventitskii's account in "Vtoroi vecher vospominanii," RGALI, f. 2723, op. 1, d. 534, ll. 9–10 ob.

Шарж Н. Радлова

М. В. Соколовский

A sketch of Mikhail Sokolovskii. *Leningradskii TRAM v Moskve* (Leningrad: Izdanie Gostrama, 1928).

formances, they were not part of the inner circle of organizers and writ-ers. By 1923, yet another collaborator joined the group—none other than Adrian Piotrovskii, the articulate advocate of united artistic circles. Well-placed in the city's cultural bureaucracies, Piotrovskii became a co-worker, promoter, and protector for the theater.[7]

The Gleron Club was simultaneously the central Komsomol club for Petrograd as a whole and a neighborhood center serving the Moscow-Narvskii District, part of the city's industrial core. It attracted factory youth from the nearby plants, like the big Skorokhod factory, the in-tended constituency for the Komsomol. The appeal of club events did not stop there, however. Well-dressed young people in straight-legged pants, starched collars, and silk handkerchiefs appeared alongside scruffy street youth of the semi-criminal demi-monde at club events. Evening performances were sometimes rowdy affairs, with fistfights breaking out between the club's different constituencies. The narrow club theater could pack in close to four hundred viewers, with the audi-ence sitting in the aisles, on window sills, and even on the stage.[8]

Participants in the Komsomol club had little or no training in the arts, but neither they nor Sokolovskii saw this lack as an obstacle. When the club was swamped with volunteers who wanted to take part in the first performance in 1922, Sokolovskii encouraged all comers. According to Pavel Marinchik, when volunteers asked what they could do, "Sokolovskii grinned and looked at them, 'You can become playwrights and actors.' "[9] This irreverence toward conventional artistic training was part of the spirit of the times. Marinchik recalls that club members laughed about the exalted connotations of the word "artist." "We went to the Gleron House, wrote and performed *instsenirovki*, conducted club evenings, and thought that all of this was just another form of Komso-mol work."[10] Some members even initially rejected the appellation of "theater" for their circle, believing that it evoked conservative notions of performance separated from life. As Sokolovskii put it, "For us it was not always clear where life ended and the performances began."[11]

From 1922 until 1925, the Komsomol theater circle was actively en-gaged in agitational work, marking the dates of the Red Calendar. On May Day 1923, it put on a performance called "Hymn to Labor" and

---

7. On Piotrovskii's first work with Sokolovskii, see "Vecher vospominanii," l. 2.
8. Marinchik, *Rozhdenie*, 43–44; "Vecher vospominanii," l. 2.
9. Marinchik, *Rozhdenie*, 38.
10. Ibid., 54.
11. "Puti razvitiia Leningradskogo TRAM'a," RGALI, f. 941, op. 4, d. 66, ll. 1–2.

participated in the city's anti-religious festivities for Komsomol Easter. In 1924, it celebrated Red Army Day with a skit called "The Dream of the Illiterate Red Army Soldier." For the Day of the Paris Commune, it staged a work by Piotrovskii devoted to the holiday. The group drew in part on folk traditions for its scripts, staging a loose adaptation of the venerable folk play *Tsar Maksimilian* at a performance in honor of Komsomol Christmas, this time with the evil father figure recast as General Kolchak, an anti-Bolshevik leader during the Russian Civil War.[12]

Like many other clubs, the Gleron House started its own living newspaper, "Gleron's Pencil," which chose its topics close to home. Its satirical performances were devoted almost exclusively to life within the club and to the role of youth in the new society. The tensions between Communist-identified youth and the other youth cultures of NEP were favorite themes, as in one performance that mocked "phony" Komsomol members who liked to go to dances instead of studying.[13] "Gleron's Pencil" developed a stock character, "Crazy Sashka" (Sashka Chumovoi), an undisciplined factory youth who was having a hard time adjusting to NEP. Bored by political education classes and the dull routine of daily life, Sashka had ties to hooligan elements. Crazy Sashka was featured in club brawls, factory settings, street scenes, and even on foreign trips. In a 1925 May Day performance of "Gleron's Pencil," he showed up unexpectedly at a meeting of German capitalists.[14] Played by the club member Vasia Kopachev, Sashka appeared in hooligan attire—bell-bottom trousers, a striped sailor's shirt, and a cap worn slightly askew.[15] Performances featuring Crazy Sashka won the circle an enthusiastic audience.

The Gleron circle also began to experiment with more tightly organized works, moving away from small forms and toward plays. *Man in a Red Wig,* written by group members and staged in 1923, examined the problem of intellectuals in the revolution. The next year the Gleron circle performed several works that were sustained investigations into a single theme, meeting the requirements for a club play. These included *The Story of the Iron Battalion (Slovo o zheleznom batal'one),* based on an Alexander Serafimovich story about the fall of the Provisional Government and *An Intellectual Marriage (Zhenit'ba intelligentnogo),* which dealt

12. "Pervoe maia v rabochikh klubakh," ZI 17 (1923): 8; "Dom Glerona," ZI 10 (1924): 19; B. Prokof'ev, "Dom Glerona," ZI 14 (1924): 19; "Vecher vospominanii," l. 2.

13. A. Garin, "Shestaia konferentsiia RLKSM v Moskovsko-Narvskom raione," ZI 7 (1925): 32.

14. A. Senzul', "Gleronovskii karandash," ZI 22 (1925): 21.

15. Pavel Marinchik, "Dalekoe-blizkoe," *Neva* 11 (1957): 171; idem, *Rozhdenie,* 62–63.

with the moderate socialist leader, Alexander Kerenskii, during the February Revolution.[16] By this time, the theater studio had gained a number of helpers, including the acrobat Fedor Knorre, who taught movement, and the avant-gardist director from the Agitational Theater, Igor Terent'ev, who gave instructions in diction.[17]

Serious efforts to turn the club circle into a theater studio with its own budget for rehearsals, scripts, and props began in 1924. The city Politprosvet division first took charge of the discussion, but conflicts quickly emerged over just who would head the circle: Sokolovskii, who had been responsible for the work thus far, or the more experienced theater worker Grigorii Avlov, from the city's Politprosvet division. But the most difficult problem proved to be money. Even after both the city government and the Komsomol had given approval for the venture, no funds materialized. The members of the Gleron circle took matters into their own hands. Turning to their protector Piotrovskii, who also worked for the Leningrad division of Sovkino, the state film trust, they volunteered to play bit parts as petty thieves and hooligans in the film *The Devil's Wheel* (*Chortovo koleso*). This film, directed by Grigorii Kozintsev and Leonid Trauberg, had a scenario by Piotrovskii. Their collective earnings—four hundred rubles—was used as capital to launch their first full-length play.[18]

The Gleron circle theater was officially reincarnated as TRAM in the fall of 1925 with the premiere of *Crazy Sashka*, based on the popular character in TRAM's living newspaper sketches. Still housed in the Gleron club, the group's original collective had been augmented by new forces chosen through auditions advertised throughout the city. By the opening, TRAM had assembled a support staff that significantly expanded its abilities to stage a polished production. The set designer Roman Ianov, with a newly minted degree from the Technicum of Stage Arts (the future Leningrad Institute of Theater, Music, and Cinema), was involved in creating the scenery. The constructivist set was built by the young artist Alexander Zonov. The musician Nikolai Dvorikov wrote the score, and the caretaker for the Gleron House, Ekaterina

16. B. S., "Raionnyi klub RKSM im. tov. Glerona," ZI 26 (1926): 21; T. R., "Dom im. Glerona," RiT 9 (1924): 15; "Tsentral'nyi dom komm. vospit. im. Glerona," ZI 24 (1924): 18; N. Nikolaev, "Zhenit'ba intelligentnogo," ZI 29 (1924): 17.

17. "U stanka," RiT 6 (1925): 15. On Knorre's background, see Marinchik, *Rozhdenie*, 85–86.

18. Sokolovskii's account in "Vecher vospominanii," l. 6. See also the Moscow TRAM leader, Pavel Sokolov's, account in "O piatiletii Leningradskogo TRAM'a," RGALI, f. 2947, op. 1, d. 18, l. 20.

Strazd, known to participants as "Aunt Katia," was placed in charge of wardrobe.[19] Certainly, in the modest posters for the production, which listed the director, set designer, music director, and costumer, it appeared that the impecunious Komsomol collective was following in the footsteps of more established theaters. But the theme of TRAM's first play, which built on its living newspaper, revealed its origins in the theater of small forms.

Staging Soviet Youth Culture

From the outset, TRAM members made it clear that the joys and sorrows of Soviet youth would be their subject matter. That meant depicting a wide range of social types, from the hooligan demi-monde to the children of White Guardists to upright Komsomol members. However, TRAM plays did not stop here. They also examined the tensions within the Komsomol milieu itself, showing unsavory bureaucrats, self-absorbed young women, and predatory young men. In the words of one reviewer, TRAM saw itself as fighting "on the barricades for a new life."[20]

As the work of Anne Gorsuch has shown, the future of Soviet youth was a major preoccupation of the Soviet regime during the 1920s. On the one hand, young people were valued for their enthusiasm and supposed pliability, which would allow them to be educated into the first true generation of Soviet men and women. On the other hand, they were feared for their volatility and lack of rational maturity. Young people, for their part, were not so easily molded into ideal Soviet citizens. During NEP a range of conflicting urban youth cultures took shape. They included the clean-living Komsomol, with their anti-alcohol and anti-religious campaigns; alienated hard-core Communists, who saw NEP as a disappointing retreat into petty-bourgeois life styles; a hooligan underworld enamored of violence; those who used the consumption possibilities of NEP to pursue fashion and imported Western culture; and a segment who rejected the anti-religiosity of the Bolsheviks to found their own new communities based on religious faith.[21]

TRAM plays acknowledged the existence of these complex urban cultures beckoning to Soviet youth. Although their purpose was obviously to draw young audiences to the "correct" solution, the upstanding life of

19. Marinchik, *Rozhdenie*, 68–72; "Vecher vospominanii," l. 6.
20. M. Skripil', "TRAM," ZI 20 (1926): 17.
21. Anne Gorsuch, *Enthusiasts, Bohemians, and Delinquents: Soviet Youth Culture, 1921–1928* (Bloomington, Ind.: Indiana University Press, forthcoming).

the Komsomol, the main characters in TRAM works are most often people caught in the middle between two worlds who feel the attraction of other possibilities. This characteristic distinguishes TRAM plays from earlier agitational works that show simple conflicts between good and evil. The entirely good Komsomol characters in TRAM plays are often not appealing; rather, the works showcase conflicted figures who eventually lose their doubts and recommit themselves to the Communist cause. Of course, this left open the possibility that audiences might sympathize with characters in their less-than-perfect form.

The first TRAM play, *Crazy Sashka*, depicted the confrontation between the hooligan underworld of NEP and the healthy, purposeful Komsomol. Sashka Chumovoi, the central figure, was part of both worlds. He was drawn to the hooligans because of old friendships and because his girlfriend, Klavka, remained in that milieu. At the opening of the play, the hooligans are holding a noisy party and also planning a smuggling venture. Their disreputable antics are contrasted with the activities of the Komsomols, headed by Sasha Delovoi (literally, "Energetic Sasha") and his girlfriend, Niura. Rather than engaging in a drunken brawl, the Komsomols are exercising, singing, and playing basketball. This contrast is an intentional one between dark and light—the "good-for-nothing, meaningless stupidity of the rabble [*shpana*]" opposed to the cheerful aspirations of Komsomol members.[22]

Sashka Chumovoi has promised to join in a Komsomol venture, to crew on a Soviet ship heading for China. Before shipping out, he comes back to his old crowd to pick up Klavka. This detour, which includes some fistfights with a rival for Klavka's attention, makes him late for the Komsomols' departure. Sashka is determined to make the boat and Klavka is equally determined to stay with him, so she decides to follow along, disguised as a boy. Unfortunately, she makes such an unconvincing boy—constantly powdering her nose and wearing her bell bottoms backward—that Sashka worries that they will be stranded somewhere on the journey. So he and Klavka intentionally pick a fight with their hosts, are placed in the hold, and escape. They wind up on the border of Russia and Estonia, which they somehow mistake for America. There they witness a smuggling attempt by Sashka's old pals, which convinces Sashka once and for all that they are a bad lot. In the meantime, Sasha Delovoi has followed the pair and brings the border guards to arrest the

22. A. Gorbenko, *Sashka Chumovoi: Komsomol'skaia komediia*, in A. Piotrovskii and M. Sokolovskii, eds., *Teatr rabochei molodezhi: Sbornik p'es dlia komsomol'skogo teatra* (Moscow: Gosudarstvennoe izdatel'stvo, 1928), 91.

smugglers. In the grand finale, Crazy Sashka gives up his ties to the life of crime and embraces the Komsomol collective, this time without his troublesome companion, Klavka.

As was often the case in TRAM plays, Sashka Chumovoi is a much more arresting figure than his clean-living counterpart. Chumovoi, who had fought in the Civil War, is bored by the dull routine of daily life and spends much of his time "making up for lost sleep."[23] At crucial intervals he recounts his war stories, adventures of questionable veracity in which he plays a leading role. In one such tale he saves Trotsky's life, recounting a scenario with detective-thriller qualities. Trotsky discovers himself alone in an exposed position on a bad horse facing five White soldiers. Suddenly, Sashka appears and Trotsky appeals to him as if to an old friend. "Hey, Sashka," he calls in the familiar voice, "They are overtaking me, come help!" "Even if I die," Sashka tells his hooligan friends, "I will save the army." Sashka puts Trotsky on his own horse, leading the Whites to chase Sashka instead. Trotsky and the army were rescued, but Sashka modestly refused credit, even turning down a medal.[24]

According to one TRAM member, Roman Ianov, who provided an assessment of the play in the Leningrad journal *Worker and Theater* (*Rabochii i teatr*), the character Sashka Chumovoi suffered from *"pinketonovshchina,"* an exaggerated interest in detective fiction (*"pinkertony,"* in Russian). It was Ianov's hope that the funny story and its edifying conclusion would lure worker youth away from popular films, which "very often poison young viewers with detective stories and petty-bourgeois venom."[25] Of course, just the opposite might have been the case—*Crazy Sashka* could have won an audience because it drew on familiar forms of popular entertainment, with viewers focusing on the wild antics and improbable, humorous plot rather on the last minute transformation of the hero. Even a team of earnest *rabkor* reporters commented that the performance's greatest asset was that it was fun to watch.[26]

For whatever reason, because it was successful transformative propaganda or because it was a fun evening's amusement, *Crazy Sashka* was a big success for TRAM. It was performed over fifty times in TRAM's first

23. Gorbenko, *Sashka Chumovoi*, 111.
24. Ibid., 96. See a similar tale with Voroshilov, 111.
25. Roman Ianov, "TRAM," RiT 46 (1925): 13.
26. M. Kudriashev, Aleksandrov, and Mirotvorskaia, "TRAM," RiT 51 (1925): 20.

season—a huge run for a club performance.[27] According to Pavel Marinchik, even the city's street youth were fans. Rumors had spread
through the city that Sashka Chumovoi was *"svoi"*—one of their own. A
gang of rowdy youth arrived on opening night, a special event for the
local press and Komsomol dignitaries, and were miffed that they were
not let in to see the play. They stormed the doors, broke windows, and
threatened a major disturbance if they were not given seats. They were
only placated when TRAM leaders offered a special performance just for
them.[28]

After the debut of *Crazy Sashka*, TRAM members prepared a number of
plays in the late 1920s that touched on contemporary problems of Soviet
young people: the Komsomol in revolution and Civil War in *Zor'ka*
(1926) and *Rowdy Cohort* (*Buzlivaia kogorta*, 1927); struggles in the workplace in *Factory Storm* (*Fabzavshturm*, 1926) and *Call the Factory Committee*
(*Zovi fabkom*, 1928); and the alienation of young people unable to make
peace with NEP in *Work Days* (*Budni*, 1926). Four of the plays—
Meshchanka (1926), *The Days Are Melting* (*Plaviatsia dni*, 1928), *Happy
Hillock* (*Druzhnaia gorka*, 1928), and *The Thoughtful Dandy* (*Klesh zadumchivyi*, 1929)—take love and marriage within the Komsomol as their central problem.

The threat of the Soviet underworld is a recurring subject of TRAM
plays. In *Crazy Sashka* hooligans are more buffoonish than dangerous.
However, in TRAM's next work, *Factory Storm*, written by Dmitrii Tolmachev, hooligans are more disruptive. The bad boy in the play, a
drunken worker who shows up late and steals factory materials, has ties
to the local gang. When he is kicked out of his job, he arranges for his
friends to beat up the Komsomol hero who had orchestrated his dis-
missal, nearly leading to the hero's death.[29] An even more dangerous underworld emerges in *Work Days*. In this work a disaffected Komsomol
member loses interest in an upright Komsomol worker and falls in love
with the daughter of a specialist, whom his colleagues suspect of shady
dealings. Their suspicions are correct; she is in fact the member of a
White Guardist family. Both her father and brother are secretly trying to
overthrow the Soviet regime. Although her sympathies lie with her
boyfriend, she is unable to inform on her own family. In the process, she

27. V. Mironova, *TRAM*, 26.
28. Marinchik, *Rozhdenie*, 73–74.
29. D. Tolmachev, *Fabzavshtorm*, in Piotrovskii and Sokolovskii, eds., *Teatr rabochei
molodezhi*, 82–84.

A scene from the Leningrad TRAM play *Work Days* (*Budni*). Bakhrushin State Central Theatrical Museum. Reproduced with permission.

entangles her boyfriend in a conspiracy that threatens his membership in the Komsomol.[30]

The appeal of materialist consumption in NEP culture is also an important subject in TRAM plays, usually presented through female characters. The troubled heroine of *Meshchanka* is revealed as an unreliable figure when her friends discover powder in her purse—her use of makeup showing that she could not be a politically conscious individual.[31] She is not the only vain woman in the play; her friends' pursuit of style has led them to get their hair scorched by an incompetent beautician.[32] While male characters often ridicule women's interest in fashion, numerous Komsomol men in TRAM plays look for affection from stylish women outside of their political milieu. This causes the rejected Komsomol

30. P. Marinchik, and S. Kashevnik, *Budni*, ibid., 56.
31. Pavel Marinchik, *Meshchanka* (Leningrad: Teakinopechat', 1929), 26.
32. Ibid., 44.

leader in *Work Days* to worry that "perhaps we are ourselves to blame . . . we factory girls are just too plain."[33]

While the appeals of fashion tempt Komsomol women, drunkenness is the most serious problem for the men. Drink drives them to bad deeds, like spending their Komsomol dues or beating up their colleagues. Minor male Komsomol members in TRAM plays constantly challenge the prohibition on alcohol at social gatherings, insisting that drinking would make them even more pleasurable. In *Meshchanka*, one male character who is particularly critical of women's interest in finery tries to convince them that his taste for vodka does not qualify as a vice. A party with only tea is a "bourgeois affair." By contrast, "Vodka is not a bourgeois drink; it is loved by all classes."[34] Very few female characters indulge in alcohol, but those that do are a particularly bad lot, leading men astray and leaving broken homes in their wake.

The widely available but, for TRAM members, disreputable commercial amusements of NEP culture are another important subtheme. When the Komsomol collective in *Work Days* want to find the hero and his frivolous girlfriend, someone suggests that they begin their search at several local restaurants; if they come up empty-handed, they should then case the yacht club.[35] The evil woman in *Meshchanka* is said to be "as beautiful as Mary Pickford," a reference to the popularity of American film in NEP and its troubling influence.[36] The extremely conflicted female heroine of *The Thoughtful Dandy* is drawn to a number of highly questionable activities. She secretly takes dancing lessons, where she learns foreign dance steps. She has considered suicide and even keeps a store of poison. In an act of desperation, she leaves her husband and home for a religious commune, an allusion to the strong religious communities that were gaining youthful followings in the 1920s.[37]

These conflicted heroines and heroes are tempted by the distractions of alternative youth cultures, yet in the end they are always drawn back to the Komsomol community. TRAM plays offer a sense of the Komsomol club as a model for a new kind of family, responsible for the nurturing,

---

33. Marinchik and Kashevnik, *Budni*, 35. For more on gender roles in TRAM, see Lynn Mally, "Performing the New Woman: The Komsomolka as Actress and Image in Soviet Youth Theater," *Journal of Social History* 30, no. 1 (Fall 1996): 79–95.

34. Marinchik, *Meshchanka*, 45.

35. Marchinik and Kashevnik, *Budni*, 39.

36. Marinchik, *Meshchanka*, 17. On American films and their following, see Denise Youngblood, *Movies for the Masses: Popular Cinema and Soviet Society in the 1920s* (Cambridge: Cambridge University Press, 1992), 50–67.

37. N. L'vov, *Klesh zadumchivyi* (Leningrad: Teakinopechat', 1930), 38–42, 58–62.

care, and discipline of its members. Pavel Marinchik's play *Meshchanka* is an example of a TRAM family drama in which the Komsomol family overcomes obstacles to create a new sense of commitment and group responsibility. It plucked its topic directly from the Komsomol press. In the mid-1920s, as part of a general investigation into why so few young women participated in the Komsomol, activists began drawing attention to the fact that women who had once taken part tended to drop out once they married. They became "petty bourgeois," giving their attention to home life rather than the public sphere. This turned them into *"meshchanki,"* petty-bourgeois women, a very derogatory term in the Soviet lexicon. The play set out to analyze this problem without offering definitive solutions.[38]

In his memoirs, Marinchik reveals that he was inspired to write the play in part by the intervention of Komsomol women, who complained about men's unwillingness to help out in the home. He quotes a member of the Skorokhod factory TRAM group, Niura Petrunina, who had spoken at a local Komsomol debate: "It is very easy to spout off charges. It is very easy for you to call us *meshchanki.* But when you go home, who fixes your dinner? Who washes your shirt? Who feeds your child? Your mother or your wife. And openly admit it, you politically advanced [*ideinye*] comrades—do any of you help to surmount the unavoidable difficulties of family life?"[39]

In the play, two young activists meet in a Komsomol club and decide to marry. Niura Panova is an important organizer at her factory; Mitia Panov belongs to both the Komsomol and the Communist Party and also leads his factory committee. The marriage, embarked upon joyfully, quickly changes their lives for the worse. Overburdened by new responsibilities, Niura applies to leave her Komsomol cell. For this she is attacked by the (male) Komsomol leaders, publicly humiliated, and ostracized as a *meshchanka.* At the same time, her marriage has become shaky. Mitia does not think that Niura is doing a good job running the household, and he is also embarrassed by her transformation into a homebody. As a result, he quickly forms a romantic liaison with another woman. Faced with public ostracism and a failing marriage, Niura is brought to the brink of suicide.

---

38. Marinchik, *Rozhdenie,* 121. For an overview of this issue, see Gorsuch, *Enthusiasts,* ch. 5, and E. Troshchenko, "Devushka v soiuze," *Molodaia gvardiia* 3 (1926): 129–35.
39. Marinchik, *Rozhdenie,* 121.

No one party is given sole responsibility for this unhappy situation. Niura is shown to be easily undone by the demands of marriage, quickly (and inexplicably) changing from a lively activist to a distraught and passive wife. "I just cannot go on this way," she tells her best friend, explaining her decision to leave the Komsomol. "During the day we are at the factory, then at the club, in the collective, and we only see each other late at night. He works very hard and wants to relax. I must, I am obligated to help him."[40] The husband also must share the blame. Instead of helping his wife, he demands a hot dinner and nicely ironed shirts, insulting her when they are not prepared to his liking. He flaunts his new girlfriend and stalks out when his wife is reduced to tears, saying he cannot stand her "petty-bourgeois scenes."[41] Nor does the Komsomol organization come off very well. Members discover Niura's intention to leave by violating her privacy, rummaging through her purse. The Komsomol cell chief does not think it is necessary to investigate why her marriage might have driven her to take such a step. "She herself is to blame," he opines. "She turned into a *baba*, a *meshchanka*. We don't need her kind."[42]

The final scene, when Niura is saved from a suicide attempt at the last minute, offers an interesting critique of male sexual behavior. A former admirer of Niura's, a returning Red Army soldier, lectures not only Niura's friends and husband but also the heartless group leaders. He criticizes men who pretend to believe that women are their equals but at the same time brag about their sexual conquests. He then turns to the audience and asks, "And you gathered here, what do you say? Should we struggle to end the barbarous, slipshod relations between young men and women?" A unanimous "We should," obviously designed to include the audience, is the last line of the play.[43]

Meshchanka offers a clear answer to the question about how the family can be integrated into the community: it must be made porous to the Komsomol collective, subsumed by the Komsomol family. In the words of a reviewer in the journal *Worker and Theater*, "A sensitive and comradely collective, that is the first element of normal domestic relations."[44] Collective oversight is needed to curb both male sexual excess and fe-

---

40. Marinchik, *Meshchanka*, 33.
41. Ibid., 49, 51.
42. Ibid., 36.
43. Ibid., 64.
44. Eres, "Igrovoi teatr," RiT 49 (1926): 16.

male masochism. The Komsomol's intervention made the husband regret his rash behavior; it saved the wife from suicide. But the price was a loss of privacy—opening domestic relations between wife and husband to public oversight.

In his fascinating study about sexual discourse in the 1920s, Eric Naiman argues that the preoccupation with sex in Komsomol political and artistic literature was part of an effort to gain greater control over the nation's youth. Debates about the "problems of daily life" fascinated young people, resulting in "a process in which discussion was first eroticized so that it could ultimately be more effectively politicized."[45] Although TRAM works do not contain the same level of sexually explicit language as more sensational works from the 1920s, they too present situations where intimate personal quandaries are ultimately solved by the intervention of the political community, effectively erasing any realm of private decision making. TRAM plays abound with invasive practices— eavesdropping, rifling of wallets and purses, and the public reading of diaries. The secret police are invoked as heroes who know everything and keep a watchful eye on the supposedly private affairs of young people. Thus, the new family is presented as a panoptical device, coming to know all so that it can solve all.

With this said, it is difficult to judge what messages viewers took from TRAM plays. By presenting a wide range of youthful types, these works offered audiences a chance to identify with the anti-heroes or with the central characters before they made their final transformation. The plays showed not only the positive aspects of youthful togetherness but also offered insights into the vulgar, bossy, and cruel side of the Komsomol collective.[46] It was Crazy Sashka—not his upstanding counterpart—who had a following among Leningrad street youth, and we can assume it was his brazen and swashbuckling side, not his last-minute transformation to the clean living Komsomol, that attracted his fans. Similarly, the new family structure proposed in TRAM works subordinated the individual to the invasive Komsomol community. However, some characters resisted integration and showed the high price of subordination. By taking on the complexities of youth culture, TRAM sketched out a variety of possible trajectories and thus ensured that a wide range of Soviet youth would see themselves and their friends reflected in its works.

45. Eric Naiman, *Sex in Public: The Incarnation of Early Soviet Ideology* (Princeton: Princeton University Press, 1997), 101.

46. Piotrovskii and Sokolovskii, "Dialekticheskaia p'esa," in N. L'vov *Plaviatsia dni* (Leningrad: Teakinopechat', 1929), 4.

"TRAMism"

The Leningrad TRAM presented itself as a theater of a new type, a "bridge" between amateur and professional theaters.[47] Rooted in the agitational theater of small forms, it embraced topical themes, thus meeting its audience's demand for works that reflected on the challenges and struggles of contemporary life. Initially, TRAM also rejected the professionalization of its worker actors. Participants kept their factory jobs in order to remain close to the problems, enthusiasms, and language of contemporary youth. TRAM's application form, distributed through the Komsomol, pointedly asked for employment information and evidence of union membership.[48] TRAM's proletarian persona was already apparent in the opening march of *Crazy Sashka*: "In the mornings we are always there by our machines, but in the evenings our job is TRAM!"[49]

Sokolovskii insisted that they would not follow the guidance of any established theatrical training program; instead, they would devise their own methods. Along the same lines, they would not use scripts created by professionals because such works could not capture the milieu of worker youth. Moreover, TRAM plays would be a collective creation, with input from all members. *Crazy Sashka* was an example of such a group process. Although the script bore Arkadii Gorbenko's name, the text was worked out in a series of late-night discussions between TRAM's young writers and Adrian Piotrovskii.[50] His two rooms in a communal apartment, filled with pictures of ancient Greek playwrights, became the unofficial meeting place where TRAM members read, discussed, and hammered out their new plays.[51] Thus, while individual authors took final credit for TRAM plays, writers, participants, and observers alike insisted that these group discussions were their main creative force.

For Piotrovskii, TRAM was the embodiment of all that was positive in amateur theater engendered by the revolution. His perceptions of the new theater fit into a grander theory about the continual historic tension between amateur and professional theatrical forms. In his view, amateur theater emerged organically from the rituals and festivals of the lower

47. A. Piotrovskii, "Teatr rabochei molodezhi," ZI 43 (1925): 13.
48. "V priemochnuiu komissiiu teatra rabochei molodezhi," TSKhDMO, f. 1 (Tsentral'nyi komitet VLKSM), op. 23, d. 396, l. 125.
49. Mironova, TRAM, 34.
50. Marinchik, Rozhdenie, 61, 69–70.
51. See the memoirs of these evenings by Piotrovskii's wife, Alisa Akimova, "Chelovek dal'nikh plavanii," in E. S. Dobin, ed., Adrian Piotrovskii: Teatr, kino, zhizn' (Leningrad: Iskusstvo, 1968), 362.

classes; it then challenged the dominant modes of expression in established theaters of the ruling class. Such a challenge was currently taking place in Soviet Russia, as working-class groups criticized the presentational style and repertoire of professional theaters that had not changed significantly since the revolution. "By constructing daily life [*byt*], by organizing it in a festive way, the working class with its 'amateur,' 'autonomous' performances lays the foundation for a radical reexamination of theatrical forms and marks the way to a theater of the future," Piotrovskii insisted.[52]

Both Piotrovskii and the TRAM director Sokolovskii were convinced that TRAM had a unique contribution to make to Soviet cultural life. Together, they began to formulate the social and aesthetic principles that they believed distinguished Komsomol theater from other forms of amateur artistic creation. As opposed to many other amateur theaters where the aim was primarily entertainment, TRAM articulated a clear political goal. The group's purpose was to change daily life, rather than to describe it. Tellingly, they referred to the collective not as a theater but as the agitational arm of the Komsomol.[53]

From this followed new roles for the TRAM actor. Rather than seeing themselves as passive observers of Soviet life, TRAM participants conceived of themselves as activists who drew their subject matter from factories and dormitories and aimed to influence the behavior of viewers. Their goal was to recreate the language and movement of present-day youth and to pose the problems of young people to the audience. Although this approach demanded training, it was directly opposed to the methods endorsed by Konstantin Stanislavsky, who encouraged his actors at the Moscow Art Theater to enter the emotional world of the characters they represented on stage. In an intentional contrast to Stanislavsky's ideas, Sokolovskii maintained that the TRAM participant was more an agitator than an actor of the old school.[54] The parts TRAM actors played were social masks, beneath which the faces of worker youth were clearly visible. "While acting on the stage," wrote Piotrovskii and Sokolovskii, "the TRAM Komsomol actor does not give up his basic character of a worker youth; he continues to express his social and

52. A. I. Piotrovskii, "Osnovy samodeiatel'nogo iskusstva," *Za sovetskii teatr!* (Leningrad: Academia, 1925), 73.

53. A. Piotrovskii, "TRAM: Stranitsa teatral'noi sovremennosti," *Zvezda* 4 (1929): 142–52; M. Sokolovskii, "V nogu s komsomolom," *Komsomol'skaia pravda*, 1 June 1928; Piotrovskii and Sokolovskii, "O teatre rabochei molodezhi," in *Teatr rabochei molodezhi*, 3–8.

54. See Sokolovskii's speech at a meeting of the Leningrad TRAM, 4 March 1929, RGALI, f. 2947 (Moskovskii teatr imeni Leninskogo komsomola), op. 1, d. 4, ll. 4–23.

class nature. He does not take a 'passive' position, embodying his role, but rather remains 'active,' as if analyzing and judging the character."[55] TRAM actors offered a critical interpretation, without entering into the character's emotional world.

This method of acting, which Piotrovskii called "the denial of illusion," articulated in the late 1920s, bears a close resemblance to Bertolt Brecht's concept of alienation, first developed in the 1930s.[56] James von Geldern has speculated that TRAM might have influenced Brecht indirectly; the great director could have heard about these concepts through his friend, the Russian avant-garde author Sergei Tretiakov.[57] Although this remains speculation, certainly there was much in common between the two methods. Martin Esslin's description of Brechtian acting techniques could serve equally well for TRAM performers: "The character who is being shown and the actor who demonstrates him remain clearly differentiated. And the actor retains his freedom to *comment* on the actions of the person whose behavior he is displaying."[58]

TRAM works were synthetic creations uniting a variety of art forms, including music, song, dance, and acrobatics. These principles grew from Piotrovskii's conception of the united artistic circle. TRAM productions were sometimes composed directly during rehearsals, with songs and dances evolving as actors learned their lines. The literary script was not the most important element of the play—nor was the actor the primary bearer of meaning.[59] TRAM works were not bound to a unilinear presentation of the story. They used flashbacks; they proposed alternative endings. "It is not hard to see the ties between TRAM's many-layered presentation of events and film montage," declared Piotrovskii. Indeed, he saw TRAM as only one piece of evidence pointing to what he called the "filmization" (*kinofikatsiia*) of all the arts.[60]

55. Piotrovskii and Sokolovskii, "O teatre rabochei molodezhi," in *Teatr rabochei molodezhi*, 4–5, quotation 4. See also *Novye etapy samodeiatel'noi khudozhestvennoi raboty* (Moscow: Teakinopechat', 1930), 98.

56. See Bertolt Brecht, "Neue Technik der Schauspielkunst," in *Schriften zum Theater I* (*Gesammelte Werke 16*) (Frankfurt am Main: Suhrkamp Verlag, 1967), 339–88.

57. James von Geldern, "Soviet Mass Theater, 1917–1927," in Bernice Glatzer Rosenthal, ed., *Nietzsche and Soviet Culture* (Cambridge: Cambridge University Press, 1994), 144.

58. Martin Esslin, *Brecht: The Man and His Work* (New York: W. W. Norton, 1971), 137, emphasis in the original.

59. See, for example, M. Sokolovskii, "Nemnogo o postanovke," in *Zor'ka: V pomoshch' zriteliu* (Moscow: Teakinopechat', 1929), 3; I. Chicherov, "O teatre rabochei molodezhi," in I. I. Chicherov, ed., *Za TRAM: Vsesoiuznoe soveshchanie po khudozhestvennoi rabote sredi molodezhi* (Moscow: Teakinopechat', 1929), 15–16.

60. A. Piotrovskii, "TRAM," *Zvezda* 4 (1929), 147. On "filmization," see his *Kinofikatsiia iskusstv* (Leningrad: Izdanie avtora, 1929), esp. 14–25.

TRAM authors did not offer simple stories with single definitions of good and evil. Instead, they opposed obvious endings and presented a "dialectical structure."[61] According to Piotrovskii and Sokolovskii, the function of a TRAM play was neither to tell a simple narrative nor to reveal the inner thoughts and feelings of the characters; rather, it was to illuminate the contradictions inherent in Soviet life and to depict the internal tensions of characters themselves.[62] "Episodes are not linked in the sequence of events," explained Piotrovskii, "but as elements of a unique 'polemic,' as supporting or opposing sides of an argument."[63] This attempt to depict problems as "many-layered, capacious and many-sided" complicated TRAM's agitational role. Too many Soviet plays, insisted the two leaders, made the tensions of Soviet life seem minor: "They often show observers' conclusions in a simplistic and one-sided way compared to the contradictory complications of our reality."[64] TRAM's goal was to heighten those tensions and to make the audience face the difficult choices they often confronted in their lives.

During the waning years of NEP, the Leningrad TRAM won an enthusiastic following in its home city. Not only was the original TRAM theater at the Gleron House a popular site, but TRAM cells [iadra] opened in eight city factories, including the Skorokhod plant, the Vera Slutskaia factory, and the Elektrosil plant. It also inspired groups in Leningrad province.[65] TRAM expanded to Moscow in 1927, first beginning in several small affiliates in different parts of the city. The Moscow Komsomol sponsored a central city organization in late 1927, under the leadership of a student from the Meyerhold Theater.[66]

As TRAM began to spread and attract attention in the national press, advocates began to define TRAM as a mass movement, as "TRAMism," something that would eventually lead to a new kind of professional theater. TRAM participants attempted to set themselves apart from traditional academic theaters, which they charged had not changed sufficiently since the revolution. TRAM members were most critical of

61. A. P-skii, "O tramizme," ZI 50 (1927): 2.
62. A. Piotrovskii and M. Sokolovskii, "Dialekticheskaia p'esa," in *Plaviatsia dni*, 3–9; idem, "Spektakl' o sotsialisticheskom sorevnovanii," in L'vov, *Klesh zadumchivyi*, 3–4.
63. Piotrovskii, "TRAM," 147.
64. Piotrovskii and Sokolovskii, "Dialekticheskaia p'esa," 5.
65. V. G-ov, "V bor'be za tramovskoe dvizhenie," ZI 19 (1928): 9.
66. Chicherov, ed., *Za TRAM*, 28; I. Chicherov, "Za teatr rabochei molodezhi," NZ 28 (1927): 2; "Teatr rabochei molodezhi," ZI 29 (1927): 14; "Akt no. 2087," TSMAN, f. 2007 (Upravlenie moskovskimi zrelishchnymi predstavleniiami), op. 3, d. 184, l. 3.

Stanislavsky's theater and theatrical method. Sokolovskii referred to the Moscow Art Theater as the "Theater of Bourgeois Youth."[67] It had played an important role in reorienting theater under the old regime but now had become isolated from the external world.

TRAM also tried to set itself apart from the theatrical avant-garde, which proved a more difficult task. By abandoning straightforward narrative structures and endorsing non-realistic acting and staging techniques, TRAM theater was clearly indebted to Meyerhold's methods. Nonetheless, TRAM members insisted that while the left avant-garde performed works with revolutionary themes, their presentational style was often difficult for new viewers to understand.[68] TRAM plays, by contrast, contained the living language of worker youth. TRAM presentations were not unilinear; instead, they followed the Marxist method of dialectical materialism.

These grand claims did not go without criticism. In a discussion about TRAM's role that erupted in the Komsomol press in 1927, many skeptics came forward to challenge the ambitious theater. They asked just how TRAM actors could hone their craft if they were still employed in the factory. The entire premise of TRAM organization was wrong, according to one author. Soviet young people were not particularly interested in special plays about youth; instead, they wanted good plays, pure and simple. The collective process—whereby all members participated in every aspect of the performance, no one was devoted to the process full time, and professional help was discouraged—could never produce first rate work.[69] These critics claimed that Soviet theater would be much better served if talented young actors and directors entered existing training programs; in the process they would help to proletarianize all of Soviet culture.[70]

Beneath these aesthetic and organizational arguments were strong political undertones. Narkompros leader Robert Pel'she warned that the concept of TRAM "smelled like syndicalism," alluding to oppositional

67. Ivan Chicherov, *Perezhitoe, nezabyvaemoe* (Moscow: Molodaia gvardiia, 1977), 176–77. Chicherov was the Komsomol representative in Narkompros and later the head of TRAM's national soviet.

68. "Teatr rabochei molodezhi: Byt-proizvodstvo-bor'ba," RGALI, f. 963, op. 1, d. 1099, l. 4.

69. A. Neks, "Protiv TRAM'a," *Komsomol'skii agitproprabotnik*, 13/14 (1927): 77–79.

70. This discussion lasted through eight issues of the journal, from number fourteen to twenty-one. Each issue presented pro and con positions. Contributors included the author Boris Ivanter; the head of the Narkompros' cultural division, Robert Pel'she; and the director of the Moscow Trade Union theater, Evsei Liubimov-Lanskoi.

tendencies that threatened Communist Party control. The entire educational system was designed to serve worker youth. Why was a special group necessary?[71] And with a reference to former battles within the Komsomol over its relationship to the Communist Party, another critic asserted that "there is not and cannot be a special path for youth."[72]

Those in favor of TRAM intoned that professional theaters were ignoring the problems of youth and that a new system was needed to represent their ideals. Because of its contemporary themes, TRAM was also significant in enlivening the political-educational work of the Komsomol as a whole. In the process, the theater had created a following of viewers who regarded TRAM as their own. Since the Komsomol leadership remained firmly behind the youth theater, TRAM's future was not really in doubt. At the Fifth Komsomol Congress in March 1927, the organization resolved that it was essential to offer worker youth theaters their support.[73] However, to some degree TRAM also integrated the most significant criticism raised in this debate. In the spring of 1928, the Leningrad TRAM professionalized, freeing its young members from their factory jobs.

Gaining professional status would seem to exclude TRAM from the purview of this book, where the focus is amateurs. However, the theater was only "professional" insofar as its actors now earned meager salaries. Financial support was so low that many took pay cuts to join TRAM full time.[74] The theater was certainly not integrated into the prestigious network of academic stages, like the Moscow Art Theater, which received support directly from Narkompros. Nor did TRAM offer official training programs. In essence, TRAM actors were *"praktiki,"* experts without credentials who had learned their skills on the job rather than through formal educational channels.[75]

Moreover, the Leningrad (and later Moscow) professional troupes remained important to amateur stages as the self-proclaimed link between professional and non-professional theater. Participants vowed to be-

71. "Nuzhen li TRAM? Iz doklada tov. Pel'she na kul'tsoveshchanii pri TsK VLKSM," *Komsomol'skii agitprorabotnik*, 18 (1927): 40–41.

72. Semen Shor, "Tataram o TRAMe," *Komsomol'skii agitprorabotnik* 20 (1927): 47.

73. "O postanovke massovoi kul'turno-vospitatel'noi raboty sredi molodezhi," in *Tovarishch komsomol: Dokumenty s''ezdov, konferentsii i TsK VLKSM*, v. 1, 1918–1941 (Moscow: Molodaia gvardiia, 1969), 301.

74. "Vtoroi vecher vospominanii rabotnikov TRAM'a ot 15/V 1930," RGALI, f. 2723, op. 1, d. 534, l. 19.

75. On *praktiki*, see Sheila Fitzpatrick, *Educational and Social Mobility in the Soviet Union 1921–1934* (Cambridge: Cambridge University Press, 1979), 125, 202.

come "professionals of a new type." Piotrovskii even insisted that the term "professional actor" did not really describe their new roles. What the young people had become were professional agitators for the Komsomol, leading discussion groups and devoting themselves to political education.[76] These declamations notwithstanding, TRAM actors in Leningrad had now removed themselves from one of the problems of the amateur circles from which they had emerged. They no longer had to struggle to balance their theatrical activity with their daily working lives.

The Vanguard of Amateur Art

TRAM achieved a national following during the early years of the First Five-Year Plan (1928–32), a period of rupture so extreme that Stalin called it the "Great Break."[77] As the state launched programs of break-neck industrialization and coerced collectivization, radical cultural projects were initiated at a feverish pace. City planners turned against the idea of cities; legal experts envisioned the withering away of law. These iconoclastic dreams had a profound effect on the broad array of amateur stages, which began to use cafeterias and dormitories as stages to enact disruptive social dramas (see chapter 5). For TRAM, this period of experimentation brought it even more public attention. Its own oxymoronic vision of a professional theater that disdained professionals fit the spirit of social leveling initiated by the plan.

As many scholars have argued, the First Five-Year Plan was to some degree a youth rebellion.[78] Given the general privileging of youth, it should come as no surprise that TRAM—a theater by and for young people—would gain notoriety. Its political guardian, the Komsomol, won much greater visibility as an initiator of cultural campaigns. Not only did the Komsomol attack conventional educational programs, it

76. Adrian Piotrovskii, "TRAM i teatral'nyi professionalizm," *Rabis* 26 (1929): 4.

77. Michael David-Fox argues eloquently that this period should be called the "Great Break" to emphasize its radical nature. I have used the more prosaic "First Five-Year Plan" because that is the appellation most common in my sources. See Michael David-Fox, "What Is Cultural Revolution?" *Russian Review* 58 (April 1999): 184.

78. Sheila Fitzpatrick has made the most persuasive case for the role of youth in the First Five-Year Plan. See her "Cultural Revolution as Class War," in *The Cultural Front* (Ithaca: Cornell University Press, 1992), 115–48; and idem, *Education and Social Mobility in the Soviet Union*, 136–57. See also William J. Chase, *Workers, Society, and the Soviet State: Labor and Life in Moscow, 1918–1929* (Urbana: University of Illinois Press, 1987), 256–92, and Hiroaki Kuromiya, *Stalin's Industrial Revolution: Politics and Workers, 1928–1932* (Cambridge: Cambridge University Press, 1988), 100–35.

also waged a war of words against the citadels of high culture. Both the
Bol'shoi Theater and the Moscow Art Theater faced stinging attacks in
the Komsomol press for their generous government funding, non-prole-
tarian social composition, and outdated, anti-revolutionary repertoires.
As the Komsomol assaulted these remnants of the old world, it championed new institutions like TRAM and attempted to win them greater financial support.[79]

The Leningrad TRAM's shift to professional status gave it much more
national visibility. With support from the Komsomol, the theater made
its first tour to Moscow in the summer of 1928, which helped to popularize TRAM plays and methods. It took *Call the Factory Committee, Happy
Cohort,* and a new play, *The Days Are Melting (Plaviatsia dni),* which examined the strains experienced by a young Komsomol couple when a
child was born.[80] The group was met by enthusiastic audiences everywhere it went: in Orekhovo-Zuevo, a textile town not far from Moscow,
they had to add extra performances; in Moscow itself, nearly twenty-
five thousand people showed up for TRAM productions.[81] As the industrialization drive began in earnest, TRAM collectives spread throughout
Soviet territory. Only a handful of TRAM circles existed outside of
Leningrad before 1928 but some observers counted up to seventy by the
end of the year and three hundred by 1932.[82] The Leningrad TRAM and
its repertoire inspired emulation across the nation, as new factory and
city-based TRAM organizations took shape. The vast majority of these
new theaters, spread from Baku to Magnitogorsk, were amateur
circles.[83]

TRAM began to attract the attention of national cultural institutions. At
the Conference on Artistic Work among Youth, which met in Moscow in
the summer of 1928, Anatolii Lunacharskii, the head of Narkompros,

79. See, for example, "Poltora goda na odnom meste," *Komsomol'skaia pravda* (henceforth
cited as KP), 13 November 1928. On the Komsomol in theatrical politics, see Nikolai A.
Gorchakov, *The Theater in Soviet Russia,* trans. Edgar Lehrman (New York: Columbia University Press, 1957), 283–85; Richard G. Thorpe, *Academic Art in Revolutionary Russia,* unpublished manuscript, ch. 7.

80. N. L'vov, *Plaviatsia dni: Dialekticheskoe predstavlenie v 3-kh krugakh* (Leningrad:
Teakinopechat', 1929). For an investigation of this play, see Mally, "Performing the New
Woman," 86–88.

81. On TRAM's repertoire, see *Leningradskii TRAM v Moskve* (Leningrad: Izdanie Gostrama,
1928); on its reception, see "Golos rabochei molodezhi," KP 6 July 1928; "Na zavodakh,"
KP 13 July 1928.

82. V. G-ov, "V bor'be za tramovskoe dvizhenie," ZI 19 (1928): 9; Mironova, 6.

83. Marinchik, *Rozhdenie,* 170, 207; F. Knorre, "Moskovskii TRAM," *Rabis* 26 (1929): 9.

«ЗОВИ ФАБКОМ»
Павлушка—артист Виноградов, А.

A sketch of the hooligan figure in the TRAM play *Call the Factory Committee* (*Zovi fabkom*). *Leningradskii* TRAM *v Moskve* (Leningrad: Izdanie Gostrama, 1928).

A scene from the Leningrad TRAM play *The Thoughtful Dandy (Klesh zadumchivyi)*.
Bakhrushin State Central Theatrical Museum. Reproduced with permission.

called TRAM a model for building a new socialist theater.[84] The following
month, he praised TRAM's work in the nation's newspaper of record,
Pravda. In a long article, Lunacharskii traced the theater's history from a
Komsomol club to its recent visit to Moscow, giving particular attention
to *The Days Are Melting*. The commissar of the arts also gave TRAM an
aesthetic endorsement by linking it to the work of Meyerhold: "It is no
accident that the great master Meyerhold expressed his admiration for
these performances, and also no accident that Mikhail Sokolovskii,
TRAM's organizer, willingly admitted that TRAM drew broadly on the
work of Meyerhold."[85]

84. A. V. Lunacharskii, "Iskusstvo molodezhi i zadachi khudozhestvennoi raboty sredi
molodezhi," in R. A. Pel'she et al., eds., *Komsomol, na front iskusstva!* (Leningrad:
Teakinopechat', 1929), 33–35.
85. A. Lunacharskii, "TRAM," *Pravda* 8 July 1928.

With the onset of the First Five-Year Plan, TRAM plays became even more topical, addressing the rapid changes in labor organization and daily life demanded by the industrialization drive. In early 1929, the Leningrad TRAM premiered *The Thoughtful Dandy* (*Klesh zadumchivyi*), which addressed the many opportunities and distractions for youth as the country underwent rapid industrialization.[86] The play introduces facts and figures of industrial expansion, a new element in TRAM works but typical of the writing of this period. "Five years!" exclaims the Komsomol cell leader. "Five years of fast-moving life. And then there will be an army of 150,000 tractors in battle position!"[87] At the center of the work is a seemingly model young couple that is almost torn apart by temptations that lead them away from the collective. The wife has been advanced from her factory to study at the university but does not like it there. She is drawn instead to the night life of the city. The husband is entranced by the prospect of earning a lot of money and winning back his partner with the lure of material possessions. Although the play has a happy ending—the young couple come back to their Komsomol group—the work examined some of the personal costs of the rapid reorganization of daily life.[88]

As the First Five-Year Plan heated up, the Leningrad TRAM also began to intensify the pace of its production and reach out for new subject matter. At the end of 1929, the theater for the first time performed a work by an author from outside the TRAM circle, Alexander Bezymenskii's *The Shot* (*Vystrel*), which showed Komsomol activists attacking bureaucratic shortcomings in the Communist Party. It also began to move outside of the urban world of Komsomol youth, staging two works on collectivization and class struggle in the countryside, *Virgin Soil* (*Tselina*) and *The Roof* (*Krysha*) in 1931. Piotrovskii's *Rule Britannia* (*Prav', Britaniia*, 1931) moved its attention to a foreign setting for the first time.

By 1929, TRAM had many branches throughout the country and began to make plans to establish a national organization framework. Local representatives came to Moscow for the first national TRAM conference, intending to articulate standardized organizational guidelines and set up

---

86. L'vov, *Klesh zadumchivyi*. Not only was this published as an individual work, but it was also distributed in the journal *Materialy dlia klubnoi stseny*, which included information on staging, lighting, and music. See *Materialy dlia klubnoi stseny* 7/8 1929.

87. L'vov, *Klesh zadumchivyi*, 13.

88. I. Beletskii, "O tvorcheskom puti Moskovskogo Tsentral'nogo Trama," *Za agitprop-brigadu i TRAM* 1 (1932): 22–24.

a national governing board, the TRAM soviet.[89] The gathering featured a congratulatory greeting from Lunacharskii, who was "made younger by 35 years and pronounced an honorary TRAM member."[90] After this cheerful beginning, serious disagreements emerged as the rapidly expanding local groups tried to discover common principles that would unite them on a national level.

At the national gathering, the Leningrad TRAM organization began to feel some of the contradictory pressures emerging from its success. What kind of theater was it—the vanguard of the amateur theater movement or a new kind of professional stage? Sokolovskii, TRAM's forefather, chose to stress its amateur heritage. "We are not a theater and do not want to be one," Moscow newspapers quoted him as saying. "Instead we are a part of the Komsomol *aktiv*, taking part in the active battle for our class ideals, for the creation of socialism."[91] By appealing to the original mission of the Leningrad TRAM, he showed that he was not entirely comfortable with its new role as a professional stage.

Platon Kerzhentsev represented the Communist Party at the conference. This chameleon-like Soviet bureaucrat had argued for the superiority of amateur theater during the Civil War in his often-republished book, *Creative Theater*.[92] Now he argued in favor of professional standards. He warned that TRAM should recognize that it had a lot to learn from professional stages, even from Stanislavsky.[93] The final decisions of this first national event were formulated in the spirit of compromise. TRAM served simultaneously as a school, an agitational cell, and a theater. The militant Sokolovskii announced that TRAM was willing to consider elements of the cultural heritage but would not follow the methods of any single school. The compromise formulation that depicted TRAM as both an organized theater and an agitational group seemed to feed leaders' grandiose ambitions; they would claim a leading role over both professional and amateur stages.

The Leningrad TRAM not only expanded its influence over its national affiliates, it also hoped to increase its power over rival cultural groups. In November 1929 it formed a theatrical alliance with the Proletkult, Red Theater, and Agitational Theater in Leningrad. The aim was to give strength to

89. *Novye etapy samodeiatel'noi khudozhestvennoi raboty*, 100–104.

90. "Vsesoiuznaia konferentsiia TRAM'ov," KG 3 July 1929.

91. B., "Printsipy i metody TRAM'a," *Vecherniaia Moskva* (henceforth cited as VM) 3 July 1929.

92. See ch. 1, pages 20, 35, 36. For Kerzhentsev's destructive role in the 1930s, see ch. 6.

93. B., "Printsipy i metody TRAM'a."

the "socialist assault" against conservative academic stages. "We refuse to follow the formal traditions of the old theater slavishly," the declaration read. "We consider the most serious danger at the moment the idealist tradition emanating from the [Moscow] Art Theater, which until this point has kept its influence on theatrical activity."[94] Endorsing TRAM's claims to more power and resources, the Komsomol's national newspaper, *Komsomol'skaia pravda*, called for a grand new structure to be built for the Leningrad organization that would house up to two thousand viewers.[95]

Under the leadership of the Leningrad organization, TRAM groups were ready to claim control over amateur circles as well. At the 1930 national conference, delegates passed a resolution claiming TRAM's preeminent position. Sokolovskii pronounced, "Only as the vanguard [*golovnoi otriad*] of all amateur art, only as the active participant and leading brigadier of all restructuring of all armies of amateur artistic forms can TRAM truly become a new, socialist phenomenon in our art."[96] TRAM's links with agitprop brigades, mobile agitational groups sponsored by trade unions, were a clear indication of a shift in its cultural role. The only difference between a TRAM cell and an agitprop brigade, proclaimed Ivan Chicherov, head of the national TRAM soviet, was that the TRAM cell emerged from the factory Komsomol organization, whereas the agitprop brigade was generated by the factory committee. By embracing these burgeoning new circles, TRAM leaders aimed to solidify their claims to lead the amateur theater movement.[97]

TRAM's influence was even spreading to other media, with the founding of groups in the visual arts (IZORAM), film (KINORAM), and music (MUZORAM).[98] It began to move outside of its urban base and adolescent core constituency, establishing a Kolkhoz TRAM in Leningrad province and a Pioneer TRAM to cater to younger children.[99] For the fifth anniver-

94. "Revoliutsionnyi dogovor," ZI 44 (1929): 7. See also "Prazdnik molodogo revoliutsionnogo teatra," *Krasnaia gazeta* 4 November 1929; Clark, *Petersburg, Crucible of Cultural Revolution* (Cambridge: Harvard University Press, 1995), 266–73.

95. "Leningradskii TRAM zadykhaetsia v tesnote," KP 2 September 1930.

96. "Novyi tramovskii god," *Sbornik materialov k tret'emu plenumu tsentral'nogo soveta TRAM'ov pri TsK VLKSM* (Moscow: Teakinopechat', 1930), 9. See also O. Litovskii, "TRAM," *Smena* 2/3 (1931): 28.

97. For more on agitprop brigades, see ch. 5.

98. "V komsomol'skom kino," *Krasnaia gazeta* 18 December 1929; "Zasedanie rabochego soveta Moskovskogo tsentral'nogo TRAM'a ot 29 ianv. 1931," RGALI, f. 2947, op. 1, d. 22, l. 5; N. Chemberdzhi, "Muzykal'nyi front TRAM'a," *Sovetskoe iskusstvo* 27 May 1932.

99. V. Ipatov, "TRAM—udarnaia brigada Komsomola v iskusstve," *Klub i revoliutsiia* 21/22 (1931): 38.

sary of the Leningrad TRAM in 1930 the national Komsomol newspaper published a full-page celebratory assessment of its accomplishments, including greetings from German groups that had been inspired by its repertoire and fulsome praise from Meyerhold. According to one commentator, TRAM was one of the few theaters in the Soviet Union that was not suffering a crisis of repertoire because it made its own.[100] For a brief and heady movement, all appeared to be within TRAM's grasp.

From Vanguard to Rear Guard

Just as the TRAM movement seemed set to assume a dominant position within the fractious world of cultural politics during the First Five-Year Plan, critics began to line up against the Leningrad organization. Its unstable position between amateur and professional stages made it an easy target from both sides. In the course of this critical onslaught, the Leningrad theater was unceremoniously ousted from its position as the head of the TRAM movement, one of those rapid reversals that were a common feature of Soviet cultural conflicts. By the time the First Five-Year Plan was over, the Moscow circle was the most important TRAM theater in the nation, a status it achieved by renouncing the distinctive artistic positions formulated in Leningrad.

In 1931, the "third and decisive year" of the industrialization drive, the Leningrad TRAM began to face attacks from the amateur circles that it claimed to lead. Many groups, now staging highly agitational works often composed directly at the performance site, argued that TRAM plays were quickly outdated. In addition, they were not specific enough to illuminate local issues. Although TRAM claimed credit for leading agit-prop brigades, its leadership was "entirely fictitious," chided one critic.[101] TRAM works were also subjected to much stricter ideological criticism. At a discussion after the collectivization play *Virgin Soil*, one viewer objected to the portrayal of the decision to turn to total collectivization. It seemed to him more a negative step to destroy the well-to-do peasant (*kulak*) than a positive decision to transform the countryside.[102] A representative at a TRAM gathering in 1931 demanded that *The Thoughtful Dandy* no longer be performed: "It takes place outside of real

100. "Piat' let Leningradskogo TRAM'a," KP 2 December 1930.
101. V. Golubov, "Bez rulia i marshruta," RiT 6 (1931): 11. See also E. Lishchinev, "TRAM—khudozhestvennoe orudie marksistsko-leninskogo vospitaniia," *Iunyi kommunist* 13 (1931): 36.
102. "Obmen mnenii posle prem'ery *Tseliny*," 10. V. 1930, RGALI, f. 2723, op. 1, d. 535, l. 33.

production, outside of a specific factory or a specific city. . . . Such plays cannot inspire cadres among viewers to fight for production in their industry or town because the play does not address concrete, specific problems."[103] The humorous tone of many TRAM productions was offensive to austere worker critics, who believed that the Soviet Union was fighting a life-or-death battle in its struggle for industrialization.[104]

Other critics challenged TRAM's claim to be a new kind of professional theater. Here the most important antagonist was the Russian branch of the Proletarian Writers' Association, known by its acronym RAPP, the most aggressive cultural organization during the First Five-Year Plan. Its members believed that TRAM was not moving in the direction of a professional theater that represented proletarian interests, citing its rejection of established professional training methods and its "formalist" aesthetic principles. The leadership of RAPP linked the TRAM movement to the ideas and practices of the Leningrad Litfront, a dissident wing of the national association of proletarian writers. Litfront members believed that literature had to become more closely tied to life. To do this, writers should abandon traditional plot structures and psychologically motivated characters; instead, they should turn to short sketches and documentation taken from the lives of workers and peasants.[105] TRAM theater, with its emphasis on illuminating the problems of youth and its opposition to the techniques of professional theater, did indeed bear similarities to the spirit of the Litfront. The Leningrad TRAM had even performed a work of one of the most vocal members of the Litfront, the playwright Alexander Bezymenskii. By late 1930, RAPP had succeeded in turning the charge of "Litfrontism" into a dangerous offense. This group, RAPP leaders argued, was essentially nihilistic and incapable of creating psychologically convincing characters. Their aesthetic errors were linked to more serious political failings: through rather strained logic, the head of RAPP charged that the Litfront was part of a bloc of highly placed critics of Stalin's social and political policies.[106]

At a January 1931 conference on theater, RAPP turned these same charges against TRAM. While recognizing TRAM's important position within the amateur theater movement, RAPP leaders charged that the

103. "Orgsoveshchanie TRAM'ov: Utrennee zasedanie 7/VII/31 g.," RGALI, f. 2723, op. 1, d. 536, l. 21.
104. V. Petushkov, " 'Krysha' v TRAM'e," RiT 4 (1931): 13.
105. See A. Kemp-Welch, *Stalin and the Literary Intelligentsia, 1928–39* (New York: St. Martin's, 1991), 82–89.
106. Ibid., 89.

theater had been led astray by the "rightist" ideas of Piotrovskii, an agent of "the now defeated Litfront."[107] These views were elaborated in greater detail in RAPP's major statement on theater, "RAPP's Duties on the Theatrical Front," published in fall 1931. In this lengthy denunciation of all current tendencies in Soviet theater, RAPP charged that the TRAM movement, inspired by the Leningrad organization, was based on faulty and harmful principles. These included the idea that amateur theater was fundamentally different than professional theater, which led TRAM to deny the theatrical heritage. Other serious criticisms included its focus on "class-alien elements within the Komsomol" and its attempt to minimize the importance of the actor and the script in plays.[108] The solution was for RAPP to assume control over TRAM and amateur theaters in general, "in order to strengthen the struggle with the contrivances, mechanical methods, and vulgar Marxism permeating the TRAM and amateur theater movements."[109]

The national TRAM leadership put up some resistance to these criticisms, protesting that RAPP did not understand their position on the art of the past or their relationship to amateur theaters. In addition, they claimed that RAPP, a literary organization, did not really understand the aesthetics of theater, an art form that integrated many different media.[110] However, their main strategy was to try to isolate the national organization from the Leningrad group.[111] Underscoring this point, the head of the national organization, Ivan Chicherov, laid all of TRAM's ills at the feet of Piotrovskii. According to Chicherov, Piotrovskii had caused TRAM to abandon a linear plot structure in favor of confusing experiments and excessive improvisation.[112] Chicherov also charged that Piotrovskii did not understand the concept of the dialectic at all, even though he had championed the so-called dialectical play. "*The Thoughtful Dandy* was based on just such a false, mechanical understanding of the dialectic," Chicherov charged. "In fact, it was completely incompre-

107. "Za proletarskii teatr!" *Sovetskii teatr* 2/3 (1931): 1.
108. "O zadachakh RAPP na teatral'nom fronte," *Sovetskii teatr* 10/11 (1931): 4–10, esp. 8–9.
109. "Za proletarskii teatr!" *Sovetskii teatr* 2/3 (1931): 1; "Ob'edinim proletarskie sily na teatral'nom fronte," RiT 6 (1931): 14.
110. "Tvorcheskii metod proletarskogo teatra," *Sovetskoe iskusstvo* 7 February 1931.
111. "Vo fraktsiiu sekretariata RAPP'a," RGALI, f. 2947, op. 1, d. 24, l. 1.
112. I. Chicherov, "Oshibki i nedostatki tramovskogo dvizheniia," 23 June 1931, RGALI, f. 2947, op. 1, d. 32, ll. 3–6. See also idem, "Za boevoi soiuz RAPP'a i TRAM'a," *Za agitpropbrigadu i TRAM* 1 (1931): 5–10.

hensible. Why did a good Komsomol girl, a good young woman, suddenly turn to sectarianism? . . . There are a whole number of completely schematic, unconvincing, and false elements in the play."[113]

Fighting to retain leadership, Sokolovskii did not defend his group or accept responsibility for its errors. Instead, he also blamed Piotrovskii. Responding to RAPP's criticism, Sokolovskii admitted that the Leningrad organization had been slow to unmask the errors of Piotrovskii, especially his ideas of dialectical materialism as the aesthetic principle behind its creative work.[114] Other Leningrad TRAM members did the same, charging that Piotrovskii had furthered harmful bourgeois ideas, urging actors to ignore psychological depth and to portray social types instead.[115]

Piotrovskii was drawn into the vortex of self-criticism, confessing at the beginning of 1932 that his ideas about amateur theater were fundamentally flawed. His theories were based on reactionary bourgeois notions—inspired by Viacheslav Ivanov and even Nietzsche. They had reduced class struggle to a struggle between different theatrical schools. Piotrovskii regretted his attempts to isolate amateur theater from the influence of professionals and to undermine the role of the actor within theatrical productions, and he apologized for his endorsement of disjointed, plotless performances. "Instead of raising the mass art of worker youth to the standards of great Bolshevik art, my 'theory' simply impeded its growth. Therefore this idealistic, bourgeois theory served the politically dangerous cause of the class enemy," Piotrovskii concluded.[116] He soon thereafter quit his position in TRAM.

By abandoning the ideas formulated in the late 1920s, the Leningrad TRAM was unfortunately left without much of a method at all. This became painfully obvious when Sokolovskii wrote and produced his play *Unbroken Stream (Sploshnoi potok)* in 1932, which was a real departure from earlier work. Based on material he had gathered on trips to new construction sites, it was a straightforward presentation of a production collective's struggle to complete the construction of a dam before the onset of the spring thaw. Stripped of any of the elements that had distin-

113. Chicherov, "Oshibki," ll. 7 ob.-8.

114. See "Ob"edinim proletarskie sily na teatral'nom fronte," RiT 7 (1931): 4; these points are elaborated in M. Sokolovskii, "TRAM na perelome," *Sovetskii teatr* 2/3 (1931): 17. See also I. Chicherov, "Za boevoi soiuz RAPP'a i TRAM'a," *Za agitpropbrigadu i TRAM* 1 (1931): 5–6.

115. O. Adamovich, "TRAM'u shest' let," RiT 32/33 (1931): 5.

116. A. Piotrovskii, "O sobstvennykh formalistkikh oshibkakh," RiT 3 (1932): 10.

guished TRAM works in the past, the play lacked song, dance, and satire, and hardly any attention was paid to the specific problems of working-class youth.[117] Valerii Bliumenfel'd, a Leningrad critic who had been very sympathetic to TRAM in the past, called the play "silent": it sparked no interaction with the audience at all, almost as if the actors played alone without viewers. Bliumenfel'd concluded that in trying to cut itself off from the influence of Piotrovskii and conceding to the criticisms of RAPP, TRAM had in fact rejected its whole heritage. It was turning to the style of Stanislavsky's Moscow Art Theater and isolating itself from the youthful worker audiences that had once been so enthusiastic about its plays.[118] Other viewers noted that this play—without the songs and dances of the old productions—made the weaknesses of TRAM actors painfully apparent.[119]

The overt assault on the Leningrad TRAM gave the Moscow organization, until that point very much in the shadow of the founding group, a chance to establish its predominance. At a national TRAM meeting in July 1931, the leader of the Moscow theater charged that all of TRAM's problems rested with Sokolovskii and the Leningrad organization. It was impossible to work in a comradely manner with Sokolovskii, he opined. Instead, the Leningrad leader wanted to dominate everything himself. Until 1931, the Moscow TRAM had been very influenced by Leningrad's repertoire. But as the original organization became more and more embattled, the Moscow central TRAM started to shape its own work. It formed a special section for playwrights under the leadership of Fedor Knorre, who had moved from Leningrad to Moscow. Knorre's work *Alarm (Trevoga)*, on the possibility of a coming foreign war, played to very good reviews in 1931 and was the focus of the Moscow TRAM's 1931 May Day celebrations.[120] "Finally," remarked one critic, "this theater has offered a large work."[121]

The Moscow TRAM's efforts to set itself apart from Leningrad intensified when the Communist Party moved to reshape cultural politics in

117. [Mikhail Sokolovskii], "Sploshnoi potok," RGALI, f. 2723, op. 1, d. 531, ll. 110–61.
118. V. Bliumenfel'd, "Za propagandistskii stil' v TRAM'e," RiT 12 (1932): 14.
119. See Marinchik, *Rozhdenie*, 240; Zograf, "Puti Leningradskogo TRAM'a," RGALI, f. 2723, op. 1, d. 220, ll. 103–4.
120. "Prakticheskii plan provedeniia pervomaiskoi kampanii Moskovskogo tsentral'nogo TRAM'a," RGALI, f. 2947, op. 1, d. 26, l. 2.
121. I. Berezark, "Novoe v moskovskikh teatrakh," RiT 8/9 (1931): 12; see also S. Podol'skii, "Dva spektaklia o voine," *Sovetskoe iskusstvo* 12 March 1931.

April 1932. The famous party pronouncement summarily dissolved self-proclaimed proletarian cultural groups, including RAPP. The decree also marked a major shift toward a cultural policy that was extremely hostile to the original ideas of the Leningrad TRAM. All amateur theater groups were urged to overcome their opposition to professional directors and professionally written plays, to institute training programs that integrated theatrical history, and to provide a better education for actors.[122] At a special plenum of the central TRAM soviet called to respond to the party decree, leaders listed TRAM's past failings, including the idea that amateur and professional theater were inevitably opposed. TRAM must work to attract good professional playwrights and begin to perform classic plays. TRAM's mistakes, insisted Chicherov, could be attributed to the "Menshevist, liquidationist" views of Piotrovskii.[123]

The Moscow TRAM used the party's announcement as the occasion for its own internal purge, spearheaded by the Moscow Komsomol.[124] Those who supported TRAM's old methods were ousted from the theater. After a protracted struggle that lasted several months, those in favor of reorganization won. At this point, the new chief administrator invited Il'ia Sudakov from the Moscow Art Theater to become the artistic director, embracing the very principles the Leningrad organization had originally opposed. This move was another step in the consolidation of cultural power in Moscow, a process so vividly depicted by Katerina Clark.[125] It also was an ironic turn for the movement that had once denounced Stanislavsky's stage as "The Theater of Bourgeois Youth."

·⤳·

TRAM was an organization that stirred up controversy. It faced aggressive criticism during the waning years of the New Economic Policy and again during the First Five-Year Plan. Its function as a lightning rod in both eras, demarcated so clearly by historians, indicates its liminal status. It also reveals that the firm distinctions historians have drawn between NEP culture and the beginnings of Stalinist culture are perhaps

122. "O perestroike tramovskogo dvizheniia. Rezoliutsiia TsS VLKSM po dokladu TsS TRAM'ov," RGALI, f. 2723, op. 1, d. 423, ll. 7–11.

123. "Otkrylsia plenum TsS TRAM," Sovetskoe iskusstvo 3 June 1932; A. K., "TRAM na putiakh perestroiki," Sovetskoe iskusstvo 9 June 1932.

124. "Resheniia sekretariata MGK VLKSM po dokladu tov. Beletskogo," RGALI, f. 2947, op. 1, d. 36, l. 1.

125. Clark, Petersburg, 297–307.

not so fixed. During NEP, the theater drew criticism from those opposed to its aggressive anti-professionalism and its swaggering cult of youth, both qualities that are usually assigned to the period of the "Great Break." Those close to the professional stage doubted its commitment to art; political overseers worried that its insistence on a unique youth culture was a coded form of political protest.

Criticism continued during the First Five-Year Plan. Now TRAM faced charges that it had not shed the traces of NEP quickly enough. Its heroes remained ambivalent when the times called for decisive action. They considered too many alternatives and were too easily tempted by decadent youth cultures. That is vividly evident in the attack on *The Thoughtful Dandy*, which addressed the pressures on youth in the industrialization drive. The characters' search for meaning was emphatically denounced as "schematic, unconvincing, and false."[126] TRAM plays offered audiences too much room to make up their own minds. Indeed, the "dialectic method," touted by Piotrovskii and Sokolovskii, made it possible for the synthesis viewers worked out for themselves to be very different than what the authors intended. Moreover, TRAM authors were not able to keep up with the broad complex of rapidly shifting issues in this period of rupture. Their skills were limited to the urban milieu that they knew.

In 1928 and 1929, TRAM stood briefly on the cusp of radical change with its attacks on staid cultural institutions and its aggressive rhetoric aimed at specialists. But the Leningrad and central TRAM organizations were inept warriors in the cultural battles of the era. They could barely shape a shared institutional identity, let alone defend themselves from external criticism. When TRAM came under attack, it immediately began to tear itself apart in a frenzy of internal incriminations. Although the assault began with RAPP, the organization's most vicious critics were its own members, who accused one another of dire political failings. The central TRAM, eventually under Moscow leadership, survived only by jettisoning its original leadership and aesthetic principles.

Moreover, the decision of the Leningrad TRAM and other affiliates to turn to theater work full time alienated them from their amateur origins, despite their heated claims to the contrary. Professional TRAM circles had very little in common with newly radicalized amateur stages. As TRAM strove for financial parity with academic theaters, these new cir-

126. I. Chicherov, "Oshibki i nedostatki tramovskogo dvizheniia," 23 June 1931, RGALI, f. 2947, op. 1, d. 32, ll. 7 ob.-8.

cles insisted that professionals writers and directors could not hope to express the ideas of the Soviet Union's workers. As TRAM struggled for adequate performance spaces, amateur circles took their works to cafeterias, dormitories, and onto the factory floor. While TRAM theorists dreamed of changing audiences' attitudes through performances, agitprop brigades actually tried to change their actions, extracting funds and pledges of work speed-ups. TRAM had made its reputation on radicalism, on being the most extreme manifestation of amateur theater, but it had to give up this reputation to new groups that called themselves shock workers on the cultural front.

5
Shock Workers on the Cultural Front

DURING THE First Five-Year Plan, a new kind of amateur theater group emerged known as the agitprop brigade. These small, itinerant circles had a hostile relationship to the drama workshops of late NEP, many of which had begun to devote themselves to honing their performance skills. Agitprop brigades loudly and aggressively rejected professional models and guidance. They not only reclaimed the performance styles of the agitational theater of small forms born during the Civil War and perfected in the early 1920s, they applied them to utilitarian purposes that earlier activists had never envisioned. In the process, participants argued that they were creating new standards for artistic expression. "Not one measure, not one step that does not serve to implement the industrial plan," intoned the Moscow trade union leader, I. Isaev.[1]

Created by the industrialization drive, agitprop brigades combined voluntarism with coercion. Participants rejected standard theatrical training; their work was task-oriented, put together at the performance site and often without any political oversight. They claimed disdain for established forms of leadership and distrusted all "experts." At the same time, however, members of the brigades saw themselves as conduits for government programs, interpreters who transformed the bureaucratic jargon of state initiatives into a language that average people could understand. Their role as the state's messengers, as enforcers of state initiatives, gave them power over their audiences that they used in oppressive ways. In a public environment suffused with messages about the

1. "Za vypolnenie lozungov TsK partii!" KS 9 (1930): 3.

production drive—with posters, banners, and placards urging harder work and chastising slackers—agitprop brigades were yet another method to incite workers to fulfill the plan.

Not willing to wait for an audience to come to them, agitprop brigades hunted down viewers in factories, in dormitories, and on the street. They took their works to the countryside in a new effort by amateurs to reach beyond the neighborhoods where groups were formed. They even found an international audience, as leftists everywhere, inspired by Soviet industrial expansion in the midst of a global depression, began to emulate Soviet performance styles. Commenting on the predominance of agitational groups in Russia, the British Communist theater leader, Tom Thomas, explained: "Experience has thus shown that this flexible, vigorous, mobile, inexpensive form is the one best adapted to Workers' Theaters in capitalist countries, if they wish to play their part in the class struggle and to be more than working class dilettantes (curse the breed!)."[2]

To understand the aggressive performance style of these groups, it is useful to return to the concepts of aesthetic and social drama introduced in chapter one.[3] Agitprop brigades rejected the conventions of aesthetic drama, the established modes of presenting a story to an audience. They eschewed makeup, elaborate costumes, sets, stages, rigorous training programs, and sometimes even scripts. More to the point, they felt the goal of aesthetic drama, namely to bring about a change of consciousness in viewers, was much too modest. Instead, they wanted to change their viewers' actions. Theirs was social drama of a particularly invasive kind; they demanded to see tangible, measurable changes in their viewers' behavior. The purpose of agitprop brigades, noted the club leader Sergei Alekseev, "was not to provide the laboring population with art, but to mobilize it through art to overcome the difficulties of socialist construction."[4]

The Formation of Agitprop Brigades

As the industrialization drive began in earnest in 1929, many amateur circles located in clubs and factories shaped small, mobile, and politi-

---

2. Tom Thomas, "World Congress of Workers' Theatre Groups," *New Masses*, November 1930, 21.

3. See ch. 1, pp. 19–20.

4. S. Alekseev, "Za khudozhestvennye proizvodstvennye agitpropbrigady," *Malye formy klubnogo zrelishcha* 16 (1930): 1.

Front cover of a program for an amateur art competition in Leningrad, May 1928.
Harvard Theatre Collection, The Houghton Library. Reproduced with permission.

Back cover of a program for an amateur art competition in Leningrad, May 1928. The caption reads: "Club art is a mighty weapon of cultural revolution." Harvard Theatre Collection, The Houghton Library. Reproduced with permission.

cally motivated touring performance groups. They set themselves apart from conventional theater circles, whose goals and methods they disdained. "The leading amateur circles, TRAM cells, and their leaders must struggle against the apolitical comfort and slavish imitation of dilettantish circles," read one of the first pronouncements in favor of these groups. "Artistic agitprop brigades, closely tied to their clubs and factories, should play a leading role in the transformation."[5]

The industrial shock work movement was a major inspiration for agitprop brigades. Begun in embryo in the waning years of NEP, shock work became a widespread phenomenon during the First Five-Year Plan. Young workers, often organized in the Komsomol, banned together to shake up old patterns of production in factories. They attacked the privileges and established labor methods of older skilled workers, developing methods to produce goods more quickly and efficiently. Operating at first without support of the factory management or union leadership, shock workers began to gain more publicity for their efforts by 1928, using Party support to raise overall production quotas.[6]

In the summer 1929, the national trade union leadership was reconstituted. The head of the organization during NEP, Mikhail Tomskii, had hoped to defend trade union autonomy during the industrialization drive. Perceived as an opponent of Stalin, he was ousted in a bid to make unions more pliable to the Party leader's vision of rapid industrialization.[7] These high-level shifts had a direct effect on amateur theaters. Tomskii had supported closer ties to experts and more conventional repertoires. Not only did the new leadership, headed by Nikolai Shvernik, give its support to shock work campaigns at the factory level, it also endorsed a more utilitarian cultural policy. An April 1930 national trade union gathering determined that all cultural work should now be directed toward production. The stress on leisure and relaxation

5. "Boi na fronte samodeiatel'nogo teatra," ZI 46 (1929): 1.

6. On shock workers, see Hiroaki Kuromiya, *Stalin's Industrial Revolution: Politics and Workers, 1928–1932* (Cambridge: Cambridge University Press, 1988), 115–28; David R. Shearer, "The Language and Politics of Soviet Rationalization," *Cahiers du Monde russe et soviétique* 32 (1991): 581–608; Louis H. Siegelbaum, *Stakhanovism and the Politics of Productivity in the USSR, 1935–1941* (Cambridge: Cambridge University Press, 1988), 40–53; idem, *Soviet State and Society between Revolutions* (Cambridge: Cambridge University Press, 1992), 209–13; and Chris Ward, *Russia's Cotton Workers and the New Economic Policy: Shop-Floor Culture and State Policy, 1921–1929* (Cambridge: Cambridge University Press, 1990), 244–52.

7. On the intricacies of these high-level changes, see Kuromiya, *Stalin's Industrial Revolution*, 40–46.

in clubs must come to an end.[8] Speaking at the Party congress later that year, Shvernik denounced the apolitical and culturally conservative direction of Tomskii's leadership and tied current cultural activity directly to shock work.[9]

As shock work gained visibility and acceptance in Soviet factories, agitprop brigades began to make their appearance in significant numbers. Participants in agitprop brigades compared themselves to shock workers in the most literal sense, calling their activities "a method of artistic shock work."[10] In the fall of 1929, the Leningrad city trade union organization was the first to embrace agitprop brigades as a method to put art to the service of the Five-Year Plan. "Instead of apolitical, imitative, dilettantish groups, we should embrace artistic agitprop brigades as the basic form of union work," read the final resolution of a city-wide cultural conference.[11]

Agitprop brigades were composed of young enthusiasts from trade unions, clubs, and factories. Touring work sites and the countryside to drum up support for the industrialization and collectivization drives, they prepared agitational skits and short plays from the raw materials at hand—newspapers, public speeches, and production statistics. Brigade participants were distrustful of professional theater workers and playwrights, who allegedly had no knowledge of daily struggle at the workplace. Instead, they tried to rely on their own experiences as laborers and political activists. With their stress on local experience and hostility to conventional repertoire and training, agitprop brigades clearly harkened back to the use of small forms on stages in the early period of NEP. The links were closest to the action circles of Moscow, with their anti-aesthetic, task-specific orientation. One commentator describing agitprop brigades employed categories used during NEP to distinguish the goals of action circles from conventional drama groups. While drama circles aimed to entertain, action circles and agitprop brigades

8. V. Kirov, "Za rabotu po-novomu," *Klub i revoliutsiia* 8 (1930): 8–9.

9. *Shestnadtsatyi s''ezd Vsesoiuznoi Kommunisticheskoi partii (B): Stenograficheskii otchet* (Moscow: OG12-Moskovskii rabochii, 1931), 662–63. See also "Zadachi profsoiuzov v rekonstruktivnyi period," *Pravda* 21 May 1930.

10. "Puti razvitiia agit-propbrigadnogo dvizheniia. Material k pervoi oblastnoi konferentsii khudozhestvennykh agitpropbrigad moskovskikh profsoiuzov," RGALI, f. 2723, op. 1, d. 419, l. 104.

11. "Ko vsem rabotnikam klubnykh khudozhestvennykh organizatsii," ZI 46 (1929): 12. See also Grigorii Avlov, *Teatral'nye agitpropbrigady v klube* (Leningrad: Gosudarstvennoe izdatel'stvo khudozhestvennoi literatury, 1931), 9–14. I found the first reference to brigades in Moscow in November, "Kul'tpokhod zrelishchnykh kruzhkov," VM 16 November 1929.

strove toward "active, practical participation in socialist construction."[12] Some of the advocates of action circles, like Moscow's Nikolai L'vov, again became very visible commentators and organizers of amateur groups during the First Five-Year Plan.

Still, there were crucial differences between the small forms of the NEP era and these new configurations. Agitprop brigades were not tied to specific club venues; they might perform on club stages, but they were ready and eager to take their shows on the road. As one advocate proclaimed, "The main arena for circles should not be the stage, but rather the factory shop, the dormitory."[13] Most brigades were fairly small, with around ten members. Club circles might have more than forty members. Although the club groups of NEP expressed open contempt for "entertainment," their work had to also be pleasurable to watch; otherwise, audiences would leave. They incorporated songs, dances, physical humor, and other methods to keep audiences entertained. By contrast, agitprop brigades often played to captive audiences. They concentrated on words to convey their messages and were not interested in their viewers' pleasure.[14] Instead, they wanted results—more money for industrialization, higher production figures, more volunteers for political causes. Accounts of agitprop performances read much like industrial production reports, filled with a blaze of figures on the number of appearances, along with statistical evidence about the transformative power of the presentation.[15]

Agitprop brigades also had different methods and goals from the expanding TRAM movement. TRAM circles, for the most part, still performed plays on stages; they met for rehearsals and did not present works until they felt they were ready for audience consumption. Although TRAM authors tried to stay up to date with their material, their fairly conventional method of first finding or preparing a script, choosing actors for the roles, and then starting rehearsals meant that the subject matter of TRAM plays could not keep up with the rapid twists and

12. B. Filippov, "Khudozhestvennye agitpropbrigady—v deistvii," KS 5 (1931): 3–5, quotation 4.

13. Georgii Polianovskii, "Za khudozhestvennuiu propagandu promfinplana," *Pravda* 14 February 1930.

14. For an analysis of the shift away from multimedia techniques, see M. V. Iunisov, "Agitatsionno-khudozhestvennye brigady," in S. Iu. Rumiantsev, ed., *Samodeiatel'noe khudozhestvennoe tvorchestvo v SSSR*, v. 1 (Moscow: Gosudarstvennyi institut iskusstvoznaniia, 1995), 250.

15. N. Gruzkov, "Po Ves'egonskomu i Volokolamskomu raionam," *Za agitpropbrigadu i TRAM* 1 (1932): 39–40.

turns of government policies. Agitprop brigades, by contrast, could change their scenarios in an instant, to incorporate the very latest news.

So widespread were agitprop brigades by the fall of 1930 that many performed at a competition sponsored by the Moscow trade union organization at the new Park of Culture and Leisure, soon to be renamed Gorky Park. It was timed to correspond with the Sixteenth Party Congress and to show how union artistic groups were turning to productive tasks. Chanting in unison, brigade members delivered a public statement of their goals: "We will transform amateur art into a weapon for our great social construction against the class enemies of the proletariat. We will restructure our work to turn our face to production. . . . Amateur art, a fighting weapon in the battle for the Five-Year Plan in four!"[16]

After the Party congress, agitprop brigades proliferated rapidly. Because the circles were ephemeral, there are no reliable composite figures on their numbers or social composition. However, judging from statistics compiled at local and national competitions, it appears that participants were primarily young shock workers.[17] Many could trace their involvement in factory cultural work back to the years before the First Five-Year Plan.[18] Very spotty figures on gender composition indicate that women constituted some thirty percent of the membership, similar to the overall figure for women shock workers.[19] The leader of the brigade at the Sickle and Hammer factory in Moscow said he judged potential members by their standing in the factory—only shock workers with excellent records on the factory floor need apply. Their performance skills received no mention at all.[20] Grigorii Avlov, the seasoned

16. E. M. Karachunskaia, "Moskovskii smotr 1931g.," in *Khudozhestvennye agitbrigady: Itogi smotra i puti razvitiia* (Moscow: Narkompros RSFSR, 1931), 12–13. See also S. Alekseev, "Smotr khudozhestvennykh sil moskovskikh profsoiuzov," *Malye formy klubnogo zrelishcha* 17 (1930): 1–5.

17. A number of sources estimates the brigades to have had at least seventy percent shock workers. See N. Strel'tsov, "Agitpropbrigadnoe dvizhenie v novoi obstanovke raboty profsoiuzov," *Za agitpropbrigadu i TRAM* 2 (1931): 5; "Samodeiatel'nyi teatr na olimpiade," KS 9 (1932): 1; "VI Plenum TsK Rabis," RiT 28 (1931): 7; V. N. Aizenshtadt, *Sovetskii samodeiatel'nyi teatr: Osnovnye etapy razvitiia* (Kharkov: Khar'kovskii gosudarstvennyi institut kul'tury, 1983), 39.

18. See E. Permiak, "Khudozhestvennye brigady piatogo dnia," *Klub i revoliutsiia* 14 (1932): 41.

19. "Brosim sily na ugol', torf v Boriki," *Za agitpropbrigadu i TRAM* 1 (1931): 52; Delegat, "Nasha stsena—khlopkovye polia," KS 9 (1932): 41.

20. D. Korobov, "Kak sozdavalas' i stroilas' serpomolotovskaia agitbrigada," *Za agitpropbrigadu i TRAM* 1 (1931): 11–12.

Leningrad cultural activist, insisted that agitprop brigades could not be simply renamed factory drama circles (although they often were). "It is quite obvious," he argued, "that an agitprop brigade, which aims to depict questions of socialist construction and necessarily must integrate actual local material, should orient itself primarily to production workers who are closely tied to their work."[21]

Agitprop advocates believed that their homemade performances, filled with details from factory life, gave their work an immediacy and relevance that material by professional authors could not possibly achieve. Moreover, they asserted that their viewers responded with enthusiasm to the portrayal of events from their daily experience. To prepare, brigade members spent time collecting local material from factory workers, union and party members on site, and even from managerial reports. One Leningrad brigade gathered information from local newspapers, factory wall newspapers, and the factory union leadership.[22] Group preparation was prized, and a few brigades even organized communal living arrangements to increase their cooperation.[23] It was not uncommon for the final script to be the work of the brigade leader or factory literary circle, with input from participants along the way. However, some circles found more innovative methods, dividing up the task of writing as if on an assembly line. One subsection would collect material, another would shape it into a rough outline, while still another was responsible for the final product. "A shock work tempo demands shock work methods," proclaimed one brigade leader.[24]

At a time when speed was valued over all else, brigades prided themselves on being able to convert local material into a performance with dazzling dispatch. In one competition among five brigades from the Moscow woodworkers' union, participants started gathering material at six in the evening; by nine they began to write, and by three in the morning they had a finished work![25] Some brigades had a rigorous performance schedule that even surpassed the fervor of club circles during

21. Avlov, *Teatral'nye agitpropbrigady*, 32.

22. M. Reznik, "Opyt vskrytiia tvorcheskogo metoda agitpropbrigady LRROP," *Za agitpropbrigadu i TRAM* 1 (1931): 16.

23. B. P., "Agitbrigada 'Krasnyi Putilovets,'" RiT 19 (1931): 9; Karachunskaia, "Moskovskii smotr," in *Khudozhestvennye agitbrigady*, 15.

24. I. Mazin, "O khudozhestvennoi agitpropgruppe," KS 1/2 (1931): 24. See also B. Filippov, "Khudozhestvennye agitpropbrigady—v deistvii," KS 5 (1931): 8–9.

25. B. Shmelev, "Agitbrigady—khudozhestvennyi tsekh zavoda," KS 7/8 (1931): 17.

early NEP. The Moscow Rusakov brigade, for example, only took shape in mid-September 1930. By the beginning of October, it had already performed sixteen times.[26]

If brigades did not have the skill or confidence to shape their own work from scratch, they could turn to outlines and examples published in the trade union and Komsomol press, which they were encouraged to alter for their own purposes. The journal *Club Stage* presented what it called "repertoire material," intended as an outline or "carcass" for local work, along with bibliographies explaining where interested readers might turn to find the material used in the scenario. One literary montage called "Face to the Industrial Plan," was composed by Aleksei Arbuzov, who would later become a famous playwright. He drew on speeches by Lenin, Stalin, and prominent economic leaders as well as bits of plays and poems by Vladimir Maiakovskii, Alexander Bezymenskii, Sergei Tretiakov, and Demian Bednyi.[27] Some of these outlines suggested places where local material could be inserted, leaving relatively little to the imagination.

Ideally, brigades also engaged in "extra-stage" (*vnestsennye*) tasks. They organized political meetings, sponsored demonstrations, and helped to write factory wall newspapers, designed to keep workers apprised of local efforts to fulfill the industrial plan. To stamp out the problem of drunkenness, one brigade held a political rally, encouraging those in attendance to share their reasons for drinking. Moscow and Leningrad brigades took trips to the surrounding countryside and nearby construction sites, where they helped to collect fuel and organize new dormitories.[28] One participant recounted that he could only keep up with his many responsibilities by drastically cutting back on sleep.[29]

The most important function of these impromptu groups was to convey the constantly changing demands economic and political organizations placed on the laboring population. According to one advocate, "Agitprop brigades closely link their activities to factory committees and party organizations, quickly reacting to problems in production and trade union work. They discuss all current political campaigns and

26. "Raport o rabote agit-brigady kluba im. Rusakova soiuza kommunal'nikov," GTSTM, f. 150, d. 37, l. 7.
27. A. Arbuzov, "Litsom k promfinplanu," KS 9 (1930): 40–49.
28. N. Gruzkov, "Po Ves'egonskomu i Volokolamskomu raionam," *Za agitpropbrigadu i TRAM* 1 (1932): 39–40; Gabaev i Lapshina, "Na novostroikakh," KS 11 (1931): 67.
29. Iunisov, "Agitatsionno-khudozhestvennye brigady," 250.

serve as a megaphone [*rupor*] for the local proletarian public."[30] Their production methods allowed them to respond almost instantly to new regime initiatives, transforming the official language of communiqués into vivid examples of how new policies could potentially aid workers who cooperated and hurt those who did not. Numerous state agencies appreciated their services and inundated them with assignments to explain factory economy measures, help with the collectivization drive, aid in national defense, and increase worker responsibility for factory production. A 1930 textile union directive, for example, instructed cultural groups that they needed to provide explanations for the raw material shortage that was plaguing the industry.[31] Thus, the spiraling demands of the industrialization drive fueled the frantic work schedule of the brigades—their tasks, it seemed, were never done.

The War on the Audience

Agitprop brigade members claimed close ties to their audiences. Since they collected material locally, viewers could recognize their own victories and defeats acted out on stage. This kind of verisimilitude made some viewers see the players as "*svoi*," as their own.[32] When brigades praised local heroes and chastised unpopular figures like managers and corrupt trade union leaders, they got an enthusiastic response. In addition, many brigades addressed true-to-life local problems—dangerous work sites, unrepaired housing complexes, and surly salespeople in stores. Sometimes their performances helped to alleviate these very real woes.

Absent managers and dirty dormitories were not the only targets of agitprop performances, however. Audience members themselves were not exempt from censure. Brigades did not shy away from ridicule, shame, and even political threats to achieve their goals. This was utilitarian art of the most extreme kind, with success measured in improved industrial output and political participation. Aiming for their own kind of production statistics, agitprop brigades became much more aggressive and invasive than earlier amateur circles had ever been. Given the

30. M. Veprinskii, "Zrelishchnye kruzhki v period rekonstruktsii," *Klub i revoliutsiia* 13/14 (1930): 58.
31. "Material dlia khudozhestvennykh kruzhkov v kampanii otpusknikov," June 1930, GTSTM, f. 150, d. 36, l. 22.
32. V. Darskii, "Agitbrigada na lesozagotovkakh," *Za agitpropbrigadu i* TRAM 1 (1931): 61; Eidinov, Polonskaia, Lekitskaia, "Chetvertaia fabrika Moskvoshvei," KS 4 (1932): 42.

many coercive methods they employed to change the actions of their viewers, it is no exaggeration to say that they declared war on the audience.

Because they did not need stages, lights, or elaborate props, agitprop brigades could perform almost anywhere that workers congregated. Rather than trying to lure viewers to clubs after the work day ended, they brought their performances to factory workshops, cafeterias, barracks, apartment courtyards, and even to underpasses linking factories to tram and train lines. Scripts were usually short, intended to fit into a lunch break or work break on the job. While such methods certainly increased the number of viewers, it also meant that many people were exposed to these performances against their will. Using aggressive methods inspired by shock workers in production, the brigades aimed to root out old habits and humiliate those who practiced them.

Many agitprop performances took the form of an urban *charivari*, where poor laborers were publicly humiliated. According to one report by Nikolai L'vov, the audience for a performance by the Rusakov agitprop brigade in Moscow only became attentive when the participants began naming names: "When the brigade began to castigate real perpetrators of the evils of laziness and shirking, etc., then the mass of viewers became lively and the guilty members of the audience began to feel uncomfortable."[33] One brigade posted pictures of workers who were chronically late, soliciting the help of the factory art circle. It began the performance by carrying in a coffin emblazoned with the name of the worst offender. Another group extended its censure beyond the performance site itself, putting up signs in front of the apartments or barracks of repeat offenders and even sending notes home to their wives.[34]

Public shaming rituals were an important part of agitprop performances. One common tactic was to prepare lists of exemplary and poor workers, known as the "red list" (*krasnaia doska*) and the "black list" (*chernaia doska*). Before performances, local leaders would provide the brigade with the names of individuals who were to be censured for infractions such as drunkenness, lateness, and disruption of labor disci-

33. N. I. L'vov, "Raport o rabote agit-brigady kluba im. Rusakova soiuza kommunal'nikov," GTSTM, f. 150, d. 37, l. 7. See also A. Gol'dman and M. Imas, *Sotsialisticheskoe sorevnovanie i udarnichestvo v iskusstve* (Moscow: Gosudarstvennoe izdatel'stvo khudozhestvennoi literatury, 1931), 65.

34. K. Barinov, "Sryvaiushchikh rabotu pod obstrel," KS 11 (1931): 68; Rumiantsev, "Agitpropbrigady zheleznodorozhnikov v boiu za chetkuiu rabotu transporta," KS 4 (1931): 8.

pline, who would find their names on the black list.[35] According to one Western observer, these public shamings had an influence on behavior: "Every factory in Russia today has its red and black boards [the literal translation of *doska*]. . . . Wives and children, friends and fellow workers, see there who has disgraced himself as a slacker. Children lecture their inefficient worker-fathers."[36] One Moscow troupe gave a factory's worst idlers a badge of shame to wear—a flag made of woven straw (or *bast*, a material typical of the peasantry) emblazoned with an empty bottle.[37] As might be expected, not all audiences were appreciative of these demeaning tactics. When one brigade performed a skit satirizing the poor quality of a factory cafeteria's offerings, some workers protested that it was none of the brigade's business.[38]

Agitprop brigades honed their aggressive style by performing in the countryside for audiences they assumed would be hostile. One of the first organized agitprop campaigns was an effort to help the 1930 spring sowing campaign. More than sixty groups from Moscow alone answered a call by trade union organizations to aid in this effort. They disseminated information about the collectivization program, organized (or in some cases reorganized) local drama groups, and took part in anti-religious agitation.[39] In the process, they sometimes met with overt resistance; unhappy viewers created disturbances and even threw rocks and bottles to disrupt performances.[40]

Judging from the arrogant tone of the reports brigades sent back to the city, the agitators maintained that they could discover and isolate problems within a village after a few hours of hasty research and then eradicate them in the course of a performance. One brigade arrived at a newly established collective farm plagued with difficulties. The problem, according to the group leader, was the resistance of local *kulaks*, better-off peasants who were blocking collectivization. Brigade members quickly isolated these offenders: "With our *chastushki* and prepared material [*karkasnyi material*] we revealed to kolkhoz members those responsible

35. V. Rudman, "Dva mesiatsa na zheleznodorozhnykh stroikakh," *Za agitpropbrigadu i* TRAM 2 (1931): 53–54.

36. Ella Winter, *Red Virtue: Human Relationships in the New Russia* (New York: Harcourt Brace, 1933), 56.

37. P. Surozhskii, "Na obshchestvennom prosmotre igro-plakata," KS 10/11 (1930): 11.

38. "Na rel'sy reorganizatsii," KS 11 (1931): 3.

39. Vas., "Khudozhestvennye agit-brigady v derevniu na pomoshch' posevnoi kampanii," KS 2 (1930): 19.

40. V. Savkin, "Na khlebnom fronte," KS 11 (1931): 70; I. Elik, "V bor'be s klassovym vragom," KS 4 (1931): 6.

for hindering their work."[41] In another village, inhabitants had been avoiding a general meeting on the issue of dekulakization. Collaborating with local authorities, a visiting agitprop brigade from Moscow gathered the population together for what viewers believed would be an evening of song and entertainment. The brigade then interrupted their performance and forced a vote on the touchy issue. "As a result," noted a proud reporter, "the village voted unanimously to rid itself of *kulaks*."[42]

These coercive techniques were perfected on urban audiences when agitprop brigades used their performances to extract funds for the industrialization drive. Since the early 1920s, the Soviet government had raised revenue through bond programs. With the turn to rapid industrialization, the regime implemented mass subscription bonds with deductions taken directly from paychecks. An expansive effort to increase participation in the bond program was launched in the spring of 1931, and agitprop brigades embraced it with enthusiasm. Not only did brigadiers themselves contribute generously, but they attempted to make audience members pledge at least the equivalent of one month's salary to the program.[43] Since the First Five-Year Plan was a period of sinking salaries and worsening living conditions for workers, getting viewers to take even more money out of their pockets was a difficult task.[44]

Agitprop brigades used considerable ingenuity in their efforts, using fear, praise, shame, and even charges of sabotage to get viewers to give part of their meager salaries. Scattered published scenarios give some idea of how brigades worked their audiences. The agitprop troupe of the Postroika Theater Collective from Moscow composed a montage of political speeches, newspaper reports, and local statistics to drum up support for the campaign. Their performance opened with the exhortation: "The Party of Lenin has a pledge every worker should make: Catch up and overtake." The players challenged cynics who did not believe that the Soviet Union could ever overtake America by presenting current production statistics from newspapers and political speeches. How will the na-

41. Shorshe, "Kak my rabotali v derevne," KS 11 (1931): 71–73, quotation 73.

42. N. Strel'tsov, "Agitpropbrigadnoe dvizhenie v novoi obstanovke raboty profsoiuzov," *Za agitpropbrigadu i* TRAM 2 (1931): 6. See also S. Bardin, "Agitflotiliia MOSPS na propolochnoi kampanii v kolkhozakh Moskovskoi oblasti," ibid., 48–49.

43. On Soviet bond programs, see James R. Millar, "History and Analysis of Soviet Domestic Bond Policy," in Susan Linz, ed., *The Soviet Economic Experiment* (Urbana: Illinois University Press, 1990), 113–19.

44. On popular protest against government loan campaigns during the Second Five-Year Plan, see Sarah Davies, *Popular Opinion in Stalin's Russia: Terror, Propaganda and Dissent, 1934–1941* (Cambridge: Cambridge University Press, 1997), 35–37, 64.

The agitprop brigade of the Rusakov Club in Moscow. The poster says: "Loan—Five-Year Plan in Four Years." Bakhrushin State Central Theatrical Museum. Reproduced with permission.

tion move even further forward? performers then asked. "Who will give the money? The capitalists? No, they will not give it and we will not take it. . . . We, we ourselves will give the money for construction." After explaining how much money was expected from each audience member, participants distributed pledge forms urging viewers to sign up. They ended their performance with statistics on local compliance.[45]

Other groups used even more forceful methods to secure support. One brigade employed a five-step scale, from "the order of the airplane" (the best) to "the order of the two-humped camel" (the worst), determined according to the speed and enthusiasm with which workers had responded to the bond campaign. During performances they would assign each factory workshop its fitting appellation.[46] Another brigade not

45. N. Sen, "S agitatsiei zaima po novostroikam," KS 7/8 (1931): 27–30.
46. These labels, with some variation, were widely used during the plan. See Valentin Kataev, *Time, Forward!*, trans. Charles Malamuth (Bloomington: Indiana University Press, 1976), 26–31; Winter, *Red Virtue*, 58–59; and the agitational films of Nikolai Medvedkin, depicted in Christopher Marker's documentary *The Last Bolshevik*.

only distributed pledge forms but also revealed the names of those who did not fill them out. Recalcitrant workers who did not bend to this pressure found their names printed on a black list. If these methods were unsuccessful, some brigades escalated their tactics still further, accusing shirkers of sabotage.[47] Clearly, all thought of entertainment had vanished from agitprop agendas.

Agitprop Aesthetics

The main goals of agitprop brigades were to inspire action, not to produce works of lasting artistic value. Nonetheless, participants did articulate principles that we could call an incipient aesthetic, ideas for what would make performances have the maximum impact on the audience. These principles were influential in many other discussions, including those affecting the design of club structures. They even had an influence on professional theaters. Moreover, they were echoed in many other branches of art during the First Five-Year Plan.

Agitprop performances were primarily a method of criticism, based on the unspoken assumption that censure was a more effective means of motivation than praise. The repertoire did have its share of exemplary railway switchmen who saved valuable shipments and plucky young workers who found better ways to install foreign technology—what Katerina Clark has called the "little heroes and big deeds" of the First Five-Year Plan.[48] But the emotional weight fell more heavily on villains than on such paragons of socialist virtue. The most ubiquitous evil figures were those in positions of authority on the shop floor; cynical factory managers who did not show any interest in their workers or their jobs, drunken and corrupt union leaders, and of course, highly trained experts like engineers, whose sympathies for the Five-Year Plan were under constant scrutiny.[49] These little villains with their bad deeds were the stock and trade of agitprop productions.

Agitprop scripts ignored the sphere of private life almost entirely. This

47. A. Ovchinnikov, "Agitpropbrigady i realizatsiia novogo zaima," Za agitpropbrigadu i TRAM 1 (1931): 27–28; N. Sen, "Agitbrigada 'Postroika' v Bobrikakh," ibid., 29–33; "Daesh' zaem!" KS 7/8 (1931): 30–33.

48. Katerina Clark, "Little Heroes and Big Deeds: Literature Responds to the First Five-Year Plan," in Sheila Fitzpatrick, ed., Cultural Revolution in Russia, 1928–1931 (Bloomington: Indiana University Press, 1984), 189–206.

49. V. Pavlov, "V polose otchuzhdenii," KS 3 (1931): 12–15; D. Korobov, "Za udarnyi zavod," KS 6 (1931): 35–40; M. B. Reznik and A. A. Fedorovich, "Vstrechnyi," Za agitpropbrigadu i TRAM 2 (1931): 29–36. See also V. Shneerson, "Spetsialisty, kul'trabota i bor'ba s vreditel'stvom," Klub i revoliutsiia 21/22 (1930): 6–14.

set them apart from TRAM plays, which stressed the interaction between work life and the home and examined new rules of romance among Soviet youth. All that mattered for agitprop brigades was accomplishment at the work site, something that can be seen already in the prosaic titles of agitprop works: *On Cost Accounting, Down with the Wreckers, Face to Production.*[50] Brigades were not alone in their hostility to the home. The youth newspaper *Komsomol'skaia pravda* launched a noisy campaign to rid the home of all remnants of cozy "domestic trash." Avant-gardists designed austere, portable furniture for a nation on the move, and the artist El Lissitzky claimed that all any person really needed in life was a mattress, a folding chair, a table, and a gramophone.[51]

Since home and family were coded as female spheres in the Soviet imagination, agitprop performance works depicted worlds almost entirely without women. This probably also reflected the overwhelmingly male composition of the brigades. Many published agitprop scripts had no female parts at all or else portrayed women as standing entirely outside the production process. The railroad drama *Counter-Plan* (*Vstrechnyi*), for example, featured only a cameo appearance by an aggrieved mother in a world otherwise populated entirely by men.[52] This was by no means a "realistic" depiction of Soviet production sites, because women entered the labor force in record numbers during this period.[53]

Participants in agitprop brigades made a virtue of the speed with which they were able to conduct their work. Many enthusiastic young people believed that conventional theater's inability to keep up with current events was one of its greatest weaknesses. "Our life goes too fast," remarked one young actress to the American communist Ella Winter. "By the time a drama reaches the stage its theme is already dead."[54] Here agitprop brigades had a clear advantage: they often performed work that had just been written from material that had only recently been collected at the factory. In the opinion of one agitprop advocate, this meant that for the first time art would not suffer from "tailism,"

50. B. V. Shmelev, "Ot liubitel'skogo dramkruzhka—k pervoi khudozhestvennoi kul't-brigade," KS 7/8 (1931): 13.

51. Svetlana Boym, *Common Places: Mythologies of Everyday Life in Russia* (Cambridge: Harvard University Press, 1994), 8–9, 35–38.

52. M. B. Reznik and A. A. Fedorovich, "Vstrechnyi," *Za agitpropbrigadu i TRAM* 2 (1931): 35. For just one of many examples of scripts without female parts, see V. Pavlov, "V polose otchuzhdeniia," KS 3 (1931): 12–15.

53. Gail Warshofsky Lapidus, *Women in Soviet Society* (Berkeley: University of California Press, 1978), 95–103.

54. Winter, *Red Virtue*, 292.

from reflecting on events after they had already happened. Instead, it could shape events.[55] Of course, the need to keep up with current events guaranteed that work was quickly outdated. Brigades could not perform the same composition over a long period, perfecting their methods, because they constantly needed to change the subject matter and consider a different audience.

This acute attention to current events turned agitprop work into what Susan Suleiman has called a "perishable genre." Her reflections about highly ideological novels that attempt to prove the validity of a certain doctrine apply equally well to agitprop scenarios: "Written in and for a specific historical and social circumstance, the *roman à thèse* is not easily exported. And even in its native land, it becomes 'ancient history' as soon as the circumstance that founded it no longer holds."[56] Agitprop performances were of vital interest only to the actors and audience for whom they were composed. Brigades made a cult of local specificity and detail as a central element of their performance. Audiences also demanded to see themselves reflected on the stage. One group of railroad workers sent an open letter to the journal *Club Stage* asking for works about their industry: "Playwrights! Give us a play about the life and times of railroad workers! Show their heroic struggle to fulfill the transport plan in three years with twin mountings and labor discipline!"[57]

The perishable genre of agitprop theater exerted a powerful influence over the practices of Communist amateur and semi-professional theater groups in Western Europe and the United States. During the Depression, left-wing theater groups applied these techniques to local situations, performing in impoverished working-class neighborhoods, at striking factories, and in city parks. Their homemade scripts, with titles like *Fight against Starvation* and *Lenin Calls*, cursed capitalists and praised worker solidarity. "Groups in the vicinity of strikes should seek to perform appropriate plays," admonished one American journal. "Groups should participate in the raising of funds for strike relief."[58] Like their Soviet counterparts, these mobile circles tried to inspire their

55. V. Sibachev, "Stat' na golovu vyshe," *Za agitpropbrigadu i* TRAM 2 (1931): 4; see also Avlov, *Teatral'nye agitpropbrigady*, 27.

56. Susan Rubin Suleiman, *Authoritarian Fictions: The Ideological Novel as a Literary Genre* (Princeton: Princeton University Press, 1983), 147.

57. "Otkrytoe pis'mo ko vsem proletarskim pisateliam, poetam, dramaturgam, stsenaristam, kinorezhisseram, khudozhnikam," KS 3 (1931): 3.

58. B. Reines, "The Experience of the International Workers' Theatre as Reported at the First Enlarged Plenum of the I.W.D.U.," *Workers' Theatre* 1, no. 9 (December 1931): 4. There

audiences to action. However, they did not have the power of the state behind them.

No matter where they took place, agitprop performances were animated by their attention to concrete detail. In the Soviet Union, this put agitprop brigades in the same camp with avant-gardists gathered around the journal *Novyi lef,* who advocated what they called a "literature of fact." Writers like Sergei Tretiakov, Boris Arvatov, and Nikolai Chuzhak wanted authors to abandon traditional large forms like the novel and base their work on short sketches, diaries, travel notes, and reports. Such works, without central heroes, would be a kind of literary montage, where the reader would be required to make meaning from the work. Not only would such a method make art relevant to the contemporary period, ideally it also opened up the process of creation to a very broad public.[59]

But during the First Five-Year Plan, "facts" were hard to come by; they were replaced by idealistic plans, projections, propagandistic statements, and even dreams. The sophisticated theorists of "literature of fact" were well aware of the tensions between straightforward documentation and inspiring propaganda, or what Osip Brik called "protocol" and "proclamation."[60] In the hands of inexperienced agitprop brigade authors, this meant that despite their works' grounding in a specific time and place, printed scripts have a remarkable similarity to them, with all industries apparently blessed with standard-issue shock workers and cursed with the same incompetent managers and loutish drunks.

Defenders of agitprop brigades were at pains to show that earlier criticisms of small forms did not apply to their efforts. Brigades did not suffer from "Blue Blouseism," a blanket term of abuse that had crystalized

is a large literature on agit-prop theater in the West. See W. L. Guttsman, *Workers' Culture in Weimar Germany: Between Tradition and Commitment,* ch. 9 (New York: Berg, 1990); Daniel Hoffman-Ostwald and Ursula Behse, *Agitprop, 1924–1933* (Leipzig: BEB Friedrich Hofmeister, 1960); Raphael Samuels, et al., eds., *Theatres of the Left, 1880–1935: Workers' Theatre Movements in Britain and America* (London: Routledge and Kegan Paul, 1985); Richard Stourac and Kathleen McCreary, *Theatre as a Weapon: Workers' Theatre in the Soviet Union, Germany and Britain, 1917–1934* (London: Routledge and Kegan Paul, 1986).

59. Hans Günther, "Einleitung," in N. F. Chuzhak, ed., *Literatura fakta* (1929; rpr. Munich, 1972), v–xvi; Fritz Mierau, ed., *Sergei Tretiakov: Gesichter der Avantgarde* (Berlin: Aufbau Verlag, 1985), 87–122.

60. Osip Brik quoted in Günther, "Einleitung," ix. See also Suleiman's assessment that highly politicized literature is an odd mixture of verisimilitude and didacticism, *Authoritarian Fictions,* 146.

by the late 1920s. Those afflicted with this aesthetic disease were overly influenced by popular entertainment styles and depended on formal innovations. In addition, Blue Blouse scripts had been written by professional authors far removed from the production site. Whereas Blue Blouse groups let the form determine the content, insisted one advocate, in agitprop brigades the content determined the form.[61] It was precisely the privileging of function over form that was the most distinctive element of agitprop brigades, determined Grigorii Avlov, one of the earliest advocates of the united artistic circle in Leningrad.[62] In Avlov's opinion, agitprop brigades were much more than a new performance style; in fact, they were a new social and organizational form.[63] Their goal was not a conventional performance but rather propagandistic action to solve a social-political problem. Through their action, they not only affected the lives of their viewers, they also molded the participants into conscious fighters for socialism.[64]

These mobile troupes challenged conventional understandings of performance space. Their ability to work anywhere helped to refine a persistent criticism of club architecture. Just as the club building boom, started in late NEP, had begun to make large stages and auditoriums available to amateur theaters, advocates of agitational art criticized their expansion. Such structures were expensive and only encouraged passive viewership at a time when amateur circles were trying to activate audiences, they argued.[65] Big performance spaces meant that clubs felt required to fill them and often resorted to inviting professional theaters or traveling troupes.[66] One critical reviewer of Konstantin Mel'nikov's structure for the Kauchuk Chemical Workers' Club insisted that the new auditorium was so large that it "ate up" the rest of the club.[67] Such shiny

61. I. Mazin, "O khudozhestvennoi agitpropgruppe," KS 1/2 (1931): 26.

62. G. Avlov, *Klubnyi samodeiatel'nyi teatr: Evoliutsiia metodov i form* (Leningrad: Teakinopechat', 1930), 17–19. Avlov saw this work as an update and correction of Tikhonovich's study on amateur theaters published during the Civil War, which had defined amateur theater as those venues where participants did not earn their living from their performances.

63. Avlov, *Teatral'nye agitpropbrigady*, 12, 25.

64. "Puti razvitiia agit-propbrigadnogo dvizheniia," GTSTM, f. 150, d. 37, l. 30.

65. See S. Tretiakov, "Esteticheskoe zagnivanie kluba," *Revoliutsiia i kul'tura* 11 (1928): 36–39; A. Perovskii, "Dvortsy kul'tury bez mass," *Pravda* 9 January 1929. For an assessment of the architectural discussion surrounding club construction, see Roanne Barris, "Chaos by Design: The Constructivist Stage and Its Reception," (Ph.D. Dissertation, University of Illinois at Urbana-Champaign, 1994), 395–400.

66. Boris Roslavlev, "Klubnyi vopros," *Revoliutsiia i kul'tura* 15 (1928): 52.

67. Ts. A., "V novom klube 'Kauchuk,' " NZ 20 (1929): 14.

new buildings did not result in new or innovative work, chided the youth newspaper *Komsomol'skaia pravda*. Instead, they offered poor films and low-quality entertainment, often for a fee.[68]

To add to the problems of conventional clubs, the introduction of the continuous work-week meant that they could no longer balance their budgets by staging popular big-ticket events on weekends.[69] This unpopular attempt to maximize factory use was introduced in the fall of 1929. The labor force for each factory was divided into five groups, each of which worked for four days, with a fifth day off in staggered schedules.[70] This upset family leisure time, since members might have different free days. It also complicated preparation time for artistic groups and caused scheduling nightmares for club directors. Critics of large halls used it as further evidence that big performance spaces were no longer needed.

To solve these many difficulties, a group of radical architects articulated ideas on a new kind of club just as agitprop brigades were taking shape in 1929–30. They argued that clubs should not contain performance spaces at all. The vast new auditoriums in many new clubs discouraged other forms of creative work. Instead, clubs should be reconceptualized as centers for cultural activists, without spaces for passive spectatorship. Some Komsomol activists even insisted that clubs should be eliminated altogether and replaced by "social-political soviets."[71] Although it is hard to know if these ideas were inspired by brigades, they certainly fit the agitprop aesthetic. Brigades did not need stages; they brought the performances to the audience. With their combative, interventionist style, they eliminated the problem of passive viewers. Instead, involvement was obligatory. If viewers did not take action on their own, their participation would be forced.

Agitprop brigades embodied radically egalitarian, anti-intellectual principles. Many refused the oversight of specialists, instead electing one of their own members to take a leadership position.[72] For Sergei Alekseev, a club leader in Moscow, this showed that agitprop brigades

68. "Net kul'tury v dvortsakh kul'tury," KP 24 April 1932.

69. Iurii Beliaev, "Klubnaia samodeiatel'nost' na zadvorkah," KS 6 (1930): 20; M. Korol'kov, "Nepreryvka v klube," NZ 42 (1929): 11.

70. On the continuous work week, see Lewis Siegelbaum, *State and Society Between Revolutions, 1918–1929* (Cambridge: Cambridge University Press, 1992), 204–14; Sheila Fitzpatrick, *Everyday Stalinism* (New York: Oxford University Press, 1999), 239.

71. V. Khazanova, *Klubnaia zhizn' i arkhitektura kluba*, v. 1 (Moscow: Rossiiskii institut iskusstvoznania, 1994), 119–127; Gorzka, *Arbeiterkultur*, 260–64. For Komsomol proposals, see "Estafeta kul'turnoi revoliutsii," KP 25 July 1930.

72. Rumiantsev, "Agitpropbrigady zheleznodorozhnikov," 7.

were really do-it-yourself collectives, playing off the literal meaning of *samodeiatel'nost'*. Older drama circles were subject to the author of the play, to the artistic director, and to the heads of artistic organizations that oversaw their work. Agitprop brigades removed these troublesome intermediaries, making their own scripts and their own formal decisions.[73] By writing their own work, concurred Avlov, brigades were able to define their own issues. "An agitprop brigade should not wait until someone writes a play," he insisted." [It] should find its own question, investigate it, pose it, work up the material, and write a text."[74] This directive put a lot of responsibility on young brigade members, who often were not used to writing. One brigade participant at the Putilov factory in Leningrad bemoaned, "It is a torturous process for young people to take up the pen for the first time and write their own plays. There was a lot of insecurity, dissatisfaction, and disillusionment."[75]

Such egalitarian strains were widespread during the First Five-Year Plan, evident in the shock work movement itself and in all artistic media. Amateur visual artists also formed brigades and moved into the factory, creating site-specific posters and satirical drawings of those falling behind in the campaign for higher work quotas.[76] Amateur photographers captured images of their co-workers on the job.[77] Scores of new writers and worker journalists were recruited by newspapers and literary organizations to document the rapid changes in industry and agriculture.[78] In the view of some observers, the rapid growth of amateur artistic movements was evidence of a seismic historical shift, where the divisions between mental and physical labor would disappear. Echoing Marx's contention that socialism would end the separation of the arts from the rest of life, one writer claimed he was witnessing such a process in the work of amateur circles.[79]

Agitprop methods even influenced professional stages. During the

---

73. S. P. Alekseev, "Agitpropbrigady—udarnaia brigada samodeiatel'nogo iskusstva," KS 4 (1931): 12; see also M. Reznik, "Opyt vskrytiia tvorcheskogo metoda agitprop-brigady LRROP," *Za agitpropbrigadu i TRAM* 1 (1931): 16.

74. Avlov, *Teatral'nye agitpropbrigady*, 24.

75. Lind, "Putilovtsy na perestroike," KS 7/8 (1930): 6.

76. D. Mirlas, "Na peredovykh pozitsiiakh," *Za proletarskoe iskusstvo* 3/4 (1931): 31–34.

77. See A. L. Sokolovskaia, "Fotoliubitel'stvo," in S. Iu. Rumiantsev and A. P. Shul'pin, eds., *Samodeiatel'noe khudozhestvennoe tvorchestvo v SSSR*, v. 1 (Moscow: Gosudarstvennyi institut iskusstvoznaniia, 1995), 215–45.

78. Harriet Borland, *Soviet Literary Theory and Practice during the First Five-Year Plan, 1928–32* (New York: King's Crown Press, 1950), 38–74.

79. Iu. Ianel', "Massovaia khudozhestvennaia samodeiatel'nost' i puti sotsialisticheskogo razvitiia iskusstva," *Literatura i iskusstvo* 3/4 (1930): 43, 59.

1930 spring sowing period, when agitprop circles took to the countryside, brigades from professional theaters joined them.[80] They performed
in urban areas as well, sometimes offering their standard repertoire
when it had some relevance to the venue. A brigade from the Meyerhold
Theater, for example, performed Bezymenskii's *The Shot* at a special performance at the Moscow factory Elektrozavod, which had close ties to
the theater. Professional groups heading to the countryside often chose
works that were originally conceived for amateur circles, such as the agitational play *Red Sowing* (*Krasnyi sev*), written hurriedly for the Moscow
House of Amateur Art.[81] Since professionals were now relying on work
designed for amateurs, some observers concluded that amateur theaters
had now gained the upper hand; professionals should come to learn
from them.

Advocates of agitprop brigades adopted an arrogant pose toward the
drama circles from which many of them had emerged. Brigades presented themselves as a "vanguard" whose task it was to transform the
work of conventional circles. However, some amateur actors were not
so easily convinced. At the Rusakov Club in Moscow, several members
left when the drama circle was transformed into an agitprop brigade.
The Putilov factory drama circle lost more than half of its members
when it turned to agitprop performance.[82] The Krasnyi Bogatyr factory,
located in Moscow, had begun an agitprop brigade already in the fall of
1929. Initially, it included about fifteen people who broke off from the
drama circle. They then attracted other interested members from the literature and music circles, all with shock worker status. Although the
brigade won distinctions for its work in the factory, it did not replace the
drama circle entirely. One reporter noted that "the old drama circle
members, having 'played' for years, mustered considerable oppositional
strength."[83]

The language agitprop circles used to distinguish themselves from
their "apolitical" rivals was filled with threats and warnings, reflecting
the turn toward purging then taking place in society at large. Groups

80. "Moskovskie teatry—v kolkhozy," *Literaturnaia gazeta* 24 February 1930; M. Imas,
"Sotssorevnovanie i udarnichestvo v teatre," *Sovetskii teatr* 13/16 (1930): 22; A. Gladkov,
"Brigada MKHATA v pokhode," ibid., 20.

81. "Udarnye brigady meierkhol'dtsev," *Literaturnaia gazeta* 29 September 1930; M. Imas,
Iskusstvo na fronte rekonstruktsii sel'skogo khoziaistva (Moscow: Gosudarstvennoe izdatel'stvo
khudozhestvennoi literatury, 1931), 23, 118.

82. Gabaev and Vronskii, "Nasha istoriia," KS 4 (1931): 25; Avlov, *Teatral'nye agitpropbrigady*, 26.

83. "Nachalsia smotr—sorevnovanie khudozhestvennykh agitbrigad," *Malye formy
klubnogo zrelishcha*, 23/24 (1930): 2.

that refused to change their repertoire should be ostracized, with their names placed on a black list, insisted one cultural worker. Another believed that such groups should be disbanded for harboring Trotskyist sympathies.[84] Critics frequently blamed theater circle directors for inhibiting change, charging that they were drawn from "opportunistic elements" and even included class enemies. Agitprop supporters called for "rigorous internal discipline," "strenuous oversight of repertoire," and a "purge of alien elements."[85] "We know of cases," wrote the editors of *Club Stage*, "where the class enemy has not only worked his way into our mines, factories, and other institutions (think of the Shakhty affair, the Industrial Party Trial, the Menshevik Trial, etc.). In addition, he has wormed his way into choirs, orchestras, and drama circles in workers' clubs."[86]

The Assault on the Small

The hegemony of agitprop brigades did not go without protest even in their heyday. Cultural bureaucrats from Narkompros, like Robert Pel'she, charged them with an appalling lack of skill. Representatives from RAPP, who admired the Moscow Art Theater, complained that they had fallen under the influence of Litfront and Blue Blouse.[87] As the First Five-Year Plan drew to a close, critics also called the political reliability of agitprop brigades into question. Although they eagerly embraced the task of presenting official positions in a palatable form, these groups were the ones in control of the process of composition. Their ability to prepare material in a hurry was the very reason for their existence. This meant that brigades often performed before their work could be previewed or censored by political authorities. According to one local observer, "Political control over the content by factory committees is practically nonexistent. The circles are left to themselves."[88] Since the brigades were more effective in presenting villains and bottlenecks than

84. I. Isaev, "Partiinye lozungi na khudozhestvennom fronte," KS 3 (1930): 1; V. Vin, "K perevyboram sovetov," KS 2 (1930): 23.

85. L. Tasin, "Blizhaishie zadachi dramkruzhkov," ZI 36 (1929): 2. See also references to a "purge" of club leaders, in *Pravda*, "Kluby—opornye punkty na fronte kul'turnoi revoliutsii," 22 April 1930.

86. "Priblizhaemsia k IX s"ezdu profsoiuzov," KS 1/2 (1931): 2.

87. "Stenogramma metosektora po zaslushannomu doklad tov. L'vova o formakh agitbrigadnykh vystuplenii," GTSTM, f. 150, d. 58, l. 5; R. Pel'she, "K itogam smotra," in *Khudozhestvennye agitpropbrigady*, 5–11.

88. N. Bespalov, "Smotr povyshaet aktivnost'!" KS 6 (1932): 34. See also Iakov Vasserman, "Chto tormozit rost?," ibid., 37.

heroes and production triumphs, their work could easily be seen as an open assault on Soviet production methods. Commentators increasingly called for more oversight over the content of performances.

Perhaps the most important mark against agitprop brigades was their aggressive stance against hierarchies based on skill, whether in the factory or the artistic community. Expert at bashing experts, many brigades had a difficult time adjusting to the new line on specialists and the turn against egalitarianism launched by Stalin in the summer of 1931.[89] At this point, the government officially rejected the anti-authoritarian spirit fostered by the First Five-Year Plan, rehabilitating once-maligned experts and establishing sizeable wage differentials based on skill. Agitprop troupes' negative portrayal of managers and factory directors began to concern critics. They also worried that these impromptu performances presented no real heroes that audiences could use as role models.[90]

By 1932, agitprop brigades had ample evidence that the cultural winds were shifting. In April the Communist Party issued its momentous decree "On the Restructuring of Literary and Artistic Organizations." This proclamation marked an important turning point in the direction of Soviet culture. With it, the Communist Party ended the aggressive dominance of self-proclaimed proletarian cultural groups that had gained considerable visibility during the First Five-Year Plan. According to the resolution, these organizations had become too narrow and sectarian, hindering the further development of Soviet culture. They would be replaced by national artistic unions open to all classes.[91] This decision meant the end for well-established groups like RAPP, the Proletkult, and the Proletarian Musicians' Union.

The Communist Party's pronouncement on the arts might have given local cultural circles like agitprop brigades some cause for concern. After all, they usually claimed to be class-exclusive groups catering primarily to workers or working-class youth. They also could be charged with narrow and sectarian pursuits. Initially, however, no one interpreted the directive in this light. Cultural journals urged participants to consider the significance of the April pronouncement in their work, and

89. J. V. Stalin, "New Conditions, New Tasks in Economic Construction," in *Problems of Leninism* (Peking: Foreign Languages Press, 1976), 532–59, esp. 552.

90. L. Sokolov, "Za vysokoe kachestvo khudozhestvennoi samodeiatel'nosti," *Za agitpropbrigadu i TRAM* 2 (1932): 10.

91. "O perestroike literaturno-khudozhestvennykh organizatsii. Postanovlenie TsK VKP(b) ot 23 aprelia 1932 g.," *Pravda* 24 April 1932.

some local clubs and factories held discussions about its possible implications, but there was no consensus about what it might mean for amateur artistic activity.[92]

For agitprop brigades, a more significant turning point marking the end of their predominance was a supposedly festive event meant to celebrate the achievements of amateur art. At the beginning of 1932, the central trade union leadership joined together with the Communist Party, Narkompros, and the Komsomol to begin plans for a national Olympiad (a term used for competitions) of amateur musical and theatrical groups recruited from all over the country. Organizers had numerous models to follow, since local unions and city cultural divisions had been hosting competitions of this kind for many years and an Olympiad of theaters from the Soviet national republics had already been staged in 1930.[93] Since agitprop brigades had come to dominate amateur theatrical work, they were the most widely represented theater circles at the competition.

By February 1932 the organizing committee began publicizing the upcoming event in the national press and specialized cultural journals. Competitions were to be held at the local level, with the best groups performing in Moscow that summer. The winners from those competitions were promised a prominent spot at the festivities surrounding the fifteenth anniversary of the revolution in November. The committee also determined appropriate topics for the theatrical presentations, choosing subjects that mirrored the kinds of themes already common in agitprop brigades, including military preparedness, the struggle for collectivization, and the successful completion of the industrial plan.[94]

In August 1932, one hundred and two amateur theater groups, choirs, and orchestras from all over the country converged on Moscow's Park for Culture and Leisure. Opening ceremonies followed the pattern of other First Five-Year Plan festivals, with their displays of military might and technical achievement.[95] Dirigibles and spotlights announced the beginning of festivities. A group of soldiers from the local garrison made its appearance, followed by a parade of the participants, all in dif-

92. "Vsesoiuznyi smotr samodeiatel'nosti," RiT 20 (1932): 1–2.

93. "Olimpiada samodeiatel'nogo iskusstva," *Sovetskoe iskusstvo* 9 February 1932; "Samodeiatel'noe iskusstvo—litsom k proizvodstvu," *Trud* 22 February 1932.

94. "Smotr sorevnovanie khudozhestvennoi samodeiatel'nosti," *Za agitpropbrigadu i TRAM* 2 (1932): 4–5.

95. On First Five-Year Plan festivals, see Vladimir Tolstoi, Irina Bibikova, and Catherine Cooke, eds., *Street Art of the Revolution: Festivals and Celebrations in Russia, 1918–1933* (London: Thames and Hudson, 1990), 167–229.

ferent colored costumes to identify their geographic regions. A huge orchestra and mass choir inaugurated the cultural competition. Estimates
of the crowd at the opening ranged from 60,000 to 100,000, with many
viewers coming from local Moscow factories.[96]

The week-long festival was elaborately scripted and included visits to
local museums and theaters, speeches by important cultural experts,
and meetings with Moscow shock workers. Proponents of amateur theater had extremely high expectations for this event. A lead editorial in
Worker and Theater predicted that the Olympiad would fulfill an ambitious artistic and ideological agenda. It would contradict Leon Trotsky,
who believed that there could be no proletarian socialist culture and no
socialism in one country. The Olympiad would also disprove the views
of Mikhail Tomskii, the recently ousted trade union leader, because it
would show that workers' cultural circles could accomplish more than
rudimentary cultural training. Finally, it would expose the false position
of the avant-garde, who argued for a total break with the culture of the
past. "Under the leadership of the party and unions, amateur art will
strike at rightist 'advisers' and 'leftist phrases.' "[97]

The politicization of theatrical groups in the course of the First Five-
Year Plan was clearly apparent at the festival. Well over half of the theater circles represented were agitprop brigades. TRAM groups were the
next most numerous. Only one group called itself a drama circle.[98] The
festival's theme was "For a Magnitostroi in Art," signaling that cultural
construction should be as successful as industrial construction in the
new city of Magnitogorsk.[99] Factory motifs and the struggle for higher
production quotas dominated festival repertoires. The transformation of
proletarian consciousness through the struggle for production was another popular subject.

Participants in the Olympiad wielded impressive political and social
credentials. According to several estimates, more than fifty percent of
them were members of the Communist Party or Komsomol, and seventy
percent called themselves shock workers, a term used with increasing

96. For reports of the opening celebration, see "Olimpiada zakonchilas', perestroiku na
polnyi khod," RiT 24 (1932): 9; "Grandioznyi prazdnik iskusstva i tvorchestva mass," KP 8
August 1932; N. Khor'kov, "Simfoniia, kotoruiu sozdaet kollektiv," *Trud* 8 August 1932.
97. "Privet Vsesoiuznoi olimpiade samodeiatel'nosti," RiT 22 (1932): 1–2, quotation 2.
See also "Vyshe ideino-khudozhestvennyi uroven' tvorchestva," KP 6 August 1932.
98. "Spisok kollektivov uchastvuiushchikh na pervoi Vsesoiuznoi olimpiade," GARF, f.
5451, op. 1, d. 789, l. 36.
99. "Zavtra otkryvaetsia olimpiada samodeiatel'nogo iskusstva," *Trud* 5 August 1932.

frequency by 1932. Youth was another common characteristic, which is hardly surprising given the age composition of amateur art circles. A full sixty-five percent of those taking part were under the age of twenty-three, with just ten percent over thirty-five.[100] Only twenty-nine percent of the performers were women, a figure well below standard estimates for female participation in union club theaters. No doubt the high percentage of shock workers, who were overwhelmingly male, help to explain women's low participation rates.[101] Despite efforts to reflect the geographic and cultural diversity of the Soviet Union, Moscow and Leningrad were overrepresented at the festival, sending eleven out of sixty-one theater groups.

The Olympiad received extensive coverage in the national press, in journals devoted to art and culture, and in local newspapers in Moscow and Leningrad. Some newspapers offered lengthy daily accounts of the festivities with elaborate descriptions of the opening ceremonies, many individual performances, and the final results of the week-long competition. The official jury included representatives from professional theaters, trade union organizations, TRAM, and Narkompros. Some familiar names showed up among the judges, including the long-time activists in amateur theater, Valentin Tikhonovich and Nikolai L'vov. One of the Communist Party's chief experts on cultural affairs, Iakov Boiarskii, also participated in the jury discussions.[102]

Most printed assessments on the event began with general words of praise. The festival had shown that the masses now had access to a world of culture that had once been denied them. "Those who before the revolution could not even dream of art, whose lot in life was only prison-like labor, now sang and acted," determined an author in *Pravda*. "The gods have been pulled down from Olympus. 'Holy Art' has become accessible to the broad masses of the country and has been put to

---

100. A. Fevral'skii, "Smotr samodeiatel'nogo teatra," *Literaturnaia gazeta* 17 August 1932; N. G. Zograf, "Zhivaia teatral'naia gazeta," RGALI f. 2723, op. 1, d. 425, l. 102; "Kto uchastvoval v olimpiade," *Trud* 17 August 1932; Iakov Grinval'd, "Vchera zakonchilas' olimpiada," VM 15 August 1932; "Sostav kollektivov uchastnikov pervoi Vsesoiuznoi olimpiady," GARF, f. 5251 (VTSSPS), op. 16, d. 789, l. 37.

101. Women were estimated to make up thirty-nine percent of the participants in union theater circles in 1929 (see Gabriele Gorzka, *Arbeiterkultur in der Sowjetunion: Industriearbeiter-Klubs 1917–1929* ([Berlin: Arno Verlag, 1990], 298). On the gender composition of shock workers, see Kuromiya, *Stalin's Industrial Revolution*, 321, and Siegelbaum, *Stakhanovism*, 170–72.

102. "Spisok chlenov zhiuri," GARF, f. 5451, op. 16, d. 789, l. 61; "Stenogramma zasedaniia zhiuri," 10 August 1932, ibid., d. 793, l. 116.

work for socialism."[103] However, these vague and formulaic words of praise were overshadowed by a barrage of complaints leveled at amateur theatrical groups in general and agitprop brigades in particular. While reporters did not always agree in their choice of good and bad performances and jury discussions were sometimes acrimonious, the overall critical consensus was remarkably similar: amateur theater needed fundamentally different aesthetic and organizational principles.[104] Moscow and Leningrad circles were in no way exempt from this critical onslaught.

Critics attacked groups for their remarkably low level of writing. The Izhorsk factory collective from the Leningrad suburb of Kolpino was a special target. It presented a homemade play called *Coal* (*Ugol'*), which showed how older workers learned the value of modern machinery while the factory management learned to appreciate the enthusiasm of the work force. Jury members charged that it offered far too much local detail. One observer was even harsher, condemning its ungrammatical speech and wooden dialogue.[105] Another work from Leningrad, *The Victors Will Judge*, written by original TRAM member Arkadii Gorbenko, received low marks for poor organization, a predictable plot, and unconvincing characters. The entire play did not have one living image, protested a critic in the trade union paper *Trud*. "From the very first act it was easy to predict the end."[106]

Critics discerned dangerous aesthetic trends and the influence of discredited approaches in many performances. Numerous Leningrad circles were accused of suffering from "Piotrovshchina," of not yet having overcome the evil influence of the Leningrad TRAM.[107] "Blue Blouseism" was another common failing. This error was revealed in the Putilov factory work *How Tom Gained Knowledge*, where all the characters spoke in slogans and used ungrammatical language. For the Moscow central

103. T. Kh., "Bogi stashcheny s olimpa," *Pravda*, 10 August 1932.

104. Disagreements were for the most part parochial—with critics defending their own local interests and organizational affiliation. Leningrad journals tended to defend Leningrad performances. Jury members from TRAM defended TRAM performances, etc.

105. "Agitpropbrigada zavoda 'Severnaia sudostroitel'naia verf'," GARF, f. 5451, op. 16, d. 767, l. 42; Al. Gladkov, "Luchshie sily professional 'nogo iskusstva na pomoshch' khudozhestvennoi samodeiatel'nosti," *Sovetskoe iskusstvo* 15 August 1932.

106. M. Iurenev, "Chemu ne aplodiruet zritel'," *Trud* 14 August 1932. See also Nik. Iu., "Otoiti ot shablonnykh 'agitmarshirovok,' " KP 11 August 1932.

107. GARF f. 5451, op. 16, d. 798, l. 94; Gladkov, "Luchshie sily"; Iu., "Otoiti ot shablonnykh 'agitmarshirovok.' "

TRAM, performing *The 10:10 Moscow Train*, Blue Blouseism was evidenced in its schematic construction and murky central narrative.[108]

The hallmark of the agitprop aesthetic, the use of local facts, was quite evident in the works presented at the Olympiad. Critics determined that such details might interest viewers from a specific factory, but they could not engage a broader audience. "Not every fact taken from real life rings true in art," determined jury members in response to a play tracing the building of a ship at the Northern Wharf in Leningrad. Their work, *RT 57*, had emerged from documentation collected in the "History of Factories and Plants" project. In the jury's view, its "photographic method" had resulted in a "naïve naturalism."[109]

The judges were also dissatisfied with the heroes presented in works at the Olympiad. Although the characters presented in the longer works by Moscow and Leningrad circles were superior to those in short sketches, they remained unconvincing. Their personal failings were poorly explained and their heroic accomplishments remained sketchy.[110] Moreover, the single-minded attention to production themes to the exclusion of other parts of life had become monotonous. Boiarskii, head of the artists' union Rabis, complained, "In the final analysis, agitprop brigades' focus on the struggle with negative elements in production (slackers, absentees, loafers, etc.); although this [topic] has great importance, it alone cannot reveal the activity and initiative of the working masses in construction. And does the life of the contemporary, cultured worker end at the construction site? . . . What about friendship, love?"[111]

The distribution of the prizes reinforced these critical judgments. Groups presenting short agitational works were slighted; instead, top honors went to those offering full-fledged plays. The recently professionalized Leningrad construction workers' theater, Stroika, received first prize for its performance of *We Are from Olonets* (*My Olonetskie*). In an interview, Stroika members stated that they had purposefully turned away from "small forms" and attempted to create a work that looked

108. A. Kasatkina, "Zametki o piatom dne," *Izvestiia* 12 August 1932. For the text of the play, see F. Knorre, *Moskovskii 10:10* (Moscow: Gosudarstvennoe izdatel'stvo khudozhestvennoi literatury, 1933); on the Putilov troupe, see "Agitpropbrigada krasnoznamennogo zavoda 'Krasnyi Putilovets,' " GARF f. 5451, op. 16, d. 798, l. 121.

109. "Agitpropbrigada zavoda 'Severnaia sudostroitel'naia verf'," GARF, f. 5451, op. 16, d. 797, ll. 40–41; "Perestroiku na polnyi khod," RiT 24 (1932): 12–13.

110. "TRAM Moskovskogo raiona," GARF, f. 5451, op. 16, d. 797, ll. 36–38; "Agitpropbrigada Izhorskogo zavoda," GARF f. 5451, op. 16, d. 798, l. 2.

111. Ia. Boiarskii, "Znachenie olimpiady—na printsipial'nuiu vysotu," KS 7/8 (1932): 4.

more like a professionally written play, even enlisting the help of professional playwrights in the process.[112] Second place went to the Moscow central TRAM. Although agitprop brigades had dominated the festivities, the most they could claim was a third-place prize.[113]

By the time the Olympiad was over, a critical consensus about the future of amateur theaters had emerged. Participants were advised to go back home and turn to the experts in order to diversify their repertoires and improve the quality of their productions. They should attempt works by contemporary Soviet playwrights and also take on classical plays, including the work of Alexander Ostrovsky, Molière, and the eighteenth-century Italian playwright Carlo Goldoni. When addressing political themes, amateur theaters had to learn to do this "artistically," which was only possible with the assistance of those trained in technique and familiar with the long history of Russian and world theater.[114] All of these strictures undercut the methods and messages of agitprop brigades.

For the national trade union organization, the indirect sponsor of most of the performing groups, the Olympiad marked a significant watershed in the history of the amateur arts. In a slim volume commemorating the festival, union leaders announced a major restructuring of amateur theatrical work: "The artistic demands of workers in the leading centers of production, demands once encouraged by agitprop brigades, can no longer be satisfied by the current level of agitprop brigade theater."[115] A lengthy list of resolutions outlined a general retreat from the militancy and intolerance of the First Five-Year Plan era. Agitprop brigades and drama circles should coexist, employing both large and small forms. All amateur circles needed to develop tolerance toward different artistic approaches; they should also strive to articulate a unique "creative personality" (*tvorcheskoe litso*). Older workers and non-Party members had to feel welcome in amateur circles, ending the social exclusivity of agitprop brigades. Perhaps the most striking recommendation was a new attitude toward the audience. The coercive tactics perfected by brigadiers were no longer appropriate. Union leaders sug-

112. "K sporam o Stroike," *Tribuna olimpiady* 13 August 1932.
113. "Peredoviki khudozhestvennoi samodeiatel'nosti," *Trud* 17 August 1932. The Izhorsk agitprop brigade won sixth place; the Moscow Trade Workers Brigade won seventh.
114. See, for example, A. Kasatkina, "Iskusstvo millionov," *Izvestiia*, 22 August 1932.
115. *Pervaia Vsesoiuznaia olimpiada samodeiatel'nogo iskusstva* (Moscow: Profizdat, 1932), 10.

gested that amateur circles "fight for the creation of cheerful, joyful performances that can bring viewers pleasure and constructive leisure."[116]
The war on the audience was over.

In a long assessment of the results of the Olympiad, one of the judges,
the club leader Sergei Alekseev, offered a very positive interpretation of
its lessons. He saw the event as the final struggle in a long "battle of
genres" between amateur drama circles performing longer works and
the agitational theater of small forms. During late NEP, drama circles
had dominated. Agitprop brigades achieved the upper hand in the years
of the First Five-Year Plan, however, driving out any other kind of work.
Alekseev—who had a few years before decried the use of professional
plays on club stages—now believed that the time for a true synthesis
had come: "[The Olympiad] will lead to the free growth of diverse forms
of amateur work. [Groups] will take from the rich experience of professional theaters and discover an independent, young, amateur theater of
the working class." While drama circles had ignored their social context,
agitprop brigades had ignored training. Now both sides would learn
from the other and bring forth something new.[117]

This call for synthesis and cooperation was common at the time, as
cultural bureaucrats and artistic practitioners struggled to define the
emerging doctrine of socialist realism, only just articulated in 1932.
Many hoped that it would bring an end to the politicized, nasty cultural
battles of the First Five-Year Plan. The practices of the avant-garde
would merge with the realists. Professional and amateur theaters would
enter into mutually enriching cooperative arrangements. Soviet artists
would finally discover how to create works that were both politically
correct and entertaining, ending the dysfunctional tendency toward one
or the other extreme.[118] The amateur arts would be open to a broad range
of approaches and training methods, announced a trade union official at
a cultural conference in late 1932.[119]

But there were also voices that questioned such a socialist happy ending. In its assessment of the Olympiad, the newspaper *Sovetskoe iskusstvo*

116. Ibid., 11, 19, 24, quotation 19.

117. S. P. Alekseev, "Samodeiatel'nyi teatr na olimpiade," KS 9 (1932): 1–7, quotation 3.

118. On the broad range of the debate about the meaning of socialist realism in its for-
mative period, see Régine Robin, *Socialist Realism: An Impossible Aesthetic*, trans. Catherine
Porter (Stanford: Stanford University Press, 1992), chs. 1 and 2. On socialist realism and
pleasure, see Richard Stites, *Russian Popular Culture: Entertainment and Society since 1900*
(Cambridge: Cambridge University Press, 1992), 64–97.

119. Ivan Chicherov, "Stenogramma Vsesoiuznogo soveshchaniia teatral'nykh rabotnikov profsoiuznykh teatrov," December 1932, GARF f. 5451, op. 16, d. 788, ll. 6, 16–18.

asserted that the time had come for "big forms" to address "big problems." While the editorial called for a multiplicity of artistic methods, it also asserted that small forms were unreliable. They could not do justice to the grandiose achievements of the Soviet Union. To make matters worse, the agitational theater of small forms had been tainted by its association with utilitarianism and Litfrontism.[120] By including these explicit warnings, the unnamed author indicated that the new system taking shape might not be so tolerant and inclusive after all.

In a now-famous article first published in 1978, Sheila Fitzpatrick delineated a unique period of "cultural revolution" within the First Five-Year Plan. Beginning with a highly publicized trial against engineers in 1928 known as the Shakhty Trial, this distinctive phase was marked by youthful dominance, attacks on established hierarchies, and a militant language of class war. While "unleashed" from above, these assaults were enthusiastically embraced by the Komsomol, student organizations, self-proclaimed proletarian cultural groups, and young workers eager to shake up factory management. It was not until Stalin's direct intervention in the summer of 1931, with a speech denouncing egalitarianism and defending expertise, that this anti-authoritarian phase in Soviet cultural life came to an end.[121]

Agitprop brigades embodied many of the values Fitzpatrick described, with their denunciations of experts and rejection of bourgeois culture, broadened to include all elements of aesthetic theater right down to the stage boards. Thus, it might seem strange that I have consciously chosen not to use the term "cultural revolution" in my analysis of these creations of the First Five-Year Plan. One reason is simple chronology; agitprop brigades do not fit neatly into Fitzpatrick's periodization. The Shakhty Trial made little impact on the repertoire of amateur stages. The big celebrations and competitions in the fall of 1928 in Moscow and Leningrad were almost no different from those staged a year before.[122] For amateur theaters, the change in trade union leadership in the summer of 1929, combined with the spread of shock work,

---

120. "Pervye itogi," *Sovetskoe iskusstvo* 21 August 1932.

121. Sheila Fitzpatrick, "Cultural Revolution as Class War," in Fitzpatrick, ed., *Cultural Revolution*, 8–40.

122. N. L'vov, "Kluby v dni Oktiabria," NZ 46 (1928): 9. See also I. V., "Kluby v oktiabr'skie dni," *Pravda* 11 November 1928.

marked the real rift from the cultural practices of late NEP. Similarly, while Stalin's 1931 panegyric to experts and expertise found an echo in the speeches of cultural organizers, it did not markedly change the radicalized repertoire of amateur stages. Not even the April 1932 decree dissolving independent proletarian cultural organizations like RAPP and the Proletkult affected the greatest swing back to more conventional forms. Rather, the crucial turning point was the national Olympiad of amateur arts in the summer of 1932. There small forms were viewed, assessed, and ultimately discredited in the most widely distributed media in the nation.

Moreover, Fitzpatrick's concept of cultural revolution highlights assaults on established authority as the cardinal marker of the era. Drawing on the research of Michael David-Fox, I see the First Five-Year Plan era, which he calls "The Great Break," as a complex of contradictory impulses that are not so easily separated. Challenges to hierarchy were combined with the great expansion of party and state power; attacks on "bourgeois" culture went hand in hand with efforts to instill the "bourgeois" values of sobriety and punctuality.[123] Agitprop brigades acted out these contradictions. They ridiculed shop managers but expected rigid compliance to new state initiatives. They disdained stages as remnants of the old world but mocked those who were unable to show up to work on time. In their attempts to instill good labor habits, agitprop brigades had similar goals to the amateur theater of small forms during NEP. What was fundamentally different about these troupes was their methods. Rather than using humor, references to mass culture, and persuasion, they chose preachy didacticism. Rather than seeing their work as the beginning of a dialogue, like TRAM authors did, these actors relied on the tactics of shame and extortion. Seeing their audience as potential enemies, agitprop brigades widened the scope of accusation and distrust fostered by state and Party agencies during this period of upheaval.

Agitprop brigades were an attempt to fuse the contradictory categories of spontaneity and consciousness in Soviet art. Performers presented the messages of the regime, but they arranged those messages themselves and decided how they were to be transmitted. In the long run, this strange fusion pleased neither the audience nor the govern-

123. See Michael David-Fox, *Revolution of the Mind* (Ithaca: Cornell University Press, 1997), 254–72; idem, "What Is Cultural Revolution," *Russian Review* 58 (April 1999): 181–201.

ment. At the end of the First Five-Year Plan, these intrusive groups—hostile to the very concept of pleasure—either disappeared or changed beyond recognition. Turning against brigades as anti-aesthetic, sponsoring agencies curtailed their interventionist tactics. However, in the process of fixing their artistic failings, these agencies also guarded against a resurgence of spontaneity. The era of the homemade play was over.

6

Amateurs in the Spectacle State

IN HIS fascinating discussion of the differences between early Soviet culture and the 1930s, the architectural historian Vladimir Papernyi argues that Stalinism was fixated on visual display.[1] The architecture of the period began first with the façade as a means of illustrating power. Interior spaces featured grand foyers and decorative objects designed to impress users. While many theaters in the 1920s tried to liberate the viewer and offer different perspectives on events, stages in the 1930s were designed to fix the spectators' point of view. Nor was this concern for display limited to architecture. The mass festivals common to the early Soviet years, dispersed throughout the streets and squares of urban centers, were now reserved for special locations—with events in Moscow's Red Square gaining preeminent importance. Spectacles of individual heroism, such as the thrilling exploits of long-distance pilots and polar explorers, were the focus of an enthusiastic national press coverage.[2]

The Stalinist emphasis on impressive forms of presentation led to the creation of what we might call a "spectacle state" in the 1930s, a polity in which power was conveyed through visual means. As James von Geldern has argued, Soviet citizens' knowledge of state policies and public affairs was communicated increasingly through spectacles during this decade, including show trials, parades, conventions, and highly

---

1. Vladimir Papernyi, *Kul'tura "dva"* (Ann Arbor: Ardis, 1985).
2. Ibid., 71, 209, 101; see also James von Geldern, "Cultural and Social Geography in the Mass Culture of the 1930s," in Stephen White, ed., *New Directions in Soviet History* (Cambridge: Cambridge University Press, 1990), 66–67.

publicized state initiatives soliciting public input. The state invested considerable funds into new venues for spectacles, building massive sports stadiums, movie theaters, workers' palaces, and public parks. In the process, contends von Geldern, the spectator became the model for the ideal Soviet citizen.[3]

This aesthetic and political turn had profound consequences for amateur theaters. Despite their many vicissitudes in the years up until the First Five-Year Plan, the ethos of amateur stages had been first and foremost participatory; it was more important what they did than how they looked. They were valued for the contributions they made to neighborhood collectives, club entertainments, and political campaigns. In the 1930s, however, standards of judgment changed radically. Amateur performances received credit primarily for their aesthetic impact on spectators—how impressive their stages and sets were, how polished their acting techniques, how well they approximated professional standards of performance. By setting professional performance standards for amateur theaters, cultural institutions aimed to raise their value as spectacle. They became visual evidence of the *kul'turnost'*, or "culturedness," of the formerly rough urban lower classes. The introduction of the aesthetic system of socialist realism, murky as it was in its first formulations, further served to guarantee a merger of amateur and professional art. If there was only one acceptable artistic method, intoned critics, then the distance between different forms of artistic expression could not be great.[4]

To effect this transformation, many circles in the capital cities established close links to professional stages and engaged a permanent professional staff. Rehearsal time increased exponentially. Amateur circles became a path to channel talented participants on to a lifetime career on the professional stage. In the process, however, amateur theaters lost any special place they might once have held in the lives of their audiences. In the 1920s, the lines between actors and spectators had not been rigid, both because of the location of the stage and the fact that one day's viewer might be included in the next day's play. But the changing architectural standards of the 1930s distanced performers from the audience; so did the much more rigorous training programs. As a result, amateur

3. Von Geldern, "Cultural and Social Geography," 71.
4. D. Marchenko, "Ocherednye zadachi khudozhestvennoi samodeiatel'nosti," *Klub* 7 (1933): 48–49.

theatricals turned into a profession of sorts, although it remained unpaid. It was no longer open to every enthusiast.

The Locus of Performance

Amateur stages began to approximate professional theaters in all aspects in the 1930s, including their physical environment. The club building boom of late NEP and the First Five-Year Plan had created spacious stages for select clubs in both capital cities. With performance halls seating thousands, large stages, and healthy financial support (sometimes stemming directly from ticket sales), these club theaters could mount elaborate productions with impressive sets. The KOR Railroad Workers' Club in Moscow accommodated an audience of twelve hundred viewers and had special seats set aside for Stakhanovites. The drama circle had a separate building for its activities, including a special library, an administrative office, and costume and set design studios. The Krasnyi Bogatyr factory club spent fifteen thousand rubles on the scenery for a single play, at a time when many club budgets were not much higher.[5]

Although the biggest building boom came in the late 1920s and the years of the First Five-Year Plan, money continued to pour into new club structures in the 1930s. *Pravda* proudly announced new club buildings at the Putilov and Sestropetskii factories in 1933. The Sickle and Hammer factory opened a new club building in the same year, with an auditorium seating one thousand.[6] Two separate architectural completions during the First Five-Year Plan had produced a wide range of designs for a Palace of Culture in Moscow's Proletarian District. They finally came to fruition in 1933, when a theater space for twelve hundred viewers opened. This hall not only provided entertainment for local neighborhoods, it also obliterated key elements of the old culture, since it was built on the grounds of the Simonovskii Monastery.[7]

But while performance spaces expanded, theater circles paradoxically became less important to the life of the club. The massive new club buildings of the 1930s contained rooms for a multitude of activities that

5. G. Goncharov, "Klub KOR," *Klub* 19 (1935): 53; "Nasushchnye voprosy khudozhestvennoi samodeiatel'nosti," *Klub* 14 (1937): 48.

6. "Novye shkoly, kino, kluby i dvortsy," *Pravda* 19 March 1933; "Po sssr" *Pravda* 18 May 1932.

7. V. G., "Dvorets kul'tury rabochikh Leninskoi slobody," *Pravda* 29 September 1933. On the competitions, see V. Khazanova, *Klubnaia zhizn' i arkhitektura kluba*, v. 1: 1917–1932 (Moscow: Rossiiskii Institut Iskusstvoznaniia, 1994), 127–37.

could take place simultaneously, unlike the serial use of space in smaller buildings. Their expanded budgets supported buffets, cafeterias, and sometimes even stores, together with a wide array of innovative amateur artistic projects, including photo circles and jazz orchestras.[8] With such a range of activities available, some club users boasted that they spent all their free time there, coming right after work and staying until it was time to sleep. Expanding entertainment opportunities made the work of amateur theater groups less central to club activities. Rising standards of performance reinforced this fact, as drama circles radically increased their rehearsal time and decreased the number of works they staged each year. Some circles planned only two plays during a season.

The decline in agitprop brigades meant that far fewer drama circles were prepared to partake in quickly organized agitational work and join in the small festivities and holidays that marked Soviet public life. As a result, the huge new halls were frequently filled with other forms of entertainment. Professional theaters could now bring their elaborate productions into workers' clubs much more easily. In fact, many of the new venues were used primarily for that purpose. The impressive new stage at the Proletarian District Palace of Culture hosted the cream of Moscow productions, including works by the Malyi Theater, the Theater of the Revolution, and the Meyerhold Theater. These new stages also facilitated visits of professional writers to working-class neighborhoods, where they read their works to assembled club members.[9]

Clubs built in the 1930s exhibited the kind of "elegant" details that marked Stalinist architecture in general in this period. The nomenclature of "workers' palace" (*rabochii dvorets*), claimed by club activists since the revolution, began to be taken literally by both architects and club users. Architects emphasized fine details in the façade. They constructed entry spaces that looked similar to hotels, with marble walls, fountains, flowers, and paintings. Some wealthy new clubs ordered furniture specifically designed for their interiors. One Leningrad club even boasted a doorman![10] Although the discussions around clubs still emphasized their importance as public space, architects stressed the need

8. On the simultaneous use of space, see Lewis Siegelbaum, "The Shaping of Workers' Leisure," unpublished ms. On the expansion of club amenities, see Khazanova, *Klubnaia zhizn'*, v. 2: 109.

9. Khazanova, *Klubnaia zhizn'*, v. 1: 151, v. 2: 9; E. Gabrilovich, "Dvadtsat' minut vos'mogo," *Pravda* 6 January 1935.

10. Khazanova, *Klubnaia zhizn'*, v. 2: 11–25. On the importance of the façade in 1930s architecture, see Papernyi, *Kul'tura "dva,"* 69–71.

to make the club cozy and inviting. The club became the image of an ideal home that individuals could not yet achieve on their own.[11]

Despite the expansive new buildings, club life continued to raise problems for those activists who had hoped they would significantly transform leisure time activities. Trade union cultural workers conducted periodic "sweeps," making surprise club visits to assess their cleanliness, comfort, and range of activities. They were invariably disappointed, finding club spaces dirty and inhospitable.[12] When national newspapers opened their culture pages to club users, their complaints sounded strikingly familiar to discontents voiced during NEP. Letters in *Pravda* about the Kauchuk Club listed a number of problems. This club was one of the premier structures of the Stalin era, boasting a building designed by the famous architect Konstantin Mel'nikov and a theater staff headed by directors from the Vakhtangov Theater.[13] But users were nonetheless dissatisfied. Tickets to evening events were not distributed according to a fair system, and the events themselves started too late to fit into the schedules of busy workers. "The club we are writing about is not bad," read one letter. "It has a new, good building, a big auditorium. It recently won a competition. Nonetheless it still has problems serving the cultural needs of workers."[14] A number of Leningrad clubs were cited for providing poor cultural resources to their members. The club "Promtekhnika" was singled out in *Krasnaia gazeta* for its lack of comfort and limited programs: "In Leningrad, there are thousands of amateur artistic circles, there is an army [of cultural workers]. But with all these massive resources, this rich material base, we need to bring club work up to a level to meet the tasks of the moment." This club had fallen sadly behind, concluded the article, not giving workers a sense that they could go there to improve themselves after working hours.[15]

While some club participants complained that their shiny new buildings had still not met their needs, others were struggling with older and more familiar problems. Not all clubs were reconfigured in the 1930s

11. On the new language surrounding clubs, see Khazanova, *Klubnaia zhizn'*, v. 2: 23–31, 137–39. On clubs as a surrogate home, see Leon Feuchtwanger, *Moskau 1937: Eine Reisebericht für meine Freunde* (1937; rpr. Berlin: Aufbau Verlag, 1993), 23.

12. See, for example, the untitled 1933 report on a variety of Moscow clubs, Tsentral'nyi munitsipal'nyi arkhiv Moskvy (TSMAM), f. 718 (MGSPS), op. 8, d. 45, ll. 92–95.

13. "Teatr kluba 'Kauchuk' pod rukovodstvom vakhtangovtsev," *Klub* 6 (1936): 33–35. On the club design, see S. Frederick Starr, *Melnikov: Solo Architect in a Mass Society* (Princeton: Princeton University Press, 1978), 140–42.

14. Bor. Levin, "V rabochem klube," *Pravda* 30 October 1934.

15. "Za kul'turnyi klub," *Krasnaia gazeta* 6 October 1934.

building boom. Participants in the drama circles at the Elektrozavod factory in Moscow were not housed in grand spaces. They retained a very modest rehearsal room that was much too small to meet their needs. They had to wait for hours to gain access to an auditorium.[16] Other clubs suffered from serious structural weaknesses, including leaking roofs, that made it difficult to continue work.[17] The cultural distance between these ordinary gathering places and the new "workers' palaces" increased exponentially.

Tensions between older and younger workers, a frequent theme in the club literature of the 1920s, continued into the next decade. Older workers complained about overcrowded rooms used by young people for their "trysts." They felt excluded from gatherings that seemed designed for young people, such as dance evenings. "At such events it is rare to see people like us, older workers and their wives," complained a group of long-time members of the Tsiurupy Club in Leningrad. The club needed a special room where older workers could go in peace.[18] Young workers brought their own complaints against the new club system of the 1930s. In order to finance the expensive new buildings, clubs began to charge fees for a variety of services, sometimes even for hanging up coats and using the library. Young people argued that this discriminated against youth, who did not have much income to spare. "The NEPman, commercial culture should be banned from houses of culture," complained young workers in a letter to *Komsomol'skaia pravda*.[19]

Enter the Experts

After the National Olympiad of Amateur Art in 1932, the status inversions of the preceding years, when amateurs were at times deemed superior or at least equal to professionals, ended abruptly. Both trade union and Narkompros bureaucracies urged amateur theaters to form solid links with professional stages. Up until 1936, it did not matter which professional method amateurs chose, as long as it provided a standardized training system. Teachers who tried to come up with their own methods, without a nod to one of the established theaters, could

16. "Na zadvorkakh," KP 23 August 1934; see also the description of rehearsal space in the Kalinin factory, "Beseda s rukovoditeliami khudozhestvennykh samodeiatel'nykh kruzhkov," GARF, f. 5451, op. 19, d. 422, l. 3 ob.

17. A. A. Nokhin, "Pochemu kluby na zamke?," *Pravda* 15 October 1936.

18. "Takoi klub nam ne nuzhen," *Krasnaia gazeta* 6 October 1934.

19. "Dom kul'tury ili torgovyi dom?," KP 15 October 1934; "Klub—mesto kul'turnogo otdykha," KP 15 October 1934. See also V. Kostin, "Vecherami v klubakh," KP 28 December 1936.

find themselves accused of "schematism."[20] Choices narrowed when the "formalism controversy," discussed below, broke in early 1936. Then groups with ties to the Meyerhold Theater began to receive negative reviews.[21]

Numerous professional theaters established patronage relationships with amateur stages in the theater-rich cities of Moscow and Leningrad. The Central Trade Union Theater (Teatr vTssPs) in Moscow took oversight over a number of groups, including the Moscow-Kursk Railroad Club and the Metro Subway Builders' Club. The Meyerhold Theater worked together with the Elektrozavod factory. The Malyi Theater claimed control over the amateur work of the Sickle and Hammer factory.[22] In Leningrad, the most active patron was the Leningrad Oblast Trade Union Theater, which sent instructors to more than fifteen local groups.[23]

The meaning of "professionalization" changed in the 1930s. During the First Five-Year Plan, a number of formerly amateur groups found funding sources to free them from their day jobs. But this step was not enough to gain them widespread recognition as a professional circle. In addition, these groups had to embrace an established professional acting method. This was strikingly evident in the reorganization of the Moscow TRAM in 1933. This circle had technically turned professional in 1930: actors were paid and expected to work full-time in the theater. However, it was only when the artistic directorship was taken over by Il'ia Sudakov from the Moscow Art Theater that TRAM began to receive critical attention as a serious professional theater. The new training program at the Moscow TRAM theater introduced key elements from Stanislavsky's method, with actors learning to "live their parts."[24] By 1934, some theater critics in Moscow were comparing the TRAM collective to the original Stanislavsky circle. "Isn't a new cherry orchard being planted with [TRAM's] laughter and jokes?" queried one newspaper review, referring to one of the Chekhov plays that had established the Moscow Art Theater's reputation.[25]

20. N. Engel', "Tvorcheskaia konferentsiia leningradskoi samodeiatel'nosti," *Klub* 3 (1934): 55–56.

21. S. Room, "Teatral'naia samodeiatel'nost' na novom etape," RiT 18 (1936): 5.

22. Engel', "Tvorcheskaia konferentsiia leningradskoi samodeiatel'nosti," 55–57; D. M., "Konferentsiia zritelei teatra vTssPs," *Pravda* 23 October 1933; "Studiia Malogo teatra na zavode 'Serp i molot,' " *Pravda* 16 October 1935.

23. "Vstrecha tvorcheskogo aktiva teatrov profsoiuzov," 14 August 1934, GARF, f. 5451, op. 18, d. 509, l. 12.

24. V. Solov'ev, "Akter—vyrazitel' idei p'esy," *Teatr i dramaturgiia* 5 (1933): 30–32.

25. D. Zaslavskii, " 'Chudesnyi splav,' " *Pravda* 15 June 1934.

As this review indicates, the Moscow Art Theater (MAT) came to hold an elevated status among Soviet theaters in the 1930s. As evidence of its prestige, MAT directors and actors gained more influence over amateur stages. In addition to the Moscow TRAM, numerous club stages could boast workers from the famous theater, including the Krasnyi Bogatyr' factory, the Kukhmisterov Drama Club, and the Iakovlev Tobacco Workers' Club. MAT actors worked informally to supervise training programs, including those at the Central Woodworkers' Club. Some very well-off factories even paid to send their best actors to train at MAT, as was the case for one amateur actor from the Stalin auto plant.[26]

Training regimens in amateur theaters became much more rigorous. The Kauchuk Theater's program, led by Vasilii Kuza from the Vakhtangov Theater, required mandatory five-hour rehearsals five nights a week. Rehearsals lasted up to eight months on a single play. A range of teachers were involved in instruction, including a balletmaster. The Vakhtangov Theater's own design studio provided costumes. Interviews with eager club actors indicated that they took the new approach very seriously and looked upon their previous efforts as a kind of "bad dream."[27] Teachers from professional theaters also wrestled with the bad dream of earlier training, as they struggled to make students adapt to the rigor of new methods.[28]

With the turn to higher professional standards, many stages attempted to present offerings with greater social and historical authenticity. That meant visits to libraries and museums to learn about the social settings of chosen plays. To prepare for their performance of *Gossiping Women (Bab'i spletni)* by the eighteenth-century Italian playwright Carlo Goldoni, the actors at Leningrad's Iakovlev Club listened to Italian music and took trips to the Hermitage museum. Another Leningrad theater began correspondence with agents from the secret police in order to deepen their presentation of criminals transformed by the Soviet crimi-

26. Ia. Moskovoi, "Na poroge odinnadtsatogo," *Klub* 13 (1933): 44–45; Malov, "Uchimsia u MKhATA," *Klub* 21/22 (1934): 43; M. Berliant, "Desiat' let," *Klub* 2 (1935): 49; Norris Houghton, *Moscow Rehearsals: The Golden Age of Soviet Theatre* (New York: Harcourt Brace, 1936), 32. For a recent assessment of the influence of the Moscow Art Theater, see A. P. Shulgin, "Samodeiatel'nyi teatr v gorode," in S. Iu. Rumiantsev et al., eds., *Samodeiatel'noe khudozhestvennoe tvorchestvo v SSSR*, v. 2 (Moscow: Gosudarstvennyi institut iskusstvoznaniia, 1995), 169–70.

27. "Rabochii teatr zavoda 'Kauchuk,' " *Klub* 2 (1932): 56–57; S. Persov, "Samodeiatel'noe iskusstvo v klube zavoda 'Kauchuk,' " *Klub* 1 (1933): 39–40; V. Kuza, "Teatr 'Kauchuk' pod rukovodstvom Vakhtangovtsev," *Klub* 6 (1936): 33–35, quotation 34.

28. "Mkhatovtsy v teatral'noi samodeiatel'nosti," *Kul'turnaia rabota profsoiuzov* 14 (1938): 46.

nal justice system, a favorite theme of drama and literature in the 1930s.[29]

The cultural press presented work in amateur theaters as a social responsibility for artistic professionals. Interviews with directors often included earnest statements about the importance of providing assistance to club stages. Some directors offered their free time and even their apartments as rehearsal space.[30] The British leftist director André Van Gyseghem was amazed at the sense of responsibility that professionals felt for amateur actors, a relationship much different from what he knew in the capitalist West.[31] Whether their motivation came from idealism or material need, well-trained theater workers could earn considerable sums in amateur circles. The musician Juri Jelagin was able to triple the salary he earned at the Vakhtangov Theater by taking jobs in clubs. One Stanislavsky student, Andrei Efremov, supplemented what he earned as an instructor at the Moscow Theater Institute by participating in club training courses.[32]

These patronage relationships served to increase the distance between a few important club stages and the rest—not to mention exaggerating the difference between club theaters in the two main cities and the provinces. While some theaters in Moscow and Leningrad could boast palatial settings and an outstanding staff, others continued to struggle with supply problems reminiscent of the 1920s—with no place to rehearse and very few props.[33] Provincial theaters were even worse off. Representatives to a trade union club conference in 1935 complained that they did not even have enough funds to buy an adequate supply of scripts, let alone be overly concerned about production techniques.[34]

Club directors had to assume much more responsibility for the quality of the finished product in the 1930s. Their work was put to the test in periodic amateur theater competitions. Those who evoked fine perfor-

29. V. Derzhavin, "Teamasterskaia kluba im. Iakovleva," *Klub* 19 (1934): 43; "Rabochii teatr Volodarskogo Doma Kul'tury," *Klub* 2 (1934): 55.

30. See, for example, Nikolai Okhlopkov, "Samodeiatel'noe iskusstvo," *Pravda* 3 November 1935; "Mastera iskusstv o khudozhestvennoi samodeiatel'nosti," *Klub* 20 (1937): 38–39; "Mkhatovtsy v teatral'noi samodeiatel'nosti," *Kul'turnaia rabota profsoiuzov* 14 (1938): 46.

31. André Van Gysegham, *Theatre in Soviet Russia* (London: Faber and Faber, 1943), 150–53.

32. Juri Jelagin, *The Taming of the Arts*, trans. Nicholas Wreden (New York: Dutton, 1951), 214; Margaret Wettlin, *Fifty Russian Winters* (New York: John Wiley, 1994), 103, 119.

33. "Beseda s rukovoditeliami khudozhestvennykh samodeiatel'nykh kruzhkov," 5 April 1935, GARF, f. 5451, op. 19, d. 422, ll. 2–3.

34. "Stenogramma soveshchaniia pri klubnoi inspektsii VTSSPS," GARF, f. 5451, op. 19, d. 404, ll. 1–3.

mances won accolades, but those who did not were singled out for their poor practices and sometimes could even lose their jobs. As one jury member at a Moscow club competition explained it, "The young people are not to blame. We have to blame the leadership."[35] Directors who chose the "wrong" plays, like the Red Woodworker Club's production of a light-hearted Kataev work in 1935, were simply barred from higher levels of competition.[36] One club director issued a long mea culpa after his group came in last in the final round of the Moscow city-wide competition in 1937.[37] This atmosphere of insecurity and distrust made skilled drama instructors even harder to find, which in turn increased suspicion against them. A commentator in *Pravda* observed, "The leaders of drama circles are often self-seekers and amateurs. They are hounded out of one position but almost immediately find a place somewhere else."[38]

Reshaping the Repertoire

During the 1930s, the repertoire of amateur stages began to mimic that of professional theaters. Gone were the homemade works generated by club members themselves or minor authors who wrote strictly for club stages. Most contemporary plays by Western authors also vanished.[39] Like their professional counterparts, club theaters chose "hit" Soviet plays—like Konstantin Trenev's *Liubov' Iarovaia* and Vladimir Kirshon's *The Miraculous Alloy (Chudesnyi splav)*; they supplemented these works with a limited list of Russian and Western European prerevolutionary classics.

Oversight of amateur theater activity in clubs fell largely to trade union organizations. Although local Narkompros affiliates and city soviets still exercised some oversight and provided occasional funding, national and city trade union bureaucracies were the most directly involved in the daily life of club theaters. Through periodic conferences of club workers, trade union leaders urged local theaters to take their cul-

35. "Protokoly," TSMAM, f. 718, op. 8, d. 49, l. 44.

36. See "Stenogramma soveshchaniia pri klubnoi inspektsii VTSSPS," GARF, f. 5451, op. 19, d. 404, l. 54.

37. L. Subbotin, "Samodeiatel'nyi teatr," *Teatr* 6 (1938): 119.

38. I. Blinkov, "Pochemu skuchno v klube," *Pravda* 19 July 1935. See also Veprinskii, "Zrelishchnaia samodeiatel'nost' na moskovskom smotre 1933 goda," *Klub* 15 (1933): 38–39, and Kobra, "Za kulisami kluba," *Literaturnyi Leningrad* 7 (8 February 1936): 4.

39. Of course, there were exceptions to these broad trends. The Klub im. Iakovleva, for example, performed *Itogi serdtsa*, written by club leader V. P. Derzhavin in 1934. See V. Derzhavin, "Teamasterskaia kluba im. Iakovleva," *Klub* 19 (1934), 43.

tural tasks more seriously and turn away from agitational methods.[40] The cultural division of the national trade union bureaucracy founded the journal *Klub* in 1933, which offered the most detailed published accounts of amateur theatrical activity during the 1930s.[41] The Central Trade Union Theater opened a special school to train actors and directors for club circles.[42] In addition, both Moscow and Leningrad had their own professional trade union stages that premiered repertoire suitable for club theaters, performed in clubs, and encouraged talented workers to make their way to the professional stage.[43]

Some trade unions sponsored methodological seminars to help their affiliates move to a new kind of repertoire.[44] Just as they had in the early 1920s, club leaders and members put forward compelling "transformation stories" tracing their about-face in aesthetic methods. This time, however, they were moving from small forms to large ones. In one such tale, the Communist Party decision of 1932 galvanized members of the Theater Collective of Red Woodworkers into action. "The big play has returned once again and occupies its former position," noted the club leader Iakov Mostovoi. "But work on big plays must follow a new path and become deeper and more serious."[45]

Agitprop brigades did not disappear entirely, although they lost their centrality to club life. Theaters affiliated with the Moscow Chemical and Rubber Workers' Union, which included the Kauchuk factory, sponsored several different levels of theatrical activity. At the top came the premier club theaters, now run by professional directors and teachers. However, they continued to support agitprop brigades that staged works with titles like *The Loan Campaign in the Second Five-Year Plan*. The factories also sponsored smaller drama circles that worked on both small and large forms, ranging from Gorky plays to "thematic literary

40. "Tvorcheskaia konferentsiia po samodeiatel'nosti," RiT 35 (1933): 17; "Stenogramma i rezoliutsii tret'ego plenuma Moskovskogo gorodskogo soveta professional'nykh soiuzov," March 1933, TSMAM, f. 718, op. 8, d. 1, ll. 90–91; "Vstrechi tvorcheskogo aktiva teatrov profsoiuzov," 14 August 1934, GARF, f. 5451, op. 18, d. 509; "Stenogramma soveshchaniia pri klubnoi inspektsii VTSSPS," 1935, GARF, f. 5451, op. 19, d. 404, ll. 1–44.

41. *Klub* began publication in 1933; it was superceded by *Kul'turnaia rabota profsoiuzov* in 1938.

42. "Tekhnikum teatra VTSSPS," *Pravda* 21 May 1934.

43. A. B. Viner, "Teatr im. MOSPS i samodeiatel'noe iskusstvo," *Klub* 6 (1933): 50–51.

44. A. Iordanskii, "Samodeiatel'noe iskusstvo po soiuzy rabotnikov kooperatsii i gostorgovli," *Klub* 3 (1933): 44–45.

45. Iak. Mostovoi, "Na poroge odinnadtsatogo," *Klub* 13 (1933): 43. This issue of the journal *Klub* is filled with similar tales of restructuring.

evenings" on topics such as Bloody Sunday.[46] Yet even when clubs and factories continued to support brigades, their performances gradually became interchangeable with drama circle offerings. A Leningrad brigade performed a Molière play for the May Day holiday in 1933, a choice that would have been unthinkable a few years before.[47]

Some critics in the early 1930s continued to defend the need for agit-prop brigades because they could provide commentary on local workplace issues and respond quickly to state campaigns. The high-level trade union official, Dmitrii Marchenko, warned against the assumption that all agitprop brigades must someday turn into drama circles; all too often, amateur groups used the circles to avoid their social responsibilities altogether. "This theory is mistaken and politically dangerous," he intoned.[48] But the turn toward a professional ethos undercut his own strictures; the professional models that amateurs were now emulating were hostile to the organizational principles of agitprop brigades.

One author sympathetic to agitational theatrical forms lamented on the shift in repertoire taking place in the course of 1933. Very few works were written specifically for club stages anymore, observed A. Kasatkina, a writer for *Pravda*. Some playwrights, such as Vladimir Bill-Belotserkovskii, were willing to adapt their work for amateur theaters. However, other big names in Soviet theater, like Alexander Afinogenov and Anatolii Glebov, ignored these venues. That meant that club repertoires looked strikingly similar to professional theaters. She estimated that twenty to thirty percent of the plays on club stages came from the classics, with fifty to seventy percent coming from the professional stage. Only ten to fifteen percent of the works performed included any local contributions. While she praised the turn away from poor-quality *agitki*, Kasatkina lamented that amateur stages were losing their separate identity and their ability to address local problems.[49]

Works written specifically for amateur stages did not disappear en-

46. "Otchet po khudozhestvennoi rabote mosgorkoma soiuza rezino-khimicheskoi promyshlennosti s 1-go ianvaria po 14 iiunia 1933 g.," TSMAM, f. 718, op 8, d. 49, ll. 58–59.

47. A. Berlin, "Tvorcheskoe sorevnovanie," *Klub* 6 (1933): 46; see also reports at a national trade union club conference, where local leaders insist that their agitprop brigades perform "big" works by important Soviet playwrights like Kirshon and Bill-Belotserkovskii, "Stenogramma soveshchaniia pri klubnoi inspektsii VTSSPS," GARF, f. 5451, op. 19, d. 404, l. 27.

48. D. Marchenko, "Khudozhestvennaia samodeiatel'nost' millionov," *Teatr i dramaturgiia* 5 (1935): 15.

49. A. Kasatkina, "Problemy klubnogo repertuara," *Teatr i dramaturgiia* 8 (1933): 52–55. This article was sharply attacked a few months later for ignoring the principles of socialist realism; see N. Engel', "Tvorcheskaia konferentsiia leningradskoi samodeiatel'nosti," *Klub* 3 (1934): 58.

tirely before the anti-formalist campaign brought much tighter scrutiny over repertoire. Popular club authors from the 1920s, such as Vladimir Severnyi, still composed plays for club audiences. Konstantin Finn and Vitaly Derzhavin wrote works aimed primarily at amateur actors. The most prominent of these authors was Aleksei Arbuzov, who won praise in Kasatkina's article. Arbuzov would become a famous playwright in the Khrushchev era; however, in the 1930s his works were mainly performed by amateur theaters or by professional theaters that had recently made the transition from amateur status. He got his start as a writer of agitprop pieces during the First Five-Year Plan. In the 1930s he made his own transition to longer works. His lighthearted *Six Lovers (Shestero liubimykh)* found an audience in amateur theaters, like the Moscow Tobacco Workers' TRAM. His more serious investigation into the building of the Moscow subway, *The Long Road (Dal'niaia doroga)*, was also staged by the Moscow Central TRAM.[50]

Some 1930s playwrights composed crossover works popular on both amateur and professional stages. One of the best examples is Ivan Mikitenko's *Girls of Our Country (Devushki nashei strany)*, first performed by the Leningrad Drama Theater early in 1933. Later the same year the Moscow Central TRAM picked this play as its debut performance under new leadership from the Moscow Art Theater. By the summer, several important amateur stages, including the Krasnyi Bogatyr factory in Moscow and the Vyborg House of Culture in Leningrad, chose this work for summer theater competitions.[51] Addressing the transformation of gender roles and romantic relationships during the First Five-Year Plan, this work centered on the formation of a female shock work brigade to lay concrete for an electrical power plant. This popular play also offered evidence of the transformation of socialist culture toward more traditional models. In it, Komsomol members read Lermontov and play the cello. They are, in Mikitenko's words, already a working-class intelligentsia.[52] Several critics objected to the portrayals of the young women in the play, who, according to one, "acted like private school girls [*institutki*] from Charskaia [the popular prerevolutionary writer of literature addressed to girls]."[53]

Another widely performed work on both amateur and professional stages was *Miraculous Alloy (Chudesnyi splav)* by Vladimir Kirshon. This

50. "Khronika khudozhestvennoi samodeiatel'nosti," *Klub* 8 (1935): 63.

51. "Otchet po khudozhestvennoi rabote," TsMAM, f. 718, op. 8, d. 49, l. 60; *Klub* 10 (1932): 48.

52. I. Mikitenko, "Plachu dolg," in *Devushki nashei strany* (Leningrad: Gosudarstvennyi teatr dramy, 1933), 10.

53. M. Berliant, "Teatral'naia samodeiatel'nost' Leningrada," *Klub* 19 (1933): 54.

A scene from the Moscow TRAM's performance of *The Girls of Our Country (Devushki nashei strany)*. *Teatr i dramaturgiia* 4 (1934).

play was a winner in a national competition for the best new work in 1934. During the 1934–35 season, it played concurrently at the Moscow Art Theater, the Theater of Satire, the Moscow TRAM, and several smaller professional theaters in the city. In addition, it was widely distributed to amateur stages. The journal *Kolkhoz Theater* sent out copies to all of its subscribers in early 1935.[54] The play offers a humorous look at scientific work among Komsomol students who are searching for a new alloy for airplane construction. In the process, the disparate group of students who come from different social strata and geographic areas, forges itself into a tightly knit collective. At the conclusion of the play, the institute director announces to the group: "You yourselves are the miraculous alloy, my friends, the most steadfast material against corrosion."[55] The play remained a favorite on amateur stages until Kirshon fell victim to the purges of 1937.

The 1934 play *Aristocrats (Aristokraty)* by Nikolai Pogodin was also popular on both professional and amateur stages.[56] It examines the

54. L. Tamashin, *Vladimir Kirshon: Ocherk tvorchestva* (Moscow: Sovetskii pisatel', 1965), 183; N. Gorchakov, "*Chudesnyi splav* v moskovskikh teatrakh," *Kolkhoznyi teatr* 2 (1935): 15.

55. Vladimir Kirshon, *Chudesnyi splav: Komediia v chetyrekh aktakh* (Moscow: Iskusstvo, 1956), 93.

56. "Teatral'naia dekada," *Klub* 5 (1936): 47.

reeducation of prisoners sent to build the White Sea Canal, a Stalinist work project administered by the secret police. The play traces the rehabilitation of thieves, prostitutes, and "wrecker" engineers who had been imprisoned for sabotaging Stalinist industrial programs. Inspired by the benevolent models of their secret police overseers, these outcasts are turned into useful, patriotic citizens through their labor. This panegyric to forced labor was even performed at the White Sea Project itself by imprisoned amateur actors.[57]

As choices among contemporary plays narrowed, amateur stages turned to the prerevolutionary classics. The Soviet regime sponsored a select list of classic authors as part of its general effort to show the cultural achievements of socialism. Public celebrations of these literary giants were a central feature of the Stalinist spectacle state. Festivities included elaborate performances, lectures, newspaper articles, carnivals, and even special consumption items. Among those fêted were Alexander Pushkin, Anton Chekhov, Maxim Gorky, Lev Tolstoi, and Lope de Vega.[58] The celebration marking the centennial of Pushkin's death went on for more than a year, from late 1935 until early 1937. Pushkin's works were integrated into the school curriculum, and special Pushkin cakes went on sale.[59] Amateur stages were drawn into the festivities. They staged a spate of short Pushkin works and even a few attempts at the opera *Evgenii Onegin*.[60] When Gorky was commemorated, Moscow amateur theaters staged a ten-day festival honoring his work.[61] The official reevaluation of Chekhov, who been rejected by many during the 1920s for offering a overly sentimental look at the dying aristocracy, brought a resurgence of his plays on club stages.[62]

57. On the significance of the play, see Cynthia A. Ruder, *Making History for Stalin: The Story of the Belomor Canal* (Gainesville: University Press of Florida, 1998), 155–73, and Natalia Kuziakina, *Theatre in the Solovki Prison Camp* (Luxembourg: Harwood Academic Publishers, 1995), 121, 138.

58. V. N. Aizenshtadt, *Sovetskii samodeiatel'nyi teatr* (Kharkov: Khar'kovskii gosudarstvennyi institut kul'tury, 1983), 54.

59. Karen Petrone, *Life Has Become More Joyous, Comrades: Celebrations in the Time of Stalin* (Bloomington: Indiana University Press, forthcoming) ch. 4.

60. L. Volkov, "Teatry v pushkinskie dni," *Pravda* 1 February 1937; "Pushkinskie dni v Moskovskikh klubakh," *Klub* 2 (1937): 46–48.

61. M. Berliant, "Dramaturgiia A. M. Gor'kogo v samodeiatel'nom teatre," *Klub* 12 (1937): 30–34; S. Valerin, "Gor'kovskaia dekada samodeiatel'nykh teatrov," *Klub* 15 (1937): 46–48.

62. M. Troianskii and P. Valentinskii, "Sed'maia Olimpiada khudozhestvennoi samodeiatel'nosti," *RiT* 14 (1933): 20; V. Bliumenfel'd, "Klassiki v samodeiatel'nom teatre," *RiT* 23 (1933): 6; Lesli, "Dramkruzhok kluba im. Kukhmisterova," *Klub* 19 (1934): 39.

By far the most popular Russian author was Alexander Ostrovsky, whose plays came to assume a greater prominence than they had enjoyed since the revolution. At a 1933 competition of amateur theaters in Leningrad, more than fifty percent of the works performed were from the classics, with Ostrovsky as the most popular playwright.[63] His plays also dominated the offerings at Moscow club theaters in the summer of 1934.[64] Amateur stages making the difficult transition from an agitational repertoire to more conventional plays often made an Ostrovsky work their first choice. When the Kukhmisterov Club theater was reorganized under new management in 1934, its opening work was *The Ward (Vospitannitsa)*.[65] Indeed, Ostrovsky's plays had made such inroads into amateur performances by 1936 that trade union club activists determined that his *Not a Cent and Suddenly a Windfall (Ne bylo ni grosha, da vdrug altyn)* and *A Family Affair (Svoi liudy—sochtemsia!)* were the most likely representatives of the classics in club repertoires.[66] The fiftieth anniversary of Ostrovsky's death, celebrated in the summer of 1936, only served to heighten his popularity. "A broad program of mass performances of Ostrovsky's work is being carried out in plants, houses of culture, and red corners," reported a Leningrad cultural journal. All the major factories sponsored lectures and performances of works by the nineteenth-century playwright.[67]

Playwright Anatolii Glebov (who had gotten his start in the club theaters of the 1920s) tried to assess Ostrovsky's central place on amateur stages. In a long article published in 1937, he cited reams of statistics showing that Ostrovsky's plays constituted almost twenty percent of all those performed on *kolkhoz* stages; in the Soviet Union as a whole, they were performed by amateurs some 150,000 times a year.[68] Glebov argued that the reason for the playwright's success was that he wrote for the broad masses: "The simplicity and strength of his composition, the richness and populism of his characters and language, and, most impor-

63. V. Bliumenfel'd, "Klassiki v samodeiatel'nom teatre," RiT 23 (1933): 6.
64. M. Berliant, "Obzor repertuara moskovskikh dramaticheskikh kruzhkov," *Klub* 9 (1934): 36.
65. "Dramkruzhok kluba im. Kukhmisterova," *Klub* 19 (1934): 39.
66. M. Berliant, "Itogi teatral'nogo soveshchaniia," *Klub* 4 (1936): 52.
67. "K 50-letiiu so dnia smerti Ostrovskogo," *Literaturnyi Leningrad* 27 (12 June 1936): 4.
68. A. Glebov, "Ostrovskii v teatral'noi samodeiatel'nosti," *Teatr* 4 (1937): 116. His figures came from the Dom samodeiatel'nogo iskusstva, which primarily monitored amateur work in the countryside. Glebov opens by arguing that Ostrovsky performances had fallen off in urban amateur theaters, but the rest of his article contradicts this.

tant, the deep understanding of the psychology of the people, his ability to think their thoughts—this is why Ostrovsky attracts the Soviet worker and collective farmer."[69] We might add that Ostrovsky's plays were published in large editions in the 1930s, making them readily available. In addition, Ostrovsky's works were one constant element of the classical repertoire that could claim an unbroken lineage on the amateur stage going back to prerevolutionary days, giving the playwright the advantage of familiarity. One participant in the Kauchuk theater production of *A Family Affair* confessed that she had a long history in amateur theater: "I've performed for a long time, ever since childhood, in many Ostrovsky plays."[70]

Amateur repertoire was policed through periodic amateur theatrical Olympiads sponsored by trade unions. These gatherings were a method to bring the practice of individual groups under the scrutiny of trade union officials and state cultural functionaries, who dispensed prizes and sanctions for winning and losing circles. Leningrad unions had instituted annual summer Olympiads already in 1926. Moscow amateur theaters never had the same kind of regularized annual competitions, but they performed in a variety of union-wide and city-wide Olympiads and "dekady," ten-day festivals, throughout the 1930s. In both cities, competitions had a celebratory spirit, allowing theater participants to show their accomplishments and win the attention of the press. These competitions were small versions of the big Stalinist festivities of the 1930s, with grand opening ceremonies, parades, and mass gatherings in central parts of the city.[71]

The 1933 summer competitions in Leningrad and Moscow were the first chance amateur theater circles had to show that they had indeed been transformed by the decisions made in the wake of the 1932 national Olympiad. The turn to the classics at the Leningrad competition, where more than half of the plays were written before the revolution, was widely interpreted as an indication that amateur circles had decided to improve their repertoire.[72] Groups in Moscow faced a rigorous panel of

69. Ibid., 118.

70. "Teatr Kauchuk pod rukovodstvom vakhtangovtsev," *Klub* 8 (1934): 34.

71. The Seventh Leningrad Olympiad, for example, opened with a gathering in the main square of the city and a mass performance of eight thousand circle members (*Pravda* 9 June 1933).

72. Gomello, "O nekotorykh tvorcheskikh itogakh VII leningradskoi olimpiady," *Klub* 10 (1933): 48; V. Bliumenfel'd, "Klassiki v samodeiatel'nom teatre," RiT, 23 (1933): 6.

judges that included the writer Fedor Gladkov. These observers sharply criticized theater circles that had not practiced enough and censured works that appeared "as if they were two years old"—a reference to overly agitational plays that still bore the stamp of the First Five-Year Plan.[73] At competitions the following year, some groups continued to disappoint critics. Five agitprop brigades performed in the annual Leningrad competition in 1934, showing what one commentator denounced as "1930-style work."[74]

Competitions vividly revealed the standardization of amateur repertoire. In the early 1930s there were still embarrassing gaffes at these events, such as when one factory circle chose to perform a long-forbidden play by Sofia Belaia, *The Abandoned Children (Besprizornye)* in a 1934 festival in Moscow's Proletarian District.[75] By 1938, such errors had been eradicated. At a Leningrad competition that year, only fifteen plays were allowed in the final competition.[76] The elaborate Moscow city competition of amateur theater in the spring and summer of 1938 featured a strikingly limited program. Half of the seventy-six theater groups that made it to the second round of the competition chose prerevolutionary works, and almost half of these were by Ostrovsky, the safest and most conventional choice.[77]

Aesthetic and Political Purges

By the second decade of the revolution, purges were a well-established fact of life within the Communist Party, which conducted periodic "cleansings" of its membership. The practice of denunciation and expulsion was integrated into universities in the 1920s. In addition, already during the First Five-Year Plan, warring artistic factions learned how to paint their opponents as political outlaws. Thus, the waves of purges that shook the nation in ever-widening circles in the 1930s were not without precedent. What was different was the extent and the consequences. Early in the decade, being "purged" from the Communist Party had significant but still non-lethal results. The victims, like the cultural director at the Kauchuk Club, lost his party membership and his

73. "Protokoly," TSMAM, f. 718, op. 8, d. 49, l. 47.

74. A. Berlin, "Vos'maia leningradskaia olimpiada," *Klub* 17 (1934): 34; M. Veprinskii, "Teatral'naia samodeiatel'nost' na moskovskom smotre," *Klub* 5 (1934): 47.

75. M. Veprinskii, "Teatral'naia samodeiatel'nost' na moskovskom smotre," 47.

76. A. Liubosh, "Smotr leningradskoi samodeiatel'nosti," *Iskusstvo i zhizn'* 2 (1938): 31.

77. L. Subbotin, "Nekotorye vyvody iz smotra teatral'noi samodeiatel'nosti," *Kul'turnaia rabota profsoiuzov* 12 (1938): 77.

job. His particular crime was "political illiteracy."[78] As the decade progressed, however, purges drew in a much wider public and ruined the lives of those caught up in the whirlwind. By 1937, the start of the Great Purges, the accused were charged with wrecking, spying, and treason. They now faced imprisonment, exile, and execution.[79]

Soviet cultural establishments also underwent ideological purges during the decade, as the government tried to shape a unified cultural doctrine for the nation. An important channel of artistic standardization was the Soviet Writers' Union, inaugurated in 1934. In early 1936, the state took an additional step by forming the National Committee of the Arts to oversee theater, film, literature, music, and the visual arts. This new body waged an aggressive battle, known as the "anti-formalist campaign," against the remnants of pre-1930s cultural ideas. As the purges progressed, accusers conflated political and aesthetic errors, linking the charge "formalist" to that of "Trotskyist."

The Arts Committee was headed by none other than Platon Kerzhentsev, author of *Creative Theater* and once a passionate advocate of a separate path for the amateur stage. He had already shown his intellectual flexibility by spearheading criticisms of TRAM during the First Five-Year Plan. Perhaps because of Kerzhentsev, the committee extended its attention beyond the professional arts to amateur work as well. It claimed "general methodological leadership" over the amateur arts and promised to coordinate the work of trade unions with other organizations sponsoring amateur artistic activity.[80]

At the same time the committee took shape, the national newspaper, *Pravda*, published an anonymous editorial attacking the work of the musician Dmitrii Shostakovich, in the first salvo of the anti-formalist campaign. Leonid Maksimenkov has compellingly argued that Kerzhentsev, acting for the committee, was the author of the *Pravda* publication.[81] Entitled "Muddle instead of Music," this document denounced Shosta-

78. "Stenogramma soveshchaniia o minimume znanii dlia zavklubov ot 7/XII/1934," GARF, f. 2306, op. 39, d. 5, l. 39.

79. There is a vast literature on the purges of the 1930s. For a recent study based on Communist Party archival sources, see J. Arch Getty and Oleg V. Naumov, *The Road to Terror: Stalin and the Self-Destruction of the Bolsheviks* (New Haven: Yale University Press, 1999). Fitzpatrick's *Everyday Stalinism* address the purges in the artistic community, *Everyday Stalinism*, 190–217.

80. Aizenshtadt, *Sovetskii samodeiatel'nyi teatr*, 44.

81. Leonid Maksimenkov, *Sumbur vmesto muzyki: Stalinskaia kul'turnaia revoliutsiia, 1936–1938* (Moscow: Iuridicheskaia kniga, 1997), 88–112.

kovich's previously acclaimed opera, *Lady Macbeth of the Mtsensk District*, as a dissonant cacophony, "a 'leftist' muddle instead of authentic, human music." As evidence that the opera was an example of petty-bourgeois, futurist experimentation, the editorial cited its popularity among bourgeois audiences in the West. In a clear sign to those involved in theater, the article called Shostakovich's errors remnants of "Meyerholdism" transferred into music.[82]

Republished in a number of key cultural journals, the attack on Shostakovich provided a basic vocabulary for the anti-formalist campaign, with its censure of works that were overly experimental, abstract, complicated, and "Western." At a national meeting of the Art Workers' Union shortly after the editorial was published, Kerzhentsev announced that the lessons of the *Pravda* article should be applied everywhere, since there were similar failings in all areas of the arts.[83] Various artistic disciplines organized public gatherings at which individuals added their own contributions. At a meeting of theater professionals in the summer of 1936, speakers not only criticized themselves but used the occasion to attack both Shostakovich and Meyerhold. The stage director Nikolai Okhlopk, for example, determined that he himself was not free of all the elements of petty-bourgeois aesthetics of the early Soviet years. But he certainly never had gone to the extremes that Meyerhold had. He never allowed a jazz band in a Gogol play or made Ostrovsky characters walk a tightrope. Sergei Radlov complained that the problem of formalism, and of Meyerhold, was essentially one of arrogance; it was a process by which the director placed himself above everything else in the play, including the actors and even the author. On this occasion, Meyerhold himself spoke and defended his right to artistic experimentation, rejecting the charge that he had neglected content in favor of form.[84]

Amateur theaters were quickly drawn into the formalism controversy. One of the foremost contributors and defenders of the theater of small forms in the 1920s, Adrian Piotrovskii, was engaged in a very direct way.

82. "Sumbur vmesto muzyki," *Pravda* 28 January 1936. On this episode in Soviet culture, see Sheila Fitzpatrick, "The *Lady Macbeth* Affair: Shostakovich and the Soviet Puritans," in idem, *The Cultural Front: Power and Culture in Revolutionary Russia* (Ithaca: Cornell University Press, 1992), 183–215; Evgenii Gromov, *Stalin: Vlast' i iskusstvo* (Moscow: Respublika, 1998), 245–53; Maksimenkov, *Sumbur vmesto muzyki*.

83. "III Plenum TsK Rabis," *Sovetskii teatr* 3 (1936): 3.

84. "Protiv formalizma i naturalizma," *Teatr i dramaturgiia* 4 (1936): 196, 198; Meyerhold's contribution is on pages 207–10.

He was denounced by name in a second *Pravda* attack on Shostakovich, "False Ballet." This renewed salvo directed at the composer was aimed at his ballet *Bright Stream (Svetlyi ruchei)*, for which Piotrovskii had written the libretto. The newspaper charged that the ballet, which was set in the Kuban, had nothing local or specific about it. The libretto depicted none of the peoples of the Caucasus with any individuality.[85]

As the campaign gained strength, amateur stages faced even greater scrutiny, especially during competitions. Theaters attempting innovative stagings of prerevolutionary plays quickly ran into trouble. Leveling the charge of formalism, critics attacked theaters that sought to update the classics. Declared one Leningrad observer, "In amateur theater the remnants of 'Meyerholdism' have not been extinguished. . . . One can find many examples of vulgar sociological approaches, especially in performances of Chekhov and Ostrovsky."[86] A substantial list of productions were singled out for their "distortions" in a long article in the trade union journal *Klub*. The Aviakhim club's staging of *The Marriage of Figaro* was censured in terms taken straight from *Pravda*. Many aspects of the opera were not combined in an organic way, leaving viewers with a "muddle." This same article denounced the Leningrad Iakovlev Club's setting of Shakespeare's *Merry Wives of Windsor* in the contemporary era and the Bolshevik factory's performance of Gogol's *The Wedding*, staged in an exaggerated grotesque style. The TRAM circle from Moscow's Elektrozavod factory, which had long-standing ties to the Meyerhold Theater, was chided for its obvious elements of "Meyerholdism." The article concluded with an ominous-sounding warning, "Amateur theatrical work and popular art [*narodnoe tvorchestvo*] is imbued with foreign influences [*chuzhdye vlianiia*] because of the low level of club directors and the weak leadership . . . exercised by trade unions."[87]

Directors of amateur theaters issued their own statements of self-criticism and denunciation, just like the professionals. One Moscow club director, A. S. Azarkh of the Financial Bank Workers' Club, confessed to elements of formalism and excessive exaggeration in his productions of a Chekhov work and a contemporary Soviet play, *The Iron Stream (Zheleznyi potok)*. He promised to devote far more preparation to each

85. "Baletnaia fal'sh'," *Pravda* 8 February 1936.

86. S. Room, "Teatral'naia samodeiatel'nost' na novom etape," RiT 18 (1936): 5.

87. "O formalizme, bezgramotnosti i khalture v teatral'noi samodeiatel'nosti," *Klub* 9 (1936): 40–42, quotation 42. See also M. Berliant, "Shekspir na rabochei stsene," *Narodnoe tvorchestvo* 1 (1937): 36.

play, only planning two different stagings a year.[88] Amateur stages run by directors trained by Meyerhold and those few Moscow venues with ties to the Meyerhold Theater were subject to particularly close scrutiny. And some authors' work, like that of Arbuzov, came under attack. Glebov, one of the most prolific critics of the amateur stage in the late 1930s, accused Arbuzov's work of containing "formalist elements" and presenting an overly symmetrical, "geometric" view of Soviet life.[89]

The anti-formalist campaign began before the political purges had made significant inroads into the artistic community. However, the beginning of the big purge trials in the summer of 1936 created an atmosphere in which aesthetic errors could easily be turned into political crimes.[90] The trial of Zinoviev and Kamenev included the theater critic and magazine editor Richard Pikel as one of the defendants. He had once worked as Zinoviev's secretary and now was branded as a member of the "Moscow Terrorist Center." In particular, his treachery in promoting "Trotskyist plays" was brought up as evidence against him.[91]

In 1937, Kirshon and Afinogenov were caught up in the purges, both accused of being Trotskyist agents. A special meeting of Moscow playwrights in April of that year was largely devoted to denunciations of their work.[92] Since Kirshon's plays in particular were very important to clubs, this posed yet another problem for circles faced with a diminishing repertoire. Those who followed the accusations closely needed to find substitutions. Those who did not were themselves at risk of accusations for "Trotskyist" sympathies. As more and more Soviet playwrights came under the sweep of the purges, including Ivan Mikitenko, Sergei Tretiakov, and Nikolai Erdman, amateur stages that had performed their work faced ostracism or worse.[93]

The political purges brought even greater scrutiny over club leader-

88. "Rabotniki khudozhestvennoi samodeiatel'nosti ob urokakh tvorcheskoi diskussii," *Klub* 13 (1936): 38.

89. A. Glebov, "Samodeiatel'nyi teatr i ego dramaturgiia," *Teatr i dramaturgiia* 6 (1936): 314.

90. Maksimenkov, *Sumbur vmesto muzyki*, 10–11.

91. "Prigovor po delu trotskistsko-zinov'evskogo terroristicheskogo tsentra," *Teatr i dramaturgiia* 8 (1936): 449–50; "Zorche vzgliad, tverzhe ruka!," ibid., 453–55. On Pikel's background, see Fitzpatrick, *Everyday Stalinism*, 197–98.

92. I. Lezhnev, "Sobranie moskovskikh dramaturgov," *Pravda* 29 April 1937.

93. On the effects of the purges in the theatrical world, see Nikolai A. Gorchakov, *The Theater in Soviet Russia* (New York: Columbia University Press, 1957), 364–65. For complaints about provincial circles that still staged plays by the "Trotskyists" Kirshon and Afinogenov in 1937, see A. Berlin, "Korennye nedostatki rukovodstva khudozhestvennoi samodeiatel'nost'iu," *Klub* 12 (1937): 25–27.

ship. In late 1937, the trade union bureaucracy conducted a "cleansing" of club theater workers, focusing primarily on their professional qualifications. But political loyalties entered into the investigation as well. Those conducting the investigation complained that club theater directors did not seem to know about the anti-formalist campaign and its attendant political ramifications. They were not aware of the exposure of Kirshon and Afinogenov as part of a Trotskyist conspiracy and still staged works by the popular authors.[94] In the course of the investigation, trade union officials determined that only fifty-one of the two thousand people investigated possessed the highest qualifications for their work. Almost four hundred people were removed from their jobs. Even after the inspection, concluded one official, artistic work in clubs continued to attract "alien and accidental people."[95]

A few club directors lost their jobs for overt political actions. One investigation determined that a small circle taking part in training courses designed for club theater leaders in 1937 sang anti-Soviet *chastushki*, defended Karl Radek, currently on trial as a spy, and denounced the show trials as an elaborate confabulation, using the term *instsenirovka* for a theatrical display concocted out of a variety of non-literary sources.[96] The ouster of factory leaderships during the purges often caused cleansings of the entire administrative structure, including club leadership. At the Red Dawn telephone factory in Leningrad, the directorship was unmasked as "Trotskyists" in 1937; the club leader, perhaps reading the handwriting on the wall, "simply disappeared."[97]

The political purges reinforced amateur stages' already existing tendency to retreat to the safety of the classics to avoid contemporary works. However, one notable exception was a purge hit entitled *The Confrontation (Ochnaia stavka)*, written by Lev Sheinin and the Brothers Tur (a pseudonym for Leonid Tubelskii and Piotr Ryzhei) in 1937. Amateur groups in Moscow and Leningrad staged it many times, and it was the single most popular play at the Moscow amateur competition in 1938.[98] Sheinin was himself a criminal investigator who had helped the notorious state prosecutor, Andrei Vyshinskii, in a number of show tri-

94. Berlin, "Korennye nedostatki rukovodstva," 24–25.

95. Ibid. For the results in Leningrad alone, see A. Liubotsh, "Deklaratsii i praktika," RiT 5 (1937): 58.

96. Glusov and Smirnov, "Dokladnaia zapiska. Sekretariu vtssps tov. Veinbergu, G. D.," GARF, f. 5451, op. 21, d. 135, ll. 23–26.

97. G. Mikhailov, "Zhivaia rabota zamerla," Klub 18 (1937): 63.

98. L. Subbotin, "Nekotorye vyvody iz smotra teatral'noi samodeiatel'nosti," Kul'turnaia rabota profsoiuzov 12 (1938): 77.

als.[99] His play offered audiences and actors a simple explanation for the political upheaval shaking the nation. The main villains are two spies trained by the Gestapo. These unsavory characters are unmasked through the vigilance of ordinary Soviet citizens, who immediately report unusual events to the secret police. A wily peasant notices strange movements along the border and manages to foil an illegal crossing. A young student who has just arrived to Moscow is given someone else's letter by mistake and takes it straight to the police. The spies come dangerously close to success because they have help from Trotskyist groups within the country. But in the end, they are no match for the collective power of the Soviet citizenry. When one of the spies warns that a massive network is ready to infiltrate the Soviet Union, the star of the show, a Soviet secret police agent, laughs off the threat. "We have one hundred seventy million willing helpers."[100]

The political message of *The Confrontation* is transparent—potential enemies are everywhere. The foreign infiltrators know Russian perfectly. They recite poems by Alexander Blok before dispatching Soviet citizens to their death. In addition, they have plenty of help from evil forces within the nation. The informants who bring their suspicions to the secret police are always correct; in each instance, their information proves crucial in cornering the spies. As one model citizen tells his doubting wife, "I am not going [to inform] in order to be thanked. I am going because it is necessary."[101] An American viewer who saw the play in Magnitogorsk commented, "They may catch some spies now, but it will take a generation to live down the fear and suspicion being created."[102]

Actors and Spectators

Reporters presented the achievements of amateur theaters to the public in a new way in the years of the Second Five-Year Plan. A decade earlier, groups were assessed for their collective performances, and individuals were rarely mentioned. Now directors, actors, and even set designers gave extensive interviews. Participants traced their humble

99. Arkady Vaksberg, *The Prosecutor and the Prey: Vyshinsky and the 1930s Moscow Show Trials*, trans. Jan Butler (London: Weidenfeld and Nicholson, 1990), 66, 68–69, 74–75.

100. Brat'ia Tur and L. Sheinin, *Ochnaia stavka* (Moscow: Iskusstvo, 1938), 79. See also Sheila Fitzpatrick's discussion of this play, *Everyday Stalinism*, 203.

101. Ibid., 60.

102. John Scott, *Behind the Urals: An American Worker in Russia's City of Steel*, ed. Stephen Kotkin (Bloomington: Indiana University Press, 1989), 203.

beginnings, charted their progress from supporting to major parts, and shared their tips for learning roles. One club star shared how he was inspired by a glimpse of a fellow bus rider to develop the proper posture for his part; another recommended attending museums to gain the necessary background for a Shakespeare play.[103] The journal *Klub* offered a venue for amateur theater workers to tell their stories, publishing short biographies and interviews. These highly selective portraits show amateur actors engaged in a self-education process, using theater as a path to a broadly defined *kul'turnost'*. Here they learned not only the classics of world drama and the contemporary stage; they were also exposed to lessons in diction and fashion. Trips to libraries and museums established these institutions as resources for the cultured individual.

Using the categories of the theorist Pierre Bourdieu, we can see how amateur theatrical training in the 1930s helped participants to accumulate valuable cultural capital.[104] It gave them access to a state-promoted list of cultural references, teaching them the importance of Chekhov and Lope de Vega. Theatrical training also offered participants cues on proper manners, speech, and deportment. In this sense, taking part in amateur theater could cultivate a sense of cultural refinement. For those who pursued professional stage careers, amateur training also became an avenue for social advancement.

This sense of the theater circle as a kind of cultural accumulation process is especially apparent in the accounts of recent migrants to the city. The 1930s was a period of heightened rural-urban migration, as industrial expansion attracted peasants from the impoverished countryside.[105] One recent female recruit to factory life, a worker at Moscow's Klara Tsetkin factory, used work in the drama circle to spark her interest in cultural life in general. Only a few months after running from her first audition in fear, she won a sizeable role. Gaining confidence from that success, she joined a music circle and began to subscribe to a newspaper. All of this led her to become a stalwart member of the Komsomol.[106] One "young country boy" attested to the importance of the club in general and theater in particular to his cultural development. He was

103. "Profsoiuznye kluby dolzhny pomogat' rostu rabotnits," *Klub* 5 (1935): 34–35; "Kak my ovladevali obrazami Shekspira," *Klub* 6 (1936): 39–41.

104. Pierre Bourdieu, *Distinction: A Social Critique of the Judgement of Taste*, trans. Richard Nice (Cambridge: Harvard University Press, 1984), 53–54, 114–15.

105. For migration to Moscow, see David L. Hoffmann, *Peasant Metropolis: Social Identities in Moscow, 1929–1941* (Ithaca: Cornell University Press, 1994), 32–72.

106. N. Filippova, "V klube rastem my i nashi deti," *Klub* 5 (1934): 30–31.

amazed at the fine appearance of other club members, whom he at first mistook for engineers and not other workers like himself. He quickly learned that to attend the club, one had to dress well (*chisto odevat'sia*). The drama circle taught him the importance of cultured, accurate speech. He was then inspired to go to the library to read "not simply for enjoyment, but to understand life." The theater circle took him on field trips to museums, planetariums, and professional stages. He eventually ended up as a union activist and tripled his starting salary.[107] One Georgian member of the Paris Commune factory TRAM attested to the importance of theater work for his Russian-language skills. Before taking part his Russian had been weak, but the theater circle had taught him to express himself freely. Another non-Russian worker, a Tatar, used amateur theater as a method to organize his fellow countrymen at the Rusakov club.[108]

These tales of the civilizing mission of the theater stressed the use value of theatrical training in participants' daily lives, teaching them labor discipline, new views on social interaction, and vital life skills. "Work in the [theater] circle has taught me a better attitude toward my own growth and my productive work," opined one member of the Proletarian Club in Moscow. "Now I am a member of the Party, a brigadier, a labor organizer, and I am always looking to improve my qualifications." A machinist at the Kukhmisterov club in Moscow claimed to be inspired by the positive heroes that he portrayed. "I want to become just like them."[109]

In these narratives of self-improvement, it is as if the dreams of prerevolutionary activists in popular theater, who saw drama as a method to tame the uneducated *narod*, had finally come true. Amateur actors testified to the theater's ability to make them well-dressed, punctual, and responsible, all part of the prerevolutionary agenda. But they also show that the Soviet stage was a means for amateurs to learn how to "speak Bolshevik," to use Stephen Kotkin's phrase.[110] They valued their work in amateur circles not only for its own sake or for the contribution that it made to their personal development as a cultured individuals. In addition, they stressed its significance for the labor productivity of the Soviet Union.

Successful amateur actors gained tangible rewards from their activi-

107. V. Nikiforov, "My vyrosli v klube," *Klub* 23/24 (1934): 3.
108. "Chto nam daet klub," *Klub* 23/24 (1934): 7.
109. Malov, "Uchimsia u MKhATA," *Klub* 21/22 (1934): 43.
110. Stephen Kotkin, *Magnetic Mountain: Stalinism as Civilization* (Berkeley: University of California Press, 1995), 198–237.

ties. More serious training programs opened up the chance to move on to the professional stage. Even if they stayed amateurs, they could win modest fame in their local work environment. The Moscow Proletarii Club hung pictures of amateur performers next to those of shock workers.[111] A few "stars" of the amateur world found notoriety in national journals, such as the Kauchuk actress, Klava Soloveva, praised in an article in *Klub* for her spirited portrayal of Kate in Shakespeare's *Taming of the Shrew*. In her own celebrity interview, Soloveva was able to discuss her progress to the top of the amateur theatrical world and to reveal how the experience of working on such a demanding part had increased her skills as an actor.[112] A year later, the Kauchuk factory sent Soloveva to study full-time at the Vakhtangov Theater School.[113]

Viewers gained a store of references to prerevolutionary culture by attending amateur performances. In addition, contemporary plays offered them instruction about appropriate manners in the restructured Soviet workplace. They showed, for example, that responsible women workers were now a force to be acknowledged. In a marked contrast to agitprop works, plays in the Second Five-Year Plan gave women important roles. *Girls of Our Country* pronounces this fact already in its title. *Miraculous Alloy* features aspiring women scientists. Arbuzov's *The Long Road* places a woman in charge of shock brigade building the Moscow subway. Konstantin Trenev's *Liubov Iarovaia*, about a woman commander in the Civil War, was written in the 1920s but only became a staple of amateur stages in the following decade.

Amateur performers had a very different relationship to their audiences than they had in the 1920s. While plays still had an obvious political agenda, the propaganda was less aggressive than during the First Five-Year Plan. Amateur productions tried to give viewers positive role models and to instill common cultural standards, but the audience's status as observers was not assaulted. No one tried to extract funds or shock work participants from the viewers seated in newly designed stately auditoriums. The raised proscenium stages gave the audience anonymity—the actors were on display, not the viewer.

The Soviet press presented the changes in amateur stages as audience-driven; the more sophisticated tastes of viewers had moved amateur

---

111. M. Veprinskii, "Teatral'naia samodeiatel'nost' fabrik i zavodov," *Kolkhoznyi teatr* 7/8 (1936): 54.

112. M. Berliant, " 'Ukroshchenie stroptivoi' v klube zavoda 'Kauchuk,' " *Klub* 6 (1936): 32; "Kak my ovladevali obrazami Shekspira," ibid., 39, 42.

113. "Rabotnitsa na stsene teatra," *Kul'turnaia rabota profsoiuzov* 3/4 (1938): 43–44.

stages to abandon simple agitational works and disjointed performances. It is difficult to confirm or deny this assertion, since the voices
of the viewers are hard to find. The scanty sources from the 1920s, such
as audience response forms and interviews by worker correspondents,
disappeared in the next decade. Judging only from the fact that the
biggest clubs filled their large halls, these performances certainly found
an audience. Yet, from the very structure of these events, we can also
conclude that amateur theatricals served a different function in the lives
of viewers than they had earlier. Performances were now a special
event, staged infrequently by well-coached actors. The rowdy evenings
of the 1920s, where actors were barely differentiated from the audience,
were a thing of the past.

Effacing the Amateur

By the late 1930s, the concept of *"samodeiatel'nost'"* was as problematic
as it had been in the first years of Soviet power. Then, leaders needed to
extract the idea of the Soviet amateur from notions of worker self-determination and autonomy put forward by factions of the trade union
movement, the Proletkult, and the Workers' Opposition. In the late
1930s, *samodeiatel'nost'* needed to be rescued from the theorists of the
1920s, who had proposed a different and separate path for amateur theater. Critics initially rejected these ideas as "leftist" and "constructivist"
notions. By 1937, the political purges brought ominous new elements to
the charges; the ideas were branded as "harmful" and sometimes even
"Trotskyist."[114] One of the most eloquent advocates of those earlier theories, Adrian Piotrovskii, was arrested as a Fascist agent in 1937.[115]

The spontaneous and imperfect aspects of amateur theaters were ef-
faced in the verbal accounts of their achievements in the late 1930s.
Samodeiatel'nost' now came to stand for the creative potential of the Soviet people, who, with proper diligence and training, could aspire to the
artistic standards of professionals. At least some participants believed
the word *samodeiatel'nost'* no longer fit their activities. They were actors
striving for the highest artistic standards who just happened to have day
jobs. Not coincidentally, the term *"narodnyi teatr,"* once rejected as a de-

---

114. Gr. Avlov, "Rost khudozhestvennoi samodeiatel'nosti," RiT 11 (1937): 52. In this remarkable article, Avlov does not once mention his own contribution to the ideas of the
1920s. See also L. Subbotin, "Samodeiatel'nyi teatr," *Teatr* 6 (1938): 114.
115. Untitled editorial, RiT 8 (1937): 1.

A 1936 photograph of Adrian Piotrovskii. E. S. Dobin, ed., *Adrian Piotrovskii: Teatr, kino, zhizn'* (Leningrad: Iskusstvo, 1969).

funct relict of prerevolutionary times, began to reemerge in discussions about the amateur stage.[116]

116. On the rise of "folk art" (*narodnoe iskusstvo*) in the 1930s, see Frank J. Miller, *Folklore for Stalin: Russian Folklore and Pseudofolklore of the Stalin Era* (Armonk, N.Y.: M. E. Sharpe, 1990), and Susanna Lockwood Smith, "Soviet Arts Policy, Folk Music, and National Identity: The Piatnitskii State Russian Folk Choir, 1927–1945," (Ph.D. Dissertation, University of Minnesota, 1997), esp. 130–36. For its application to theater, see "Teatr narodnogo tvorchestva gotovitsia k otkrytiiu," *Pravda* 12 March 1936.

That amateurs had abandoned any claims to a unique approach to theatrical performance was graphically illustrated in the Moscow competition of amateur theaters held in the spring and summer of 1938. *Pravda* celebrated the sheer numbers of people drawn to the festivities: "At the Aviakhim factory, 395 new participants in the amateur arts were included. . . . No one knew there were so many talented people until now."[117] The first prize went to the Gorbunov factory theater's performance of Maxim Gorky's *The Philistines (Meshchane)*. In a long article assessing the results of the festival, the theater critic Leonid Subbotin presented this group as a stellar example of the path amateur theaters had followed in the 1930s. It began its existence as a TRAM circle in 1932 and continued in that guise until 1935, when its work was finally put on the right track by two directors from the Theater of Revolution, who began training the group in Stanislavsky's methods. "Here we see the typical biography of a collective decisively turning in the direction of serious study and education," opined Subbotin. This transformation process had yielded outstanding results. Its performance of Gorky's play was "of unusual quality for an amateur group."[118]

Subbotin's lengthy account of this circle's accomplishments offered a vivid example of the aesthetic values now applied to amateur circles. The collective "presented itself as a lively, well-coordinated ensemble," he determined. "The performance was marked by the collective's sincere, moving relationship to theatrical art."[119] In others words, any trace of "amateurism" had disappeared. Subbotin was not the only commentator to erase any references to the troubling imperfections of amateurism. In his review of the festival, the professional director Il'ia Sudakov spelled out what he believed to be the task of directors of amateur theaters, namely "to teach people to discover the deep, authentic truth in art. Then they will work with a real fire in their spirit, with deeply felt creativity, and without any false elements or tricks."[120]

The 1938 festival also reveals the declining role of amateur theater within the Stalinist spectacle state. Although the number of amateur stages in general continued to rise, and the festival itself was a much larger event than the 1932 gathering, it hardly generated any publicity in the press and was covered primarily in specialized journals. Grander

117. "Smotr khudozhestvennoi samodeiatel'nosti v Moskve," *Pravda* 19 April 1938.
118. L. Subbotin, "Nekotorye vyvody iz smotra teatral'noi samodeiatel'nosti," *Kul'turnaia rabota profsoiuzov* 12 (1938): 73–74.
119. Ibid., 73.
120. I. Sudakov, "Klubnyi spektakl'," VM 25 May 1938.

spectacles, including polar expeditions, technical feats, and the purge trials themselves, offered stiff competition. Stalinist culture, in Richard Stites' words, was "the greatest show on earth," attracting consumers with its range and diversity—from restaurants with stylish jazz bands, popular movies at accessible prices, and newly available radio entertainment that brought concert music, sports coverage, adventure stories, and political trials into people's homes.[121] Amateur theater occupied only a small niche in this grandiose display.

•➤

At the end of his famous essay, "The Work of Art in the Age of Mechanical Reproduction," Walter Benjamin argues that the essence of Fascism was its aestheticization of politics. "Communism has responded by politicizing art," he concludes.[122] Although his assessment of Fascism has been very influential, I believe that Benjamin's observations about Communism, at least the Soviet variety, require revision. Soviet Communists politicized art starting with the revolution; this tendency was hardly called forth by the rise of Fascism. And while the regime's approach to political art changed in the 1930s, if anything it became more "aesthetic." The Soviet arts establishment wanted to prove that their cultural products, including amateur performances, deserved to be considered as serious art.

To this end, cultural agencies overseeing amateur stages engaged in an extensive effort to reclaim amateur performance as aesthetic drama. They revamped repertoires, improved physical facilities, and brought in professional help. This process offered real advantages to viewers, who had a chance to see the same plays current on more expensive professional stages at a location probably more convenient to their homes. Although the acting might not have been as polished, the experience was similar. The performance was a separate event, marked off from other activities. "Here too, as in the central stages of the capital, you can hear the rustle of new theater programs at seven-thirty," wrote one commentator on amateur theatrical life in Moscow.[123] The actors also had a

121. Richard Stites, *Russian Popular Culture: Entertainment and Society since 1900* (Cambridge: Cambridge University Press, 1992), 64–97, quotation 94.

122. Walter Benjamin, *Das Kunstwerk im Zeitalter seiner technischen Reproduzierbarkeit* (Frankfurt am Main: Suhrkamp, 1972), 51. See Linda Schulte-Sasse, *Entertaining the Third Reich* (Durham, N.C.: Duke University Press, 1996), 17, for Benjamin's importance in the analysis of fascist culture.

123. E. Gabrilovich, "20 minut vos'mogo," *Pravda* 1 January 1935.

chance to benefit from the change. Many offered written testimonials detailing the importance of rigorous training programs in their lives. They knew that they were learning special skills; they were not just propagandists who could be pulled directly from the production line.

Yet, in this era of purges, it is also possible to see the aestheticization of amateur theater as a process of cleansings. Amateur stages lost troublesome leaders, who represented what were now considered to be dangerous artistic trends. They severed contact to earlier ideas of amateurism, which had seen non-professionals as the main source of vitality for all of Soviet culture. They no longer generated their own works, a process that had provided them a chance, however modest, to reflect on the problems of their daily lives. In other words, they were left with very little space in which to "do it themselves."

Conclusion

IN THE 1927 film *The House on Trubnaia Square (Dom na Trub-noi)*, a young peasant woman named Praskovia makes her way to Moscow. Instead of finding good employment, she ends up working as a maid for a couple quite contented with NEP. A trade union organizer discovers her and signs her up to join a union, also encouraging her to come to a theater performance at the local club. This marks the young woman's entry into urban public life. Even though the performance space is shabby and viewers sit on hard benches, club members flock to see the play, Romain Rolland's *The Taking of the Bastille*. Just about everything that could go wrong does. At first there are no wigs to complete the period costumes. The event starts very late because the main actor shows up drunk. Nonetheless, the crowd is riveted by the play. Praskovia is so engaged that when the hero is killed by an evil general, she jumps onto the stage and urges the onlookers to continue the revolution. Although the actors and the club director are horrified, the audience loves the unexpected ending and greets her with cheers. It is Praskovia's first happy moment in Moscow.

The hit film *Volga, Volga*, released in 1938, shows the amateur arts as the main occupation of the Soviet citizenry. It depicts the residents of a small town passionately engaged in artistic activities, complete with singing waiters, dancing mechanics, and a classical orchestra led by an accountant. The star of the film is once again a young woman, the postal carrier Strelka, who has composed a song about the beauty of life along the Volga under Soviet power. When a call comes from Moscow for the town to send a representative to a national Olympiad of amateur arts,

Strelka's folk music group enters into a madcap competition with the local orchestra to be the first to arrive. The two groups eventually combine forces, writing down and orchestrating Strelka's creation. When native talent is combined with classical training, the result is a song that wins first prize.

The heroines in these contrasting films offer very different images of the amateur in Soviet society. In *The House on Trubnaia Square*, the victimized maid becomes an actor, and then an activist, by taking part in amateur theatricals. In the process, she challenges standard guidelines for artistic creation. Rebelling against the club director, Praskovia's entrance on stage turns a conventional performance into a mass activity, changing its form and meaning. The film celebrates how do-it-yourself theater, open to all, facilitates a sense of local community. In *Volga, Volga*, Strelka's many talents are not restricted to the confines of a club. She dances, sings arias, and declaims poetry in public for all to see. Her main occupation is not delivering the mail; instead, she devotes herself to revealing the innate talents of her fellow citizens. But Strelka, unlike Praskovia, is seeking national recognition of her gifts. She wants to meet, not question, prevailing artistic standards. In order for that to happen, she must work together with conventionally trained artists before she can perform on the national stage.[1]

These two films reveal how the meaning of amateurism changed from the 1920s to the 1930s. In the early Soviet period, amateur performances were open to all comers. Directors complained that their participants were constantly changing; it was almost impossible to stage a performance with the same group that had been in rehearsals from the beginning. There were no set training methods; indeed, there might have been little training at all. Praskovia goes onstage because she wants to act out the revolution, not follow a script. But by the twentieth anniversary of the revolution, the makeshift origins of Soviet amateur theater had been erased. Amateur actors now put in long hours in preparation under the direct or indirect supervision of serious artists. Strelka's long trip to Moscow along the Volga is a continual rehearsal session. Her work is subjected to tougher scrutiny because it is put on display to represent the talents of the nation.

---

1. For a discussion of *Dom na Trubnoi*, see Denise Youngblood, *Movies for the Masses* (Cambridge: Cambridge University Press, 1992), 135–38. On *Volga, Volga* see Evgeny Dobrenko, "Soviet Film Comedy, or the Carnival of Authority," *Discourse* 17, 3 (Spring 1995): 49–57, and S. Iu. Rumiantsev and A. P. Shul'pin, "Samodeiatel'noe tvorchestvo i 'gosudarstvennaia kul'tura,' " in *Samodeiatel'noe khudozhestvennoe tvorchestvo v SSSR*, v. 1 (Moscow: Gosudarstvennyi institut iskusstvoznania, 1995), 18–20.

Writing on the significance of amateur theater in the mid-1930s, Bertolt Brecht determined that one needed to distinguish between amateurs and dilettantes. "A dilettante is someone who copies professionals. An amateur must find his own art."[2] Brecht's statement evokes the principles of early Soviet writers on amateur theater, such as Adrian Piotrovskii, who believed that amateurs had something new to bring to theatrical art. Early Soviet theorists, however, went further than Brecht, insisting that amateur art would serve as a source of inspiration and renewal for all of Soviet theater. But by the late 1930s, this concept of amateurism had been discredited. Amateurs were only valued insofar as they followed the lead of professionals and provided a credible surrogate for professional performances.

This ideal of the amateur as proto-professional was not entirely an invention of the Stalin era. Key elements were already articulated in the second half of NEP, when the trade union cultural leadership declared the participatory methods of the theater of small forms an artistic and political failure. At the 1927 Agitprop conference on theater, Party and union bureaucrats urged professionals to come to the aid of amateurs. Already at this point, the ideas of Piotrovskii and his colleagues were denounced by some as dangerous nonsense that was threatening the cultural advancement of the nation. Trade union leaders and a segment of the viewing public demanded a more tightly controlled repertoire, more of the classics, more lessons, and more skill. They wanted plays instead of agitational sketches, heroes instead of stereotypes. Key elements of Stalinist culture were set even before the massive upheaval of the First Five-Year Plan or the forceful imposition of state agencies in the early 1930s.[3] Nonetheless, the ideal of the amateur in the 1930s was much narrower than the version proposed at the 1927 conference. A decade later, amateurs had a very limited repertoire at their disposal. And while their training had improved, it was also homogenized. The Stalinist version of Stanislavsky's approach, which one commentator called the "accepted laws of stage work," dominated both the professional and amateur stage.[4]

Stalinist cultural politics contributed mightily to the narrowing of the cultural horizons of the amateur. Even before the anti-formalist cam-

2. Bertolt Brecht, "Über den Beruf des Schauspielers," in *Schriften zum Theater 1 (Gesammelte Werke 15)* (Frankfurt am Main: Suhrkamp, 1967), *Anmerkungen,* 11.

3. Katerina Clark, "The 'Quiet Revolution' in Soviet Intellectual Life," in Sheila Fitzpatrick et al., eds., *Russia in the Era of NEP* (Bloomington: Indiana University Press, 1991), 226–27.

4. M. Berliant, *Samodeiatel'nyi teatr* (Moscow: Profizdat, 1938), 23.

paign was launched in 1936, the Soviet theatrical establishment had rejected almost all repertoire from Western Europe and the United States. Through any number of official anniversaries and celebrations, the government promoted a limited classical heritage of the great prerevolutionary playwrights and those foreign authors who (at least in theory) represented capitalism in its revolutionary stage. With the founding of the National Committee of the Arts, control of repertoire grew even tighter. In addition, critics turned against all forms of presentation they considered unrealistic, "formalist," or strange. There were no more surprise endings in amateur theaters. Even surprise stagings were extremely rare.

These constraints on amateur theater in the 1930s were not set only by the state. The improvised theater of small forms, which was itself in part imposed by cultural agencies, had its enemies from the outset. Although small forms offered many avenues for group participation, they were based on the principle that leisure time had to be made useful and serve as a conduit for political education. The relentless lessons about state and local policies proved tiring to audiences who were either uninterested or, as one viewer remarked, "could read newspapers themselves." Therefore, we can imagine that a sizeable segment of the viewing public was eager to see Ostrovsky's *The Storm*, with its compelling story of love, betrayal, and suicide, instead of *Face to Production*, compiled from Party speeches and official documents.

The early model of Soviet amateur theater, emerging from the participatory theater of small forms, realized one of the central ideas of the theatrical avant-garde, who attempted to dissolve the lines between performers and the passive viewing audience.[5] Meyerhold's significant involvement in club theaters in Moscow shows that avant-gardists found the amateur stage a fruitful forum for experimentation. Their belief that theater should activate the audience was fulfilled to its full nightmarish potential by agitprop brigades during the First Five-Year Plan. Then the audience had little choice but to take part in the coercive project of participatory theater, facing shaming rituals or censure if they refused. The extreme methods used to encourage audience participation discredited any merits of this approach. Although isolated critics during the Second Five-Year Plan lamented that amateur stages no longer addressed themselves to local issues, no one called for a return to the So-

5. For a sophisticated examination of the relationship between the stage and audience in different forms of Soviet theater, see Lars Kleberg, *Theatre as Action: Soviet Russian Avant-garde Aesthetics*, trans. Charles Rougle (London: Macmillan, 1993).

viet-style *charivari*. The amateur stage that emerged after the Stalin revolution was in part created by the success, and then rapid rejection, of such repressive methods of audience engagement.

In a contentious essay on the history of Soviet art, Boris Groys has argued that avant-garde artists were not the innocent victims of Stalinism, as they have often been described in Western scholarship. Instead, he insists that socialist realism was in many ways a realization of the avant-garde's vision of organizing society into monolithic forms, using art as a method to transform reality.[6] These conclusions, based on a narrow sampling of artistic manifestos by visual artists and writers, do not hold true for theater. Certainly, it is false to see the theatrical avant-garde as innocent victims, but it is difficult to see them as victors either. Their visions were not realized in the theater of the 1930s. The lines between actors and audience, which they had hoped to erase, were more sharply drawn than ever.

It is tempting to depict amateur theaters of the 1930s as a fulfillment of the ideas of activists in popular theaters before the revolution, another example of many prerevolutionary institutions and values reborn in the Stalin era.[7] The Soviet state established and supported a wide network of stages devoted to educating viewers in the classics and providing them models of civilized behavior, a goal put forward long before the revolution. A significant part of the repertoire, based heavily on Ostrovsky, was very similar; so was the rhetoric of cultural enlightenment. The resurgence of the term *"narodnyi teatr"* (*popular theater*), abandoned in the early Soviet period, seems to settle the argument.

Nonetheless, I contend that the Soviet regime's commitment to nurturing and training amateurs sets it apart from prerevolutionary models. The network created by intellectuals before 1917 was designed to provide fine performances of respected work to the lower classes. The performing troupes they favored were not composed of amateurs at all. The people's theater movement began to direct more attention to amateurs in the last years of the Imperial regime, sponsoring local stages and aiding with repertoire and set designs. Nonetheless, the main goal of participants in the movement was to bring good art to the people, not to encourage the people to make it themselves.

6. Boris Groys, *The Total Art of Stalinism: Avant-Garde, Aesthetic Dictatorship, and Beyond*, trans. Charles Rougle (Princeton: Princeton University Press, 1992), 9, 36.

7. This argument about the resurgence of prerevolutionary values and institutions has been made most forcefully in Nicholas S. Timasheff, *The Great Retreat: The Growth and Decline of Communism in Russia* (New York: E. P. Dutton, 1945), esp. chs. 9 and 10.

Nor can the club stages of the 1930s be easily equated with their pre-revolutionary factory and club precedents, although all had ties to trade unions. The oppositional tendencies of worker's theaters before 1917 vanished by the Stalin era. Before the revolution, amateur actors sought out plays that expressed an implicit critique of the dominant economic order. Such intentions were gone by the 1930s, although critics made hypersensitive by the political climate of the purges still discovered hidden oppositional messages. Live performance always carries the potential for unexpected interpretation; through gestures and intonation actors can insert subversive messages in their work. The overseers of Stalinist amateur theater struggled mightily to limit alternative meanings by controlling the repertoire, training methods, and venues where performances took place.

By the Stalin era, urban amateurs also attempted to sever any links to the theater of the fairground and the countryside. Gone were the variations on *Tsar Maksimilian* and *The Boat*. Gone were the references to carnival barkers and red-haired clowns, unifying features of living newspapers in the 1920s. Stages in the two capitals no longer tried to offer images that would resonate with new arrivals from the countryside. Instead, amateur actors used their training to shed all traces of country origins in their speech patterns, clothing styles, and deportment.

The Soviet government's determination to attract and train the amateur also distinguish it from other regimes that attempted to bring theater into the lives of their citizenry in the 1930s. In Germany the amateur theater movement had been closely associated with the Social Democratic and Communist opponents of Nazism. Rather than building new opportunities for amateurs, the Hitler state shut down many of the stages built by its political rivals. Instead, it expanded the number of traveling theatrical troupes and integrated amateurs as bit players in large theatrical festivals, the so-called Thingspiele.[8] While the Italian Fascist government encouraged clubs that sponsored amateur theatricals, its greatest support went to touring theaters that brought the classics to remote villages. Its most distinctive theatrical product, a theatrical spectacle called "18BL," named after a Fiat truck, was performed by soldiers organized along military lines.[9]

8. Cecil W. Davies, *Theatre for the People* (Manchester: Manchester University Press, 1977), 113–16; Jutta Wardetsky, *Theaterpolitik im faschistischen Deutschland: Studien und Dokumente* (Berlin: Henschelverlag, 1983), 79–99, 138–64.
9. On Fascist art policies, see Victoria de Grazia, *The Culture of Consent: Mass Organization of Leisure in Fascist Italy* (Cambridge: Cambridge University Press, 1981), 203–4; Mabel Berezin, "The Organization of Political Ideology: Culture, State, and the Theater in Fascist

Nor was the Federal Theatre Project in the United States devoted to training non-professional actors. This massive state cultural program, which flourished from 1935–39, gave work to unemployed professional actors whose livelihood had been undermined by the Depression. It was an innovation in American arts policies, remarkable as an attempt to provide contemporary drama in a wide variety of venues. The repertoire was new and challenging. The program distributed funds to all parts of the nation and worked to encourage theatrical expression among ethnic and racial minorities. It did provide some services to help amateur stages, including a list and synopsis of labor plays. Nonetheless, amateurs were explicitly excluded from the program. Despite its many innovations, the Federal Theatre Project was designed to rejuvenate and expand professional theater.[10]

The Soviet regime's commitment to the amateur arts was one of its most distinctive cultural features. Through direct and indirect state funding, it supported institutions where amateurs could train and perform. The government encouraged professionals to lend their services to amateur stages. Although the number of journals devoted specifically to amateurs declined in the 1930s, mainstream theater publications set aside considerable space to events on the amateur stage. When the National Committee of The Arts took shape in 1936, it included amateur production in its purview. As André Van Gyseghem, active in left-wing theater circles in Britain, observed, "The Soviet State considers the encouragement and increase of amateur acting groups an important part of the educational system and so allots it a definite place in its programme."[11]

Amateurs are typically marginal figures, argues one scholar of amateurism in the United States. They are isolated from others engaged in leisure-time pursuits because of their serious commitment to their craft. At the same time, they are isolated from professionals because they do not have the time to perfect their skills in order to raise them to the high standards they admire.[12] It was precisely this marginal status that the Soviet regime, and the Soviet amateur, hoped to overcome. During the revolution and Civil War, amateurs drew attention to themselves by

Italy," *American Sociological Review* 56 (1991), 639–51; and Jeffrey T. Schnapp, *Staging Fascism: 18BL and the Theater of Masses for Masses* (Stanford: Stanford University Press, 1996).

10. On the policy of the Federal Theatre Project toward amateurs, see Hallie Flanagan, *Arena* (New York: Duell, Sloan and Pearce, 1940), 15–16.

11. André Van Gyseghem, *Theatre in Soviet Russia* (London: Faber and Faber, 1942), 153.

12. Robert A. Stebbins, *Amateurs: On the Margin between Work and Leisure* (Beverly Hills: Sage Publications, 1979), esp. 257–72.

their enthusiastic embrace of artistic performance. In the 1920s advocates of the amateur arts placed themselves at the center of artistic debates, deprecating the accomplishments of professionals and pointing to amateurs as a unique source of artistic renewal. During the First Five-Year Plan, amateur theater gained a reputation as a particularly effective transmiter of political information, a way to act out the radical transformations underway in the country at large. And even in the 1930s, when professionalism was reinstated to its traditionally privileged status, amateurs were integrated into the professional system. They received praise and support as an important channel to promote a unified artistic culture.

By supporting amateurs, the Soviet government projected the image of a culturally enlightened state. Not only did it strive to share the fruits of prerevolutionary culture with the population at large, it also nurtured the creative potential of all its citizens, turning mail carriers into composers. However, the Soviet government's solicitous concern for the amateur can also be seen as a tacit recognition of the dangers of amateur creation. By bringing it in from the margins, Soviet cultural leaders tried to guarantee that amateur art would offer no surprises. This goal proved elusive. We can see this illustrated in a long 1938 article examining the past and present of Soviet amateur stages by Leonid Subbotin, head of the former Polenov House of Amateur Art, renamed the Center of Amateur Art. Published in the prestigious journal *Teatr (Theater)*, the article presents an optimistic narrative of political and cultural progress for the Soviet amateur stage. Surviving through phases of constructivist and formalist influence, amateur theater had finally become a powerful force serving the healthy cultural instincts of the Soviet viewer, contended Subbotin. Recent competitions had shown that club stages chose to perform the best of contemporary works along with the finest representative of the classics. Serious collaboration with theatrical professionals had raised the quality of the best amateur work almost to the level of the professional stage.[13]

Yet, Subbotin's cheerful story was periodically interrupted by dire warnings about the necessity for heightened vigilance and control. Enemies of the people had wormed their way into select amateur circles and even into the leadership of the National Committee of the Arts. There was no effective central guidance, no single system of rules outlining training and repertoire, no rigid standards to train and test club instruc-

13. L. Subbotin, "Samodeiatel'nyi teatr," *Teatr* 6 (1938), 113–22.

tors. "Only a single, authoritative leadership can raise amateur theater to the level where it can meet the demands of the Soviet viewer and allow it to develop its full, rich artistic potential," he insisted.[14] Even at the height of Stalinism, amateur theater remained a possible source of danger for state authorities, a form of cultural expression that could slip off into the margins and evade central control.

This study ends with the period when Soviet amateur stages had accepted the repertoire, training methods, and oversight of professionals. However, they did not always remain in such an abject state. After Stalin's death, amateur theaters experienced a reinvigoration. Select stages became a site for cultural experimentation once more. Housed again on the margins of Soviet cultural life, in basements and warehouses, amateur studio theaters in Moscow and Leningrad solicited an original repertoire and attracted a distinctive audience. By the Gorbachev era, there was a lively network of amateur stages shaping a conscious alternative to state-supported professional theater.[15] Soviet amateur theater's oppositional potential, initially employed against remnants of the old regime, now turned against established Soviet culture.

14. Ibid., 120, 122, quotation 122.
15. On these theaters, see Susan Constanzo, "Reclaiming the Stage: Amateur Theater-Studio Audiences in the Late Soviet Era," *Slavic Review* 57 (Summer 1998): 398–424.

Glossary

agitka (plural *agitki*)—agitational play

Agitprop Division—The Agitation and Propaganda Division of the Communist Party

agitsud—agitational trial or mock trial

Glavpolitprosvet—The Central Agency for Political Education within Narkompros

instsenirovka—material originally not intended for the theater that has been shaped into a performance text

Narkompros—People's Commissariat of Education

NEP—The New Economic Policy, 1921–28

Politprosvet divisions—local agencies for political education

Proletkult—Proletarian Culture Organization

rabkor (*rabochii korrespondent*) a worker correspondent supplying criticism and reportage for newspapers and journals

RAPP—The Russian Association of Proletarian Writers

samodeiatel'nost'—amateurism; independent action

smychka—union or cooperation

TRAM (*Teatr rabochei molodezhi*)—The Theater of Working-Class Youth

Vneshkol'nyi otdel—The Division for Extra-curricular Education within Narkompros

Bibliography

Archival Sources

Gosudarstvennyi Arkhiv Rossiiskoi Federatsii (GARF)
  f. 628. Tsentral'nyi dom narodnogo tvorchestva im. N. K. Krupskoi
  f. 2306. Narkompros
  f. 2313. Glavpolitprosvet
  f. 5451. Vsesoiuznyi tsentral'nyi sovet profsoiuzov (VTSSPS)
  f. 7952. Istoriia fabrik i zavodov
Gosudarstvennyi Tsentral'nyi teatral'nyi muzei im. A. A. Bakhrushina (GTSTM)
  f. 150. N. L'vov. Lichnyi fond
Rossiiskii Gosudarstvennyi arkhiv literatury i iskusstva (RGALI)
  f. 645. Glaviskusstvo
  f. 941. Teatr Leninskogo Komsomola
  f. 963. Gosudarstvennyi Teatr im. Meierkhol'da
  f. 1230. Proletkul't
  f. 2723. N. G. Zograf
  f. 2947. Moskovskii Teatr im. Leninskogo Komsomola
Tsentral'noe khranenie dokumentov molodezhnykh organizatsii (TSKhDMO)
  f. 1. Tsentral'nyi Komitet Vsesoiuznogo Leninskogo Kommunisticheskogo Soiuza Molodezhi
Tsentral'nyi munitsipal'nyi arkhiv Moskvy (TSMAM)
  f. 718. Moskovskii gorodskoi sovet professional'nykh soiuzov (MGSPS)
  f. 2007. Upravlenie moskovskimi zrelishchnymi predstavleniiami (UMZP)

Newspapers and Journals

Gorn
Griadushchee

Gudki
Iskusstvo kommuny
Iunyi kommunist
Klub
Klub i revoliutsiia
Klubnaia stsena
Kolkhoznyi teatr
Komsomol'skaia pravda
Komsomol'skii agitproprabotnik
Krasnaia gazeta
Kul'turnaia rabota profsoiuzov
Literatura i iskusstvo
Literaturnaia gazeta
Literaturnyi Leningrad
Malye formy klubnogo zrelishcha
Materialy dlia klubnoi stseny
Molodaia gvardiia
Narodnoe tvorchestvo
Novyi zritel'
Plamia
Pravda
Prizyv
Proletarskaia kul'tura
Rabis
Rabochii i teatr
Rabochii klub
Rabochii zritel'
Repertuarnyi biulleten'
Siniaia bluza
Smena (journal)
Sovetskii teatr
Sovetskoe iskusstvo
Teatr
Teatr i dramaturgiia
Trud
Vecherniaia Moskva
Vestnik teatra
Vestnik zhizni
Vneshkol'noe obrazovanie
Za agitpropbrigadu i TRAM
Za proletarskoe iskusstvo
Zhizn' iskusstva

Primary Sources

Andreev, Boris. *Sud nad starym bytom: Stsenarii dlia rabochikh klubov ko dniu rabotnitsy 8-go marta.* Moscow-Leningrad: Doloi negramotnost', 1926.

Apushkin, Ia. *Zhivogazetnyi teatr.* Leningrad: Teakinopechat', 1930.

Avlov, Grigorii, ed. *Edinyi khudozhestvennyi kruzhok: Metody klubno-khudozhestvennoi raboty.* Leningrad: Izdatel'stvo knizhnogo sektora Gubono, 1925.

———. *Igry v klube: Trenirovochnye razvlecheniia.* Leningrad: Teakinopechat', 1929.

———. *Klubnyi samodeiatel'nyi teatr: Evoliutsiia metodov i form.* Leningrad: Teakinopechat', 1930.

———. *Sud nad khuliganami.* Moscow: Doloi negramotnost', 1927.

———. *Teatral'nye agitpropbrigady v klube.* Leningrad: Gosudarstvennoe izdatel'stvo khudozhestvennoi literatury, 1931.

Benjamin, Walter. *Das Kunstwerk im Zeitalter seiner technischen Reproduzierbarkeit.* Frankfurt am Main: Suhrkamp, 1972.

Bergman, S. *Teatral'naia rabota v klube.* Kharkov: Proletarii, 1925.

Berliant, M. *Samodeiatel'nyi teatr.* Moscow: Profizdat, 1938.

Boiarskii, Ia., A. Vigalok, M. Lenau, and P. Segal, eds. *Professional'nye soiuzy na novom etape: Sbornik materialov k XVI s''ezdu VKP(b).* Moscow: Izdatel'stvo VTSSPS, 1930.

Brecht, Bertolt. *Schriften zum Theater,* v. 1. Frankfurt am Main: Suhrkamp, 1967.

Brown, Ben W. *Theatre at the Left.* Providence, R.I.: The Booke Shop, 1938.

Bulgakov, A. S., and S. S. Danilov. *Gosudarstvennyi agitatsionnyi teatr v Leningrade.* Leningrad: Academia, 1931.

Carter, Huntley. *The New Spirit in the Russian Theatre, 1917–28.* London: Chapman and Dodd, 1924.

Chicherov, I. I. *Perezhitoe, nezabyvaemoe.* Moscow: Molodaia gvardiia, 1977.

———, ed. *Za TRAM: Vsesoiuznoe soveshchanie po khudozhestvennoi rabote sredi molodezhi.* Moscow: Teakinopechat', 1929.

Dal'tsev, Z. G. "Moskva 1917–1923: Iz vospominanii." In *U istokov: Sbornik statei.* Moscow: VTO, 1960.

Desiat' Oktiabrei. Leningrad: Bol'shoi dramaticheskii teatr, 1927.

Devushki nashei strany. Leningrad: Gosudarstvennyi teatr dramy, 1933.

Diament, Kh. *Organizatsionnye formy profsoiuznoi kul'traboty.* 2nd ed. Moscow: Trud i kniga, 1927.

Dobin, E. S., ed. *Adrian Piotrovskii: Teatr, kino, zhizn'.* Leningrad: Iskusstvo, 1969.

Dolinskii, S., and S. Bergman. *Massovaia rabota v klube.* Moscow: Rabotnik prosveshcheniia, 1924.

Dune, Eduard. *Notes of a Red Guard.* Trans. and ed. Diane Koenker and Steven Smith. Urbana: Illinois University Press, 1993.

Edel'son, Z. A., and B. M. Filippov, eds. *Profsoiuzy i iskusstvo: Sbornik statei s prilozheniem rezoliutsii pervoi leningradskoi mezhsoiuznoi konferentsii po vo-prosam khudozhestvennoi raboty.* Leningrad: Izdatel'stvo leningradskogo gubprofsoveta, 1927.

Ehrenburg, Ilia. *People and Life, 1891–1921.* Trans. Anna Bostock. New York: Knopf, 1962.

Erdman, Nikolai. *Two Plays.* Trans. Marjorie Hoover. Ann Arbor: Ardis, 1975.

Feuchtwanger, Leon. *Moskau 1937: Ein Reisebericht für meine Freunde.* 1937. Reprint. Berlin: Aufbau Verlag, 1993.

Filippov, V. *Puti samodeiatel'nogo teatra: Ocherk.* Moscow: Gosudarstvennaia Akademiia khudozhestvennykh nauk, 1927.

Flanagan, Hallie. *Arena.* New York: Duell, Sloan and Pearce, 1940.

Fülöp-Miller, Rene, and Joseph Gregor. *The Russian Theatre.* Trans. Paul England. 1930. Reprint. New York: Benjamin Blom, 1968.

Gol'dman, A., and M. Imas. *Sotsialisticheskoe sorevnovanie i udarnichestvo v iskusstve.* Moscow: Gosudarstvennoe izdatel'stvo khudozhestvennoi literatury, 1931.

Gorbenko, A. N. "Krysha." RGALI, f. 2723, op. 1, d. 531, ll. 190–245.

——. *Sashka Chumovoi: Komsomol'skaia komediia.* In A. Piotrovskii and M. Sokolovskii, eds. *Sbornik p'es dlia komsomol'skogo teatra.* Moscow: Gosudarstvennoe izdatel'stvo, 1928.

Griffith, Hubert, ed. *Playtime in Russia.* London: Methuen, 1935.

Gvozdev, A. A. "Klassiki na sovetskoi stsene." *Literaturnyi sovremennik* 6 (1933): 127–46.

——. *Teatral'naia kritika.* Ed. A. Ia. Al'tshuller et al. Moscow: Iskusstvo, 1987.

Houghton, Norris. *Moscow Rehearsals: The Golden Age of Soviet Theatre.* New York: Harcourt Brace, 1936.

Gvozdev, A. A., and A. Piotrovskii. "Petrogradskie teatry i prazdnestva v epokhu voennogo kommunizma." In *Istoriia sovetskogo teatra,* vl. 1. Ed. V. E. Rafailovich. Leningrad, 1933.

Imas, M. *Iskusstvo na fronte rekonstruktsii sel'skogo khoziaistva.* Moscow: Gosudarstvennoe izdatel'stvo khudozhestvennoi literatury, 1931.

Isaev, I. *Osnovnye voprosy klubnoi stseny.* Moscow: VTSSPS, 1928.

Iskusstvo v rabochem klube. Moscow: Vserossiiskii Proletkul't, 1924.

Iufit, A. Z., ed. *Russkii sovetskii teatr, 1917–1921.* Leningrad: Iskusstvo, 1968.

Ivanter, B. and V. *Zemlia zazhglas': P'esa v trekh chastiakh.* Moscow: Molodaia gvardiia, 1924.

Jelagin, Juri. *The Taming of the Arts.* Trans. Nicholas Wreden. New York: Dutton, 1951.

Kabo, E. O. *Ocherki rabochego byta: Opyt monograficheskogo issledovaniia domashnego rabochego byta.* Moscow: VTSSPS, 1928.

Kagan, A. G. *Molodezh' posle gudka.* Moscow: Molodaia gvardiia, 1930.

——. *Sorok piat' dnei sredi molodezhi.* Leningrad: Priboi, 1929

Kak ia stal rezhisserom. Moscow: Goskinoizdat, 1946.

Karzhanskii, N. *Kollektivnaia dramaturgiia*. Moscow: Gosizdat, 1922.

Kataev, Valentin. *Time, Forward!* Trans. Charles Malamuth. Bloomington: Indiana University Press, 1976.

Kerzhentsev, P. M. *Revoliutsiia i teatr*. Moscow: Dennitsa, 1918.

——. *Tvorcheskii teatr*. 5th ed. Peterburg: Gosizdat, 1923.

Khudozhestvennye agitbrigady: Itogi smotra i puti razvitiia. Moscow: Narkompros RSFSR, 1931.

Kirchon [Kirshon], V., and A. Ouspensky. *Red Rust*. Adapted by Virginia and Frank Vernon. New York: Bretano's, 1930.

Kirshon, Vladimir. *Chudesnyi splav: Komediia v chetyrekh aktakh*. Moscow: Iskusstvo, 1956.

Klub kak on est'. Moscow: Trud i kniga, 1929.

Kluby Moskvy i gubernii. Moscow: Trud i kniga, 1926.

Knorre, F. *Moskovskii 10:10*. Moscow: Gosudarstvennoe izdatel'stvo khudozhestvennoi literatury, 1933.

Kobrin, Iurii. *Teatr im. Vs. Meierkhol'da i rabochii zritel'*. Moscow: Moskovskoe teatral'noe izdatel'stvo, 1926.

Kommunisticheskaia partiia Sovetskogo Soiuza v rezoliutsiiakh i resheniiakh s''ezdov, konferentsii i plenumov TsK. vol. 2: *1917–1924*. Moscow: Izdatel'stvo politicheskoi literatury, 1970.

Komsomol'skaia paskha. Moscow: Novaia Moskva, 1924.

Korev, S. *Zhivaia gazeta v klube*. Ed. R. Pel'she. Moscow: Novaia Moskva, 1925.

Korovkin, I., and S. Erkov. *Zovi fabkom: P'esa v 3-kh deistviiakh*. Leningrad: Teakinopechat', 1929.

Kriuchkov, Nikolai. "Khudozhestvennyi agitprop komsomola." *Teatral'naia zhizn'* 14 (July 1970): 1–3.

Krupskaia, Nadezhda. *Pedagogicheskie sochineniia*. Moscow: Izdatel'stvo Akademii pedagogicheskikh nauk, 1956.

Krylov, S. M., ed. *Puti razvitiia teatra: Stenograficheskii otchet i resheniia partiinogo soveshchaniia po voprosam teatra pri Agitprope TsK VKP(b) v mae 1927 g.* Moscow: Kinopechat', 1927.

Lebedev-Polianskii, V. I., ed. *Protokoly pervoi Vserossiiskoi konferentsii proletarskikh kul'turno-prosvetitel'nykh organizatsii*. Moscow: Proletarskaia kul'tura, 1918.

Leningradskii TRAM v Moskve iiun' 1928g. Leningrad: Gostram, 1928.

Lissitzky, El. *Russia: An Architecture for World Revolution*. Trans. Eric Dluhosch. Cambridge: MIT Press, 1970.

L'vov, N. [F.] *Klesh zadumchivyi: Dialekticheskoe predstavlenie v 3-kh krugakh*. Leningrad: Teakinopechat', 1930.

——. *Plaviatsia dni: Dialekticheskoe predstavlenie v 3-kh krugakh*. Leningrad: Teakinopechat', 1929.

——. *Zor'ka: P'esa v trekh deistviiakh*. In A. Piotrovskii and M. Sokolovskii, eds. *Sbornik p'es dlia komsomol'skogo teatra*. Moscow: Gosudarstvennoe izdatel'stvo, 1928.

L'vov, N. [I.] "P'esa ili stsenarii." *Vestnik rabotnikov iskusstv* 2/3 (1920): 53–54.
———. *Postroenie agitzrelishcha.* Moscow: Teakinopechat', 1930.
Maksimov, P., and N. L'vov. *Druzhnaia gorka: Komsomol'skaia operetta v 3-kh deistviiakh.* Leningrad: Teakinopechat', 1929.
Marinchik, Pavel. "Dalekoe-blizkoe." *Neva* 11 (1957): 169–173.
———. "Khudozhestvennyi agitprop komsomola." *Neva* 11 (1965): 202–205.
———. *Meshchanka.* Leningrad: Teakinopechat', 1929.
———. *Rozhdenie komsomol'skogo teatra.* Leningrad: Iskusstvo, 1963.
———, and S. Kashevnik. *Budni.* In A. Piotrovskii and M. Sokolovskii, eds. *Teatr rabochei molodezhi.* Moscow: Gosudarstvennoe izdatel'stvo, 1928.
Markov, P. A. *The Soviet Theatre.* London: Victor Gollancz, 1934.
Marx, Karl, and Friedrich Engels. *Literature and Art.* New York: Progress Press, 1947.
Massovye prazdnestva. Leningrad: Academia, 1926.
Mierau, Fritz, ed. *Sergei Tretiakov: Gesichter der Avantgarde.* Berlin: Aufbau Verlag, 1985.
Mikitenko, I. K. *Devushki nashei strany: P'esa v 4 deistviiakh.* Leningrad: Izdanie Kul'tkabineta Gosdramy, 1932.
Na putiakh iskusstva: Sbornik statei. Moscow: Proletkul't, 1926.
Novye etapy samodeiatel'noi khudozhestvennoi raboty. Leningrad: Teakinopechat', 1930.
Oktiabr' v klube. Moscow: Trud i kniga, 1924.
Oktiabr' v rabochikh klubakh. Moscow: Krasnaia nov', 1923.
Orlovsky, Sergei. "Moscow Theater, 1917–1941," in Martha Bradshaw, ed. *Soviet Theater 1917–1941.* New York: Research Program on the USSR, 1954.
Pel'she, R., ed. *Komsomol, na front iskusstva!* Moscow: Teakinopechat', 1929.
———. *Nasha teatral'naia politika.* Moscow: Gosudarstvennoe izdatel'stvo, 1929.
Pervaia Vsesoiuznaia olimpiada samodeiatel'nogo iskusstva. Moscow: Profizdat, 1932.
Pervichnaia komsomol'skaia organizatsiia: Dokumenty i materialy s''ezdov, konferentsii komsomola, Tsentral'nogo Komiteta VLKSM, *1918–1971.* Moscow: Molodaia gvardiia, 1972.
Petrogradskaia obshchegorodskaia konferentsiia rabochikh klubov. Petrograd: Izdatel'stvo Leningradskogo gubprofsoveta, 1920.
Pletnev, V. *Rabochii klub.* Moscow: Proletkul't, 1925.
Pimenov, V. F., ed. *Pervye sovetskie p'esy.* Moscow: Iskusstvo, 1958.
Piotrovskii, A. I. "K teorii 'samodeiatel'nogo teatra.'" *Problemy sotsiologii iskusstva.* Leningrad: Academia, 1926.
———. *Kinofikatsiia iskusstv.* Leningrad: Izdanie avtora, 1928.
———, ed. *Krasnoarmeiskii teatr: Instruktsiia k teatral'noi rabote v Krasnoi Armii.* Petrograd: Izdatel'stvo Petrogradskogo voennogo okruga. 1921.
———. "TRAM: Stranitsa teatral'noi sovremennosti." *Zvezda* 4 (1929): 142–52.

———. *Za sovetskii teatr! Sbornik statei*. Leningrad: Academia, 1925.

———, and M. Sokolovskii, eds. *Teatr rabochei molodezhi: Sbornik p'es dlia komsomol'skogo teatra*. Leningrad: Teakinopechat', 1928.

Politprosvetrabota i teatr. Moscow: Doloi negramotnost', 1927.

Rabochie o literature, teatre i muzyke. Leningrad: Priboi, 1926.

Ravenskikh, Boris Ivanovich. "Istochnik novoi energii." *Teatral'naia zhizn'* 24 (1964): 17–18.

Reines, B. "The Experience of the International Workers' Theatre as Reported at the First Enlarged Plenum of the I.W.D.U." *Workers' Theatre* 1, no. 9 (December 1931):1–4.

Repertuarnyi ukazatel': Sbornik otzyvov o p'esakh dlia professional'nogo i samodeiatel'nogo teatra. Moscow: Glavpolitprosvet, 1925.

Romashov, Boris Sergeevich. *Konets Krivoryl'ska*. In *P'esy*. Moscow: Khudozhestvennaia literatura, 1935.

Rostislavlev, N. *Dai piat': P'esa v 3 krugakh i 10 kartinakh*, Leningrad: Teakinopechat', 1930.

Savvin, I. D., ed. *Komsomol i teatr*. Moscow: MK VLKSM, 1933.

Sbornik instsenirovok: Opyty kollektivnoi dramaturgii. Leningrad: Izdatel'stvo Knizhnogo sektora Gubono, 1924.

Sbornik materialov k III plenumu Tsentral'nogo soveta TRAM'ov pri TsK VLKSM, Moscow: Teakinopechat', 1930.

Sbornik rukovodiashchikh materialov po rabote klubov. Moscow: Profizdat, 1930.

Scott, John. *Behind the Urals: An American Worker in Russia's City of Steel*. Ed. Stephen Kotkin. Bloomington: Indiana University Press, 1989.

Sed'moi s''ezd professional'nykh soiuzov. Moscow: Profizdat, 1926.

Shcheglov, Dmitrii. *Chetyre kepki*. In *Krasnyi teatr: Komsomol'skie p'esy*. Moscow: Gosizdat, 1926.

———. *Teatral'no-khudozhestvennaia rabota v klubakh: Metodika i praktika*. Leningrad: Gubprofsovet, 1926.

———. "U istokov." In *U istokov: Sbornik statei*. Moscow: VTO, 1960.

Shestnadtsatyi s''ezd Vsesoiuznoi Kommunisticheskoi partii (B): Stenograficheskii otchet. Moscow: OGIZ-Moskovskii rabochii, 1931.

Shishigin, F. E. "Khudozhniki, kotorykh sleduet vspomnit'," *Teatral'naia zhizn'*. 24 (1964): 15–16.

Shishigin, F. E., A. Piotrovskii, and M. Sokolovskii. "Zelenyi tsekh: Operetta v 3-kh deistviiakh." RGALI f. 2723, op. 1, d. 531, ll. 246–94.

Shklovskii, Viktor. *Khod konia: Sbornik statei*. Moscow: Gelikon, 1923.

Skorinko, I. *Buzlivaia kogorta: P'esa v 4 deistviiakh*. Leningrad: Priboi, 1928.

Slukhovskii, M. *Ustnaia gazeta kak vid politiko-prosvetitel'noi raboty*. Moscow: Krasnaia zvezda, 1924.

Sokolovskii, M. "Sploshnoi potok." RGALI, f. 2723, op. 1, d. 531, ll. 110–61.

———. *Za novyi byt: Zhivaia gazeta*. Moscow: Gosudarstvennoe izdatel'stvo, 1927.

Sostav rabochei molodezhi: Po massovym dannym profperepisi. Moscow: Molodaia gvardiia, 1931.

Stalin, J. V. *Problems of Leninism*. Peking: Foreign Languages Press, 1976.

Tikhonovich, V. V. *Narodnyi teatr*. Moscow: V. Magnussen, 1918.

———. *Samodeiatel'nyi teatr*. Vologda: Oblastnoi otdel Gosizdata, 1922.

———. *Teatr i sovremennost'.* Moscow: Doloi negramotnost', 1928.

Thomas, Tom. "World Congress of Workers' Theatre Groups." *New Masses* (November 1930): 21.

Tolmachev, D. *Fabzavshturm*. In A. Piotrovskii and M. Sokolovskii, eds., *Teatr rabochei molodezhi*. Moscow: Gosudarstvennoe izdatel'stvo, 1928.

Tolstoi, V. P., ed. *Agitatsionno-massovoe iskusstvo: Oformlenie prazdnestv, 1917–1932.* 2 v. Moscow: Iskusstvo, 1972.

Tolstoi, V. P. et al., eds. *Street Art of the Revolution: Festivals and Celebrations in Russia, 1918–33*. London: Thames and Hudson, 1990.

Tovarishch komsomol: Dokumenty s''ezdov, konferentsii i TsK VLKSM 1918–1968, v. 1. Moscow: Molodaia gvardiia, 1969.

Trabskii, A. Ia., ed. *Russkii sovetskii teatr, 1921–1926*. Leningrad: Iskusstvo, 1975.

———. *Russkii sovetskii teatr, 1926–1932*. Leningrad: Iskusstvo, 1982.

Troianskii, A. V., and R. I. Egiazarov. *Izuchenie kino-zritelia*. Moscow: Gosudarstvennoe izdatel'stvo, 1928.

Trotsky, Leon. *Problems of Everyday Life*. New York: Monad Press, 1973.

Tur, Brat'ia [pseud.], and L. Sheinin. *Ochnaia stavka*. Moscow: Iskusstvo, 1938.

Van Gysegham, André. *Theatre in Soviet Russia*. London: Faber and Faber, 1943.

Veprinskii, M. *Khudozhestvennye kruzhki i krasnyi kalendar'*. Moscow: Gosudarstvennoe izdatel'stvo, 1926.

———. *Zhivaia gazeta*. Moscow: Doloi negramotnost', 1927.

Von Geldern, James, and Richard Stites, eds. *Mass Culture in Soviet Russia*. Bloomington: Indiana University Press, 1995.

Voprosy kul'tury pri diktature proletariata. Moscow: Gosudarstvennoe izdatel'stvo, 1925.

Vsevolodskii-Gerngross, V. N. *Istoriia russkogo teatra*. Leningrad: Teakinopechat', 1929.

———. *Russkaia ustnaia narodnaia drama*. Moscow: Akademiia Nauk, 1959.

Wettlin, Margaret. *Fifty Russian Winters: An American Woman's Life in the Soviet Union*. New York: John Wiley, 1994.

Winter, Ella. *Red Virtue: Human Relationships in the New Russia*. New York: Harcourt Brace, 1933.

Wolkonsky, Serge. *My Reminiscences*. 2 v. Trans. A. E. Chamot. London: Hutchinson, 1924.

Zadykhin, Ia. L. *Khuligan*. Leningrad: Izdatel'stvo MODPiK, 1925.

Zamoskvoretskii, V. *Klub rabochei molodezhi*. Moscow: Novaia Moskva, 1924.

Zor'ka: V pomoshch' zriteliu. Moscow: Teakinopechat', 1929.

Secondary Sources

Aizenshtadt, V. N. *Sovetskii samodeiatel'nyi teatr: Osnovnye etapy razvitiia*. Khar-kov: Khar'kovskii gosudarstvennyi institut kul'tury, 1983.

Amiard-Chevrel, Claudine. "La Blouse Bleue." In *L'Théâtre d'agit-prop de 1917 à 1932*, v. 1. Lausanne: La Cité—L'age d'homme, 1977.

——. "Le théatre de la Jeunesse Ouvrière (TRAM)." In *Le Théâtre d'agit-prop de 1917 à 1932*, v. 1. Lausanne: La Cité—L'age d'homme, 1977.

Aston, Elaine, and George Savona. *Theatre as Sign-System*. London: Routledge, 1991.

Barris, Roanne. "Chaos by Design: The Constructivist Stage and Its Reception." Ph. D. Dissertation, University of Illinois, Champaign-Urbana, 1994.

Berezin, Mabel. "The Organization of Political Ideology: Culture, State, and Theater in Fascist Italy." *American Sociological Review* 56 (1991): 639–51.

Blok, V. B. "Khudozhestvennoe tvorchestvo mass." In A. Ia. Zis', ed., *Stranitsy istorii sovetskoi khudozhestvennoi kul'tury*. Moscow: Molodaia gvardiia, 1989.

Bodek, Richard. *Proletarian Performance in Weimar Berlin: Agitprop, Chorus, and Brecht*. Columbia, S.C.: Camden House, 1997.

Bonnell, Victoria. *Iconography of Power: Soviet Political Posters under Lenin and Stalin*. Berkeley: University of California Press, 1997.

——. *The Roots of Rebellion*. Berkeley: University of California Press, 1983.

Booth, Wayne. *For the Love of It: Amateuring and Its Rivals*. Chicago: University of Chicago Press, 1999.

Borland, Harriet. *Soviet Literary Theory and Practice during the First Five-Year Plan, 1928–32*. New York: King's Crown Press, 1950.

Bourdieu, Pierre. *Distinction: The Social Critique of the Judgement of Taste*. Trans. Richard Nice. Cambridge: Cambridge University Press, 1984.

Bown, Matthew Cullerne. *Art under Stalin*. New York: Holmes and Meier, 1991.

Boym, Svetlana. *Common Places: Mythologies of Everyday Life in Russia*. Cambridge: Harvard University Press, 1994.

Bradby, David. "The October Group and Theatre under the Front Populaire," in David Bradby et al., eds. *Politics and Performance in Popular Drama*. Cambridge: Cambridge University Press, 1980.

Bradby, David, and John McCormick. *People's Theatre*. London: Croom Helm, 1978.

Bradshaw, Martha, ed. *Soviet Theatres, 1917–1941*. New York: Research Program on the USSR, 1954.

Braulich, Heinrich. *Die Volksbühne*. Berlin: Henschelverlag, 1976.

Brooks, Jeffrey. *When Russia Learned to Read: Literacy and Popular Literature, 1861–1917*. Princeton: Princeton University Press, 1985.

Brooks, Peter. *The Melodramatic Imagination: Balzac, Henry James, Melodrama, and the Mode of Excess*. New Haven: Yale University Press, 1976.

Brown, Edward J. *The Proletarian Episode in Russian Literature, 1928–1932*. New York: Columbia University Press, 1953.

Cassiday, Julie. "The Theater of the World and the Theater of State: Drama and the Show Trial in Early Soviet Russia." Ph.D. dissertation, Stanford University, 1995.

Chase, William J. *Workers, Society and the Soviet State: Labor and Life in Moscow, 1918–1929*. Urbana: University of Illinois Press, 1987.

Clark, Katerina. "Little Heroes and Big Deeds: Literature Responds to the First Five-Year Plan." In Sheila Fitzpatrick, ed., *Cultural Revolution in Russia, 1928–1931*. Bloomington: University of Indiana Press, 1984.

——. *Petersburg, Crucible of Cultural Revolution*. Cambridge: Harvard University Press, 1995.

——. "The 'Quiet Revolution' in Soviet Intellectual Life." In Sheila Fitzpatrick et al., eds., *Russia in the Era of NEP*. Bloomington: Indiana University Press, 1991.

——. *The Soviet Novel: History as Ritual*. Chicago: University of Chicago Press, 1981.

Corbesero, Susan. "If We Build It, They Will Come: The International Red Stadium Society." Unpublished manuscript.

Cosgrove, Stuart. "From Shock Troupe to Group Theatre." In *Theatres of the Left, 1880–1935*. Ed. Raphael Samuels. London: Routledge, 1984.

Costanzo, Susan. "Reclaiming the Stage: Amateur Theater-Studio Audiences in the Late Soviet Era." *Slavic Review* 57 (Summer 1998): 398–424.

Curtiss, J. A. E. "Down with the Foxtrot! Concepts of Satire in the Soviet Theatre of the 1920s." In *Russian Theatre in the Age of Modernism*. Ed. Robert Russell and Andrew Barratt. London: Macmillan, 1990.

David-Fox, Michael. *Revolution of the Mind: Bolshevik Strategies of Higher Education*. Ithaca: Cornell University Press, 1997.

——. "What Is Cultural Revolution?" *Russian Review* 58 (April 1999): 181–201.

Davies, Cecil W. *Theatre for the People: The Story of the Volksbühne*. Austin: University of Texas Press, 1977.

Davies, Sarah. *Popular Opinion in Stalin's Russia: Terror, Propaganda, and Dissent*. Cambridge: Cambridge University Press, 1997.

Deak, Frantisek. "Blue Blouse (1923–1928)." *Drama Review* 17: 1 (1973): 35–46.

De Grazia, Victoria. *The Culture of Consent: Mass Organization of Leisure in Fascist Italy*. Cambridge: Cambridge University Press, 1981.

Dictionary of Russian Women Writers. Westport, Conn.: Greenwood Press, 1994.

Dobrée, Bonamy. *The Amateur and the Theatre*. London: Hogarth Press, 1947.

Dobrenko, Evgeny. *The Making of the State Reader: Social and Aesthetic Contexts of the Reception of Soviet Literature*. Stanford: Stanford University Press, 1997.

——. "Soviet Film Comedy, or the Carnival of Authority." *Discourse* 17, no.3 (Spring 1995): 49–57.

Ermolin, E. A. *Materializatsiia prizraka: Totalitarnyi teatr sovetskikh massovykh aktsii 1920–1930kh godov*. Iaroslavl: IAGPU im. K. D. Ushinskogo, 1996.

Esslin, Martin. *Brecht: The Man and His Work*. Rev. ed. New York: Norton, 1971.

Filtzer, Donald. *Soviet Workers and Stalinist Industrialization: The Formation of Modern Soviet Production Relations, 1928–1941*. London: Pluto, 1986.

Fisher, Ralph Talcott, Jr. *Pattern for Soviet Youth: A Study of the Congresses of the Komsomol, 1918–1954*. New York: Columbia University Press, 1959.

Fitzpatrick, Sheila. *The Commissariat of Enlightenment: Soviet Organization of Education and the Arts under Lunacharsky*. Cambridge: Cambridge University Press, 1970.

———. *The Cultural Front: Power and Culture in Revolutionary Russia*. Ithaca: Cornell University Press, 1992.

———, ed. *Cultural Revolution in Russia, 1928–1931*. Bloomington: Indiana University Press, 1984.

———. *Education and Social Mobility in the Soviet Union, 1921–1934*. Cambridge: Cambridge University Press, 1979.

———. "The Emergence of Glaviskusstvo." *Soviet Studies* 32 (October 1971): 236–53.

———. *Everyday Stalinism*. New York: Oxford University Press, 1999.

Frank, Stephen. "Popular Justice, Community, and Culture among the Russian Peasantry, 1870–1900." *Russian Review* 46, no. 3 (1987): 239–65.

———. " 'Simple Folk, Savage Customs?' Youth, Sociability, and the Dynamic of Culture in Rural Russia, 1856–1914." *Journal of Social History* 25 (1992): 711–36.

Gerould, Daniel. "Gorky, Melodrama, and the Development of Early Soviet Theatre." *Theatre Journal* 7 (Winter 1976): 33–44.

Getty, J. Arch, and Oleg V. Naumov. *The Road to Terror: Stalin and the Self-Destruction of the Bolsheviks, 1932–1939*. New Haven: Yale University Press, 1999.

Gilman, Christopher. "The Fox-Trot and the New Economic Policy." *Experiment* 2 (1996): 443–75.

Golomstock, Igor. *Totalitarian Art in the Soviet Union, the Third Reich, Fascist Italy, and the People's Republic of China*. New York: Harper Collins, 1990.

Gorchakov, N. A. *The Theater in Soviet Russia*. Trans. Edgar Lehrman. New York: Columbia University Press, 1957.

Gorsuch, Anne. *Enthusiasts, Bohemians, and Delinquents: Soviet Youth Culture, 1921–1928*. Bloomington Indiana University Press, forthcoming.

———. "Soviet Youth and the Politics of Popular Culture." *Social History* 17, no. 2 (1992): 189–201.

Gorzka, Gabriele. *Arbeiterkultur in der Sovietunion: Industriearbeiter-Klubs, 1917–1929*. Berlin: Arno Spitz, 1990.

Gromov, Evgenii. *Stalin: Vlast' i iskusstvo*. Moscow: Respublika, 1996.

Groys, Boris. *The Total Art of Stalinism: Avant-garde, Aesthetic Dictatorship, and Beyond*. Trans. Charles Rougle. Princeton: Princeton University Press, 1992.

Gruber, Helmut. *Red Vienna: Experiment in Working-Class Culture, 1919–1934*. New York: Oxford University Press, 1991.

Günther, Hans. "Einleitung." In N. F. Chuzhak, ed., *Literatura fakta*. Munich: W. Fink, 1972.

Guttsman, W. L. *Worker's Culture in Weimar Germany: Between Tradition and Commitment*. New York: Berg, 1990.

Hatch, John. "The Formation of Working Class Cultural Institutions during NEP: The Workers' Club Movement in Moscow, 1921–1923." *Carl Beck Papers in Russian and East European Studies*, no. 806, 1990.

——. "Hangouts and Hangovers: State, Class and Culture in Moscow's Workers' Club Movement, 1925–1928." *Russian Review* 53 (1994): 97–117.

——. "The Politics of Mass Culture: Workers, Communists, and Proletkul't in the Development of Workers' Clubs, 1921–1925." *Russian History* 13, nos. 2/3 (1986): 119–48.

Hoffman-Ostwald, Daniel, and Ursula Bekse. *Agitprop, 1924–1933*. Leipzig: VEB Friedrich Hofmeister, 1960.

Hoffmann, David L. *Peasant Metropolis: Social Identities in Moscow, 1929–1941*. Ithaca: Cornell University Press, 1994.

Hoover, Marjorie. *Alexander Ostrovsky*. Boston: Twayne Publishers, 1981.

Huyssen, Andreas. *After the Great Divide: Modernism, Mass Culture, Postmodernism*. Bloomington: Indiana University Press, 1986.

Ivashev, V., ed. *Ot "zhivoi gazety" do teatra-studii*. Moscow: Molodaia gvardiia, 1989.

Kakhnovich, A. D. "Rol' khudozhestvennoi samodeiatel'nosti rabochikh v podgotovke kadrov professional'nogo iskusstva, 1933–1937." In *Iz istorii sovetskoi kul'tury*. Moscow: Mysl', 1972.

Kelly, Catriona. *Petrushka: The Russian Carnival Puppet Theatre*. Cambridge: Cambridge University Press, 1990.

Kemp-Welch, A. *Stalin and the Literary Intelligentsia, 1928–1939*. New York: St. Martin's, 1991.

Kenez, Peter. *The Birth of the Propaganda State: Soviet Methods of Mass Mobilization, 1917–1929*. Cambridge: Cambridge University Press, 1985.

——. *Cinema and Soviet Society, 1917–1953*. Cambridge: Cambridge University Press, 1992.

Khaichenko, G. A. *Russkii narodnyi teatr kontsa XIX–nachala XX veka*. Moscow: Nauka, 1975.

Khan-Magomedov, Selim O. *Rodchenko: The Complete Work*. Cambridge: MIT Press, 1987.

Khazanova, V. *Klubnaia zhizn' i arkhitektura*. 2 vols. Moscow: Rossiiskii institut iskusstvoznaniia, 1994.

Kino: Entsyklopedicheskii slovar'. Moscow: Sovetskaia Entsiklopediia, 1986.

Kleberg, Lars. "The Nature of the Soviet Audience: Theatrical Ideology and Audience Research in the 1920's." In Robert Russell and Andrew Barratt, eds., *Russian Theatre in the Age of Modernism*. London: Macmillan, 1990.

——. " 'Peoples' Theatre' and the Revolution: On the History of a Concept before and after 1917." In A. A. Nilsson, ed., *Art, Society, Revolution: Russia, 1917–1921*. Stockholm: Almqvist and Wiksell International, 1979.

——. *Theatre as Action*. Trans. Charles Rougle. London: Macmillan, 1993.

Koenker, Diane. "Class and Class Consciousness in Socialist Society." In Sheila Fitzpatrick et al., eds., *Russia in the Era of NEP*. Bloomington: Indiana University Press, 1991.

Kolesova, A. K. "Prakticheskaia deiatel'nost' rabochego kluba v 1917–1920 godakh." *Uchenye zapiski Moskovskogo instituta kul'tury* 17 (1968): 231–49.

Konechnyi, Al'ban M. "Popular Carnivals during Mardi Gras and Easter Week in St. Petersburg." *Russian Studies in History* 35, no. 4 (Spring 1997): 52–91.

Kotkin, Stephen. *Magnetic Mountain: Stalinism as a Civilization*. Berkeley: University of California Press, 1995.

Kukaretin, V. M. *Nasledniki "Sinei bluzy"*. Moscow: Molodaia gvardiia, 1976.

Kuromiya, Hiroaki. *Stalin's Industrial Revolution: Politics and Workers, 1918–1932*. Cambridge: Cambridge University Press, 1988.

Kuziakina, Natalia. *Theatre in the Solovki Prison Camp*. Luxembourg: Harwood Academic Publishers, 1995.

Lane, Christel. *The Rites of Rulers*. Cambridge: Cambridge University Press, 1981.

Lapidus, Gail Warshofsky. *Women in Soviet Society*. Berkeley: University of California Press, 1978.

Lebina, Nataliia Borisovna. *Rabochaia molodezh' Leningrada: Trud i sotsial'nyi oblik, 1921–1925gg*. Leningrad: Nauka, 1982.

Levina, L. P. and T. B. Chirikova. *Russkii sovetskii dramaticheskii teatr: Annotirovannyi ukazatel' bibliograficheskikh i spravochnykh materialov, 1917–1973*. Moscow: Ministerstvo kul'tury SSSR, 1977–78.

Levine, Ira A. *Left-Wing Dramatic Theory in the American Theatre*. Ann Arbor: UMI Research Press, 1985.

Leyda, Jay. *Kino: A History of the Russian and Soviet Film*. Princeton: Princeton University Press, 1983.

Maksimenkov, Leonid. *Sumbur vmesto muzyki: Stalinskaia kul'turnaia revoliutsiia, 1936–1938*. Moscow: Iuridicheskaia kniga, 1997.

Mally, Lynn. "Autonomous Theater and the Origins of Socialist Realism: The 1932 Olympiad of Autonomous Art." *Russian Review* 52 (April 1993): 198–212.

——. *Culture of the Future: The Proletkult Movement in Revolutionary Russia*. Berkeley: University of California Press, 1990.

——. "Performing the New Woman: The Komsomolka as Actress and Image in Soviet Youth Theater." *Journal of Social History* 30, no. 1 (1996): 79–95.

——. "The Rise and Fall of the Soviet Youth Theater TRAM." *Slavic Review* 51, no. 3 (1992): 411–30.

——. "Shock Workers on the Cultural Front: Agitprop Brigades in the First Five-Year Plan." *Russian History* 23, no. 1/4 (1996): 263–75.

Mazaev, A. I. *Prazdnik kak sotsial'no-khudozhestvennoe iavlenie.* Moscow: Nauka, 1978.

Millar, James R. "History and Analysis of Soviet Domestic Bond Policy." In Susan Linz, ed., *The Soviet Economic Experiment.* Urbana: Illinois University Press, 1990.

Miller, Frank J. *Folklore for Stalin: Russian Folklore and Pseudofolklore of the Stalin Era.* Armonk, N.Y.: M. E. Sharpe, 1990.

Mironova, V. "Rezhisser i akter v spektakliakh Leningradskogo TRAM'a." In *Teatr i dramaturgiia,* v. 5. Leningrad: Iskusstvo, 1976.

——. TRAM: *Agitatsionnyi molodezhnyi teatr, 1920–1930kh gg.* Leningrad: Iskusstvo, 1977.

Naiman, Eric. "The Case of Chubarov Alley: Collective Rape, Utopian Desire and the Neutrality of NEP." *Russian History* 17. (1990): 1–30.

——. *Sex in Public: The Incarnation of Early Soviet Ideology.* Princeton: Princeton University Press, 1997.

Nekrylova, A. F. *Russkie narodnye gorodskie prazdniki, uveseleniia i zrelishcha.* Leningrad: Iskusstvo, 1984.

——, and N. I. Savushkina. "Russkii fol'klornyi teatr," in L. M. Leonov, ed., *Narodnyi teatr.* Moscow: Sovetskaia Rossiia, 1991.

Neuberger, Joan. *Hooliganism: Crime, Culture, and Power in St. Petersburg, 1900–1914.* Berkeley: University of California Press, 1993.

Papernyi, V. *Kul'tura "dva."* Ann Arbor: Ardis, 1985.

Peris, Daniel. *Storming the Heavens: The Soviet League of the Militant Godless.* Ithaca: Cornell University Press, 1998.

Petrone, Karen. *Life Has Become More Joyous, Comrades: Celebrations in the Time of Stalin.* Bloomington: Indiana University Press forthcoming.

Pinegina, L. A. *Sovetskii rabochii klass i khudozhestvennaia kul'tura.* Moscow: Izdatel'stvo Moskovskogo Universiteta, 1984.

Rabiniants, N. A. *Teatr iunosti: Ocherk istorii Leningradskogo teatra imeni Leninskogo komsomola.* Leningrad: Iskusstvo, 1959.

——. "Teatry, rozhdennye revoliutsiei: Leningradskii TRAM." In *Teatr i zhizn': Sbornik,* ed. M. O. Iankovskii. Leningrad: Iskusstvo, 1957.

Razumov, V. A. "Rol' rabochego klassa v stroitel'stve sotsialisticheskoi kul'tury v nachale revoliutsii i v gody grazhdanskoi voiny." In *Rol' rabochego klassa v razvitii sotsialisticheskoi kul'tury.* Moscow: Izdatel'stvo "Mysl'," 1976.

Robin, Régine. "Popular Literature of the 1920s." In Sheila Fitzpatrick et al., eds., *Russia in the Era of NEP.* Bloomington: Indiana University Press, 1991.

——. *Socialist Realism: An Impossible Aesthetic.* Trans. Catherine Porter. Stanford: Stanford University Press, 1992.

——. "Stalinism and Popular Culture." In *The Culture of the Stalin Period,* ed. Hans Günther. London: Macmillan, 1990.

Ruder, Cynthia A. *Making History for Stalin: The Story of the Belomor Canal.* Gainesville: University Press of Florida, 1998.

Rudnitsky, Konstantin. *Russian and Soviet Theatre: Tradition and the Avant-Garde*. Trans. Roxane Permar. London: Thames and Hudson, 1988.

Rumiantsev, S. Iu., and A. P. Shul'gin, eds. *Samodeiatel'noe khudozhestvennoe tvorchestvo v SSRR*. 2 v. Moscow: Gosudarstvennyi institut iskusstvoznaniia, 1995.

Russell, Robert. "The First Soviet Plays." In Robert Russell and Andrew Barratt, eds., *Russian Theatre in the Age of Modernism*. London: Macmillan, 1990.

———. "People's Theatre and the October Revolution." *Irish Slavonic Studies* 7 (1986): 65–84.

———. *Russian Drama of the Revolutionary Period*. London: Macmillan, 1990.

Samuels, Raphael, Ewan MacCall, and Stuart Cosgrove, eds. *Theatres of the Left, 1880–1935: Worker's Theatre Movement in Britain and America*. London: Routledge and Kegan Paul, 1985.

Sartorti, Rosalinde. "Stalinism and Carnival: Organization and Aesthetics of Political Holidays." In Hans Günther, ed., *The Culture of the Stalin Period*. New York: St. Martin's, 1990.

Savov, S. "Stanovlenie." In I. K. Sidorina and S. S. Sovetov, eds., *Narodnye teatry: Sbornik statei*. Moscow, 1962.

Schechner, Richard. *Performance Theory*. Rev. ed. New York: Routledge, 1988.

Schnapp, Jeffrey T. *Staging Fascism: 18BL and the Theater of Masses for Masses*. Stanford: Stanford University Press, 1996.

Schulte-Sasse, Linda. *Entertaining the Third Reich*. Durham, N.C.: Duke University Press, 1996.

Segel, Harold B. *Twentieth-Century Russian Drama from Gorky to the Present*. 2nd ed. Baltimore: Johns Hopkins University Press, 1993.

Senelick, Laurence. "Theatre." In Nicholas Rzhevsky, ed. *Cambridge Companion to Modern Russian Culture*. Cambridge: Cambridge University Press, 1998.

Shearer, David R. "The Language and Politics of Socialist Rationalization: Productivity, Industrial Relations, and the Social Origins of Stalinism at the End of NEP." *Cahiers du Monde russe et soviétique* 34, no. 4 (1991): 581–608.

Siegelbaum, Lewis. "The Shaping of Workers' Leisure." *International Labor and Working Class History*, Forthcoming.

———. *Soviet State and Society between Revolutions, 1918–1929*. Cambridge: Cambridge University Press, 1992.

———. *Stakhanovism and the Politics of Productivity in the USSR, 1935–1941*. Cambridge: Cambridge University Press, 1988.

Smith, Susanna Lockwood. "Soviet Arts Policy, Folk Music, and National Identity: The Piatnitskii State Russian Folk Choir, 1927–1945." Ph.D. dissertation, University of Minnesota, 1997.

Starr, S. Frederick. *Melnikov: Solo Architect in a Mass Society*. Princeton: Princeton University Press, 1978.

———. *Red and Hot: The Fate of Jazz in the Soviet Union*. New York: Limelight Editions, 1985.

Stebbins, Robert A. *Amateurs: On the Margin between Work and Leisure.* Beverly Hills: Sage Publications, 1979.

Steinberg, Mark D. *Moral Communities: The Culture of Class Relations in the Russian Printing Industry, 1867–1907.* Berkeley: University of California Press, 1992.

Stepanov, Z. V. *Kul'turnaia zhizn' Leningrada 20-kh, nachala 30-kh godov.* Leningrad: Nauka, 1976.

Stephan, Halina. *"Lef" and the Left Front of the Arts.* Munich: Verlag Otto Sagner, 1981.

Stites, Richard. *Revolutionary Dreams: Utopian Vision and Experimental Life in the Russian Revolution.* New York: Oxford, 1989.

———. *Russian Popular Culture: Entertainment and Society since 1900.* Cambridge: Cambridge University Press, 1992.

Stourac, Richard, and Kathleen McCreery. *Theatre as a Weapon: Workers' Theatre in the Soviet Union, Germany and Britain, 1917–1934.* London: Routledge, 1986.

Suleiman, Susan Rubin. *Authoritarian Fictions: The Ideological Novel as a Literary Genre.* Princeton: Princeton University Press, 1983.

Swift, E. Anthony. "Fighting the Germs of Disorder: The Censorship of Russian Popular Theater, 1888–1917." *Russian History* 18, no. 1 (1991): 1–49.

———. "Theater for the People: The Politics of Popular Culture in Urban Russia, 1861–1917." Ph.D. dissertation, University of California, Berkeley, 1991.

———. "Workers' Theater and 'Proletarian Culture' in Pre-Revolutionary Russia." *Russian History* 23 (1996): 67–94.

Tamashin, L. N. *Sovetskaia dramaturgiia v gody grazhdanskoi voiny.* Moscow: Iskusstvo, 1961.

———. *Vladimir Kirshon: Ocherk tvorchestva.* Moscow: Sovetskii pisatel', 1965.

Thorpe, Richard G. "Academic Art in Revolutionary Russia." Unpublished manuscript.

Thurston, Gary. "The Impact of Russian Popular Theatre, 1886–1915." *Journal of Modern History* 55 (June 1983): 237–67.

———. *The Popular Theatre Movement in Russia, 1862–1919.* Evanston, Ill.: Northwestern University Press, 1998.

Timasheff, Nicholas. *The Great Retreat: The Growth and Decline of Communism in Russia.* New York: Dutton, 1946.

Turner, Victor. *Dramas, Fields, and Metaphors.* Ithaca: Cornell University Press, 1974.

Uvarova, E. D. *Estradnyi teatr: Miniatiury, obozreniia, miuzik-kholly, 1917–1945.* Moscow: Iskusstvo, 1983.

———, ed. *Russkaia sovetskaia estrada, 1930–1945.* Moscow: Iskusstvo, 1977.

Vaksberg, Arkady. *The Prosecutor and the Prey: Vyshinsky and the 1930s' Moscow Show Trials.* Trans. Jan Butler. London: Weidenfeld and Nicolson, 1990.

Van Erven, Eugène. *Radical People's Theatre.* Bloomington: Indiana University Press, 1988.

Von Geldern, James. *Bolshevik Festivals, 1917–1920*. Berkeley: University of California Press, 1993.

——. "Cultural and Social Geography in the Mass Culture of the 1930s." In *New Directions in Soviet History*, ed. Stephen White. Cambridge: Cambridge University Press, 1992.

——. "Nietzschean Leaders and Followers in Soviet Mass Theater, 1917–1927." In Bernice Glatzer Rosenthal, ed., *Nietzsche and Soviet Culture: Ally and Adversary*. Cambridge: Cambridge University Press, 1994.

von Hagen, Mark. *Soldiers in the Proletarian Dictatorship*. Ithaca: Cornell University Press, 1990.

Ward, Chris. *Russia's Cotton Workers and the New Economic Policy: Shop Floor Culture and State Policy, 1921–1929*. Cambridge: Cambridge University Press, 1990.

Wardetsky, Jutta. *Theaterpolitik in faschistischen Deutschland: Studien und Dokumente*. Berlin: Henschelverlag, 1983.

Warner, Elizabeth. *The Russian Folk Theatre*. The Hague: Mouton, 1977.

White, Anne. *Destalinization and the House of Culture*. London: Routledge, 1990.

Wood, Elizabeth. *Performing Justice in Revolutionary Russia: Agitation Trials, Society, and the State*. Berkeley: University of California Press, forthcoming.

Youngblood, Denise. *Movies for the Masses: Popular Cinema and Soviet Society in the 1920s*. Cambridge: Cambridge University Press, 1992.

Zernitskaia, E. I., E. D. Loidina, and N. V. Skashkova. *Molodezhnyi teatr v SSSR*, v. 1. Moscow: Gosudarstvennaia tsentral'naia teatral'naia biblioteka, 1968.

Zimmermann, Patricia R. *Reel Families: A Social History of Amateur Film*. Bloomington: Indiana University Press, 1995.

Zograf, N. G., Iu. S. Kalashnikov, P. A. Markov, and V. I. Rostotskii, eds. *Ocherki istorii russkogo sovetskogo dramaticheskogo teatra v trekh tomakh*. Moscow: Akademiia Nauk, 1954–1960.

Zolotnitskii, D. *Sergei Radlov: The Shakespearean Fate of a Soviet Director*. Luxembourg: Harwood Academic Publishers, 1995.

——. "Teatry revoliutsionnoi satiry." In *Teatr i dramaturgiia: Trudy Leningradskogo gosudarstvennogo instituta teatra, muzyki i kinematografii*. Leningrad: Iskusstvo, 1967.

——. *Zori teatral'nogo Oktiabria*. Leningrad: Iskusstvo, 1976.

Index